Developing Orthographies for Unwritten Languages

SIL International®
Publications in Language Use and Education
6

Publications in Language Use and Education is a serial publication of SIL International. The series began as a venue for works covering a broad range of topics in sociolinguistics and has been expanded to include a broad range of topics in education, including mother tongue literacy multilingual education, and informal education. While most volumes are authored by members of SIL, suitable works by others will also form part of the series.

Series Editor
Michael Cahill

Volume Editor
Mickael Cahill and Keren Rice

Production Staff
Bonnie Brown, Managing Editor
Dirk Kievit, Content Editor
Judy Benjamin, Compositor
Lois Gourley, Composition Supervisor
Barbara Alber, Cover Design

Developing Orthographies for Unwritten Languages

Edited by

Michael Cahill and Keren Rice

SIL International®
Dallas, Texas

Library of Congress Catalog No: 2013955368
ISBN: 978-1-55671-347-7
ISSN: 1545-0074

Printed in the United States of America

Copies of this and other publications of SIL International® may be obtained from:

SIL International Publications
7500 W. Camp Wisdom Road
Dallas, TX 75236-5629

Voice: 972-708-7404
Fax: 972-708-7363
publications_intl@sil.org
sil.org/resources/publications

Contents

Introduction

Keren Rice and Michael Cahill

1.1 Why this orthography book?

Documentary linguistics was a major theme of the 2010 meeting of the Linguistic Society of America (LSA), and as I (Cahill) listened to discussions on community involvement, computer technology, dictionaries, methodology, and the occasional passing reference to literacy, it struck me that literacy among endangered languages deserved a more thorough discussion. Orthography seemed to be a manageable piece of that, although when I broached the idea to one linguist at LSA, he reacted with astonishment and disbelief. He had enough experience to know that orthographies are quite complex, not only linguistically but also politically. However, there was so much encouragement from others who felt the time was indeed ripe for this that the two editors of this volume organized an LSA Symposium in 2011 in which several of the papers here were initially presented.[1]

[1] The symposium took place on January 7, 2011, as part of the 85th annual meeting of the LSA held January 6–9, 2011, in Pittsburg, Pennsylvania (see http://www.sil.org/linguistics/2011LSASymposium/).

An orthography is a system for representing a language in written form. The first thought that comes to most people's minds is individual characters (graphemes), but an orthography is much more than that. It also includes word breaks, punctuation, diacritics, rules on how to split and hyphenate words at the end of lines, and capitalization, and is sometimes thought to include spelling as well.

There has been a trend toward increased attention to orthographies in recent years. See, for example, Taylor and Olson 1995; Daniels and Bright 1996; Tabouret-Keller et al. 1997; Coulmas 2003; Rogers 1995, 2005; Anderson 2005; Joshi and Aaron 2006; Seifart 2006; Sebba 2007; Jaffe et al. 2012. Consider also the new journals *Written Language and Literacy* and *Writing Systems Research* (first published in 1998 and 2009, respectively), as well as workshops taught at InField (now known as CoLang) in recent years.[2] This trend is the result of a number of reasons, beyond just academic interest. For one thing, the past twenty years has seen an increased awareness of endangered languages, with funds being made available for the study of these languages. Literacy is a factor in language vitality, and of course orthographies are a necessary component of that. Furthermore, there is increased sensitivity to universal human rights (including significant UNESCO attention[3]), which relates to education, including mother-tongue education. Finally, besides these humanitarian concerns, there is the technical development of Unicode and fonts based on that, which has made accessing different symbols easier as well as an increased number of characters more readily available.[4] These issues have been discussed in more detail in Karan 2006.

This volume, like the 2011 LSA Symposium where several of these papers were presented, has limited goals. We focus here on development of orthography, but we need to keep in mind that orthography is only one part of a

---

[2] For the InField/CoLang workshops, see, for example, Keren Rice and Kristine Stenzel, "Orthography: The 'midwife' approach," Institute on Field Linguistics and Language Documentation (Santa Barbara: UCSB, 2008), www.rnld.org/orthography (accessed January 4, 2013).

[3] See, for example, UNESCO, "Intangible Heritage" http://portal.unesco.org/culture/en/ev.php-URL_ID=34325&URL_DO=DO_TOPIC&URL_SECTION=201.html (accessed January 7, 2013).

[4] Increased availability and use of even basic cell phones, let alone smartphones, is also having an impact on orthographies. As with English texting, those who text in other languages, for example major African languages, use shortcuts to spelling out full words. What long-term effect this may have is still to be seen. Also, what characters are available on cell phones is starting to affect development of orthographies in minority languages, as Cahill notes in an example from Papua New Guinea (see Cahill, this volume).

viable literacy. Other aspects include developing primers, teaching reading *and* writing, facilitating a variety of reading materials, training teachers, holding writers' workshops, and a host of other activities that are necessary for vibrant and continuing literacy in a hitherto-unwritten language. Besides this bare list of activities, one needs to be attuned to sociolinguistic and cultural factors that will determine what time of day would be optimal to hold classes, whether even to have formal classes or not, and who would teach and be taught first (children are usually not the first ...).

1.2 The papers

Certain themes can be seen running through the papers in this volume. First, in these times, local people are often intimately involved in orthographic choices. The days when an outside linguist unilaterally establishes an orthography are fading, at least in many areas of the world. Part of this is due to the increase in educational levels in many areas of the world, along with accompanying multilingualism. Even if a person's mother tongue is a small minority language, it is increasingly likely that that person knows a major language which has been written, and perhaps has some education in that language. The very idea of literacy is not foreign, as it frequently was in some areas in the past century. Second is the ambivalent role of linguistics in orthography development. There is no question that a solid phonological analysis is of great assistance in initial orthography proposals. The distinct phonemes must be identified, and criteria for word breaks applied. However, we see—not only in Cahill's chapter explicitly labeled "Non-Linguistic Factors in Orthographies," but running throughout the volume—that acceptability and usability of an orthography hinges on powerful social and political factors which cannot be ignored. Third, and related to the above, we see that the "one symbol per sound and one sound per symbol" rule, held up as the ideal, is deliberately not always applied. Sometimes this is because recent studies have shown it to be linguistically inadequate in some situations (Snider's paper), but often other issues have had the deciding influence.

The contributions to this volume can be roughly divided into two parts: (1) papers outlining foundational principles and (2) case histories. We say "roughly" divided, because the principles papers are rich in examples from real situations, and the case histories often explicitly present the principles that they exemplify.

Chapter 2, by Cahill ("Non-Linguistic Factors in Orthographies") is in some ways a warning to the linguists who were the primary audience at the original LSA Symposium. It is tempting for a linguist, especially one who is a novice in working in a field situation, to imagine that if the linguistic analysis is right, then the main barrier to orthography is overcome. In practical terms, this is not so, and the case studies in the remainder of the book illustrate this amply. Legal factors such as government rules, practical factors such as ability to print a particular orthography, and over all, the social and local political factors which highly influence people, are all discussed.

In spite of the foregoing, phonological analysis is still seen as important in orthography development. Chapter 3, by Snider ("Orthography and Phonological Depth") gives an explicit theoretical proposal for the phonological level that an orthography should aim for. Snider points out that there has been remarkably little effort to apply more recent phonological theory to orthography development—in fact, very little beyond Chomsky and Halle 1968. He shows with examples that neither the traditional phonemic level nor a morphophonemic level gives consistently desirable results. He proposes invoking the basic insights of Lexical Phonology, especially the fundamental distinction between lexical and post-lexical processes. The output of the lexical level is psychologically real and should be the basis of an initial orthography proposal.

Chapter 4, by Kutsch Lojenga ("Orthography and Tone: A Tone-System Typology and its Implications for Orthography Development") is a result of the author's extensive experience in Africa, where most languages are tonal (she has personally consulted in over two hundred languages). Kutsch Lojenga reviews the different ways that people have marked tone. She then proposes a typological distinction between languages with more stable tone (which also tend to have shorter words and more tone levels) and languages with more changeable and mobile tone. Languages of the first type often have a heavy functional load of tone both in the lexicon and in the grammar. It is often necessary to mark tone on every syllable. In languages of the second type, tone often marks grammatical contrasts, and this is where tone should then be marked in the orthography. Kutsch Lojenga reviews various possibilities of marking tone in contrastive grammatical constructions. Chapter 5, also by Kutsch Lojenga ("Basic Principles for Establishing Word Boundaries") takes up the thorny issue of word breaks. Readers of this volume are so accustomed to standard English word divisions that it may come as a shock to realize that this topic is not a trivial one. Words do not break in the same places in all languages. This paper examines the impact that syllable structure and knowledge of various types of morpheme categories can have on word-boundary decisions. Especially helpful are explicit criteria for writing different types of morphemes as separate words or conjoined to another word.

Chapter 6, by Karan ("Standardization: What's the Hurry?") presents a different point of view than the usual "let's get it done *now*" approach. Probably surprisingly to some, Karan advocates slowing down the process of orthography development under certain conditions, illustrating how European orthographies, for example, were not developed overnight. She presents a variety of factors that would indicate a slow-down is called for. Involving a wide variety of people, and taking time to let them digest different possibilities, can be helpful not only in developing a psycholinguistically sound writing system, but also in fostering people's acceptance of it. Karan references others who have felt uncomfortable with rushed standardization and presents several case studies which support taking a slower approach in certain contexts.

Chapter 7, by Hinton ("Orthography Wars") is the first case study, but also serves as a bridge between the two types of papers. Hinton focuses on North America, where several Native American communities (Navajo, Kumeyaay, Big Valley Pomo, and Yurok) debate which kind of orthographies to use. The main choices are between those developed by linguists, which incorporate local sounds more directly, and those using only English alphabetic symbols with English orthography interpretations. Hinton details the linguistic backgrounds of these orthographies, and also the various non-linguistic factors involved, especially the dominant English orthography which surrounds all groups and is pushing them toward English-based practical orthographies.

Chapter 8, by Munro ("Breaking Rules for Orthography Development") reviews some of the "normal" approaches to orthographies, such as the one-to-one correspondence between symbols and sounds (i.e., generally graphemes and phonemes, respectively). After a brief presentation of how Cherokee and English disobey these rules, Munro presents in more detail the cases of Tlacolula Valley Zapotec and Gabrielino/Tongva/Fernandeño, languages of Mexico and California, respectively. She shows that other factors have overridden the usual and expected considerations.

Chapter 9, by Wise ("A Yanesha' Alphabet for the Electronic Age") is a very detailed examination of the process the Yanesha' of Peru have gone through to have their orthography developed and approved. The complex phonological issues that affect orthography are meticulously presented, and also a history of the orthographic proposals and struggles of the Yanesha'. The Yanesha' themselves and the Peruvian government have had multiple interactions, and only recently, with an alphabet congress in 2011, have the issues been resolved, with a "resulting alphabet that enables Yanesha' speakers to write their language on any computer with a Spanish keyboard."

Chapter 10, by Hyslop ("Kurtöp Orthography Development in Bhutan") is largely the story of a difficult *script* in an orthography. What would have been a relatively straightforward orthography in a Roman script turns out to be quite challenging in the 'Ucen script, which was originally developed for an older variety of Tibetan. Phonological challenges included tone and vowel length. Centuries of language change have obscured the original sound-symbol correspondences, and the religious environment played a significant role as well in challenges the developers faced.

Chapter 11, by Adams ("Case Studies of Orthography Decision Making in Mainland Southeast Asia") illustrates what can go wrong in orthography development and literacy programs in general when certain principles (his rather innovative nine "observations") are not applied. His three case histories from Asia illustrate the very human side of orthographies, both in negative outcomes (where a project had to be abandoned) and in positive ways where there were excellent success stories. Scripts, religion, identity issues, local politics, and many other factors are seen to come into play quite powerfully in these studies.

Six of these papers—those by Cahill, Snider, Munro, Hyslop, Adams, and Kutsch Lojenga's contribution on tone—were first presented at the LSA Symposium in 2011.[5]

In this volume, lesser-known languages are identified by their ISO language codes (if they have one), e.g., [kma] for Konni.[6] The following conventions are used: /a/ phonemic representation; [a] phonetic transcription; and <a> graphemic representation, i.e., the actual symbols in an orthography.

---

[5] The LSA 2011 Meeting Handbook lists Hinton as one of the presenters but Hyslop took her place at the last minute.

[6] For a complete list of ISO language codes, see http://www.sil.org/iso639-3/default.asp (accessed January 7, 2013). These same language codes are also used in the *Ethnologue* (http://www.ethnologue.com).

References

Anderson, Deborah. 2005. Recommendations for creating new orthographies. *Unicode Technical Note* 19. Unicode Inc. http://www.unicode.org/notes/tn19/ (accessed January 7, 2013).

Chomsky, Noam, and Morris Halle. 1968. *The sound pattern of English.* New York: Harper and Row.

Coulmas, Florian. 2003. *Writing systems: An introduction to their linguistic analysis.* Cambridge: Cambridge University Press.

Daniels, Peter, and William Bright, eds. 1996. *The world's writing systems.* New York: Oxford University Press.

Jaffe, Alexandra, Jannis K. Androutsopoulos, Mark Sebba, and Sally Johnson, eds. 2012. *Orthography as social action: Scripts, spelling, identity, and power.* Language and Social Processes [LSP] 3. Berlin: De Gruyter.

Joshi, R. Malatesha, and P. G. Aaron, eds. 2006. *Handbook of orthography and literacy.* Mahwah, N. J.: Lawrence Erlbaum Associates, Publishers.

Karan, Elke. 2006. Writing system development and reform: A process. M.A. thesis. University of North Dakota. http://arts-sciences.und.edu/summer-institute-of-linguistics/theses/_files/docs/2006-karan-elke.pdf (accessed February 18, 2013).

Rogers, Henry. 1995. Optimal orthographies. In Taylor and Olson, 31–43.

Rogers, Henry. 2005. *Writing systems: A linguistic approach.* Blackwell Textbooks in Linguistics. Oxford: Blackwell Publishing.

Sebba, Mark. 2007. *Spelling and society: The culture and politics of orthography around the world.* Cambridge: Cambridge University Press.

Seifart, Frank. 2006. Orthography development. In Jost Gippert, Nikolaus Himmelmann, and Ulrike Mosel (eds.), *Essentials of language documentation,* 275–299. Berlin: Mouton de Gruyter.

Tabouret-Keller, Andrée, Robert B. Le Page, Penelope Gardner-Chloros, and Gabrielle Varro, eds. 1997. *Vernacular literacy: A re-evaluation.* Oxford: Clarendon Press.

Taylor, Insup, and David R. Olson, eds. 1995. *Scripts and literacy: Reading and learning to read alphabets, syllabaries and characters.* Dordrecht, the Netherlands: Kluwer Academic Publishers.

2

Non-Linguistic Factors in Orthographies

Michael Cahill

The acceptability (and therefore actual use) of orthographies in newly written languages depends on non-linguistic factors as much as on linguistic ones. Governmental policy may be one such factor, but inevitably a host of sociolinguistic issues are also present. These include choice of which dialect to use as standard (based on geography, clan, religion, etc.). An orthography that facilitates transfer to a major language is often a goal, but this can conflict with choices of symbols or even entire scripts that emphasize group identity. Educational issues such as teachability (for level of readers aimed at) and readability (involving, for example, resemblance of characters and diacritic density) must also be considered. Technical issues include local printability and Unicode-compliance of every symbol, with preference for sans serif fonts for beginning readers. These factors often conflict with each other as well as with linguistic factors, and thus decisions on orthographies must necessarily balance these, with the local speakers' input being decisive.

2.1 Introduction*

In this paper, I focus on the non-linguistic factors that make an orthography "effective." Those who wish their orthographies to actually be used will find a useful and crucial list of issues to consider here. An effective orthography is not only (a) linguistically sound, but is also crucially (b) acceptable to all stakeholders, and (c) usable. This approximately translates into scientific, political, and practical factors.[1] Note that these factors *often,* perhaps *always,* conflict with each other! Other papers in this volume, particularly those by Snider and Kutsch Lojenga, focus on linguistic issues, while Karan's in particular deals with nonlinguistic ones as well.

This paper focuses on the last two factors, that is, acceptability (political factors) and usability (practical factors). I build the paper around a number of brief examples in each area. In the second half of the book, featuring specific case studies, we will see more extended outworkings of the principles that are but briefly mentioned here.

2.2 Governmental policies and restrictions

Countries which have few, if any, undeveloped languages may not have stated policies on new orthographies; such policies are not needed in those situations. Many researchers come from home countries like these. However, countries which have dozens or, in some cases, hundreds of undeveloped languages often have policies governing orthographic development. An outside researcher or other facilitator, not being used to the existence of such, may not give any thought to what governmental policies may exist in the country of that language. This can be a serious oversight. Ignoring such policies is, to put it mildly, not a good idea. A government may see such non-compliance as deliberately flaunting government laws, and the

*This paper is the result of tapping the practical experience of co-workers in SIL International who have more knowledge than I. SIL has been working for several decades in literacy (e.g., Pike 1947, Powlison 1968, Gudschinsky 1973, Simons 1977, Lee 1982, Litteral 1999, SIL International 1965–2001, Karan 2006). In that time, SIL has helped develop orthographies for over 1,300 previously unwritten languages and has helped produce various literacy and community development materials, including traditional folk tales and proverbs, Bible translations, and materials on AIDS, clean water, avian flu, etc.

[1] Smalley (1963) lists a somewhat different set of criteria (maximum motivation for the learner, maximum representation of speech, maximum ease of learning, maximum transfer, and maximum ease of reproduction), but his criteria can be subsumed under these three headings. See Hinton, this volume, for a discussion of Smalley's criteria.

result could be a prohibition against working with that language group, or even expulsion from the country. Another possible consequence is a forced change in the orthography when the government becomes aware, with all the attendant disruption. Orthography developers must be aware of what policies exist in the situation in which they are working.

2.2.1 Nationwide governmental policies

Sometimes the government has national policies one must follow if continued work in the country is a goal. For example, for some years in Ghana, the Bureau of Ghana Languages disallowed all tone markings in orthographies.[2] Effects of this policy continue to this day, even though the policy was relaxed some years ago. Orthographies established under that policy now have an established body of literature in place, and, therefore, changing these orthographies would require an enormous effort, if it is feasible at all.

Another example comes from Cameroon. In 1979, Cameroon established a unified alphabet (Tadadjeu and Sadembouo 1984) and required all new orthographies to conform to it by drawing their characters from that standard set. This applies to Roman-based orthographies, not to the Arabic-based ones which exist in some parts of the country.

2.2.2 Governmental approval of individual orthographies

Some governments go beyond a national policy and require approval of each new individual orthography. This is the case in the Central African Republic, where the national government must approve new orthographies. A variation on this is seen in Ethiopia, where there is no single uniform approval agency, but one of several possible agencies must approve new orthographies.

[2] The policies discussed in this section were current at the time I acquired the information from various individuals. Since governmental policies predictably change over time, it is possible that these particular policies are not current at the present time. However, they still illustrate the point.

2.3 Sociolinguistic factors: "All orthographies are political"

"Politics" takes many forms in language communities of the world. Here we examine some of these forms. For another perspective on these, see Eira (1998), and for a previous formulation of many of the relevant issues, see Cahill and Karan (2008).

2.3.1 Dialects

For efficiency's sake, it is often felt desirable to devise an orthography that will serve all of a language group, even one with fairly divergent dialects (see also Karan, this volume, and Adams, this volume). Pragmatically speaking, this makes it easier to produce materials than when each dialect has its own standard orthography. That is, you are producing only one set of materials, not several sets, each having a slightly different orthography that addresses a particular dialect. A single orthography may not be desirable in all cases (and computer adaptation may aid in easily transferring materials written in one orthography to another one), but where it is, here are some factors to consider.

There are two major approaches to a single orthography for multiple dialects: a unilectal approach and a multilectal approach. Which one is chosen will depend on local circumstances.

The first approach is the unilectal one. In this approach, the most prestigious dialect is chosen as the standard for orthography, and other dialects will adapt to it. The advantage is that once the dialect is chosen, then orthography developers can focus on that dialect, without expending effort on the others. Challenges abound in this approach, of course. It may be that there is no generally agreed-upon prestige dialect. And what constitutes "prestige"? Is it the dialect of the biggest clan or village? Of the oldest chief? Or of some group that has status for some other historic, social, or religious reason? But again, if this approach is feasible, then the savings in effort and expense can be significant.

One small example of this comes from my experience with the Koma [kma] people of northern Ghana (language often called Konni). The Koma people, at the time of my residence there, had five villages, with a total population of about 3,000. The biggest village, where I lived, is Yikpabongo, which had about 900 people and was clearly recognized by all the other villages as having the purest Konni. The village of Nangurima has a distinctly different dialect. One mark of this is that where the main dialect has /h/, Nangurima has /ŋ/, as in *hɔ̀gʊ́~ŋɔ̀gʊ́* 'woman'. My proposed orthography, now in use for almost twenty years, used /h/ for the entire group, with people from Nangurima being taught to pronounce orthographic <h> as [ŋ].

In the multilectal approach, the orthography has elements of *several* dialects, not just one. This means that the orthography does not fully represent anyone's actual speech, which may be seen by some as a disadvantage. The obvious advantage, especially in sociopolitically sensitive situations where no single group is dominant, is that one group is not favored. With sensitive negotiation, all parties can be seen to have a share in the actual writing system.

In some cases, local people may not be amenable to combining dialects into a single orthography, and if literacy is to be established, then multiple dialects must be accommodated (see the Trique example in §2.3.2.2).

2.3.2 Attitudes toward other languages

In the modern world, it is increasingly rare to find a language group that has no steady contact with another language. This could be an official language of the country. More likely in the case of small minority languages, it could be other neighboring minority languages, which may be stronger or weaker than the language in question. The history of contact between the languages, as well as the felt prestige of the other language, will predispose a positive or negative attitude toward another language.

2.3.2.1 "We want the orthography to 'look like' another language"

Most Ghanaian languages have a phonetic flap [ɾ]. However, in some languages, [ɾ] is contrastive with [d], and in others it is not (see discussion in Cahill 2007). But all Ghanaian languages I am aware of have <r> in their orthography. This is because of the pervasive influence of English, the official language of Ghana. Having <r> helps in transitioning a reader into the national language, whatever its phonemic status.

Another influence of English in Africa involves the paucity of tone marks in anglophone countries as contrasted with francophone countries. In several parts of Africa, local and sometimes governmental people have resisted tone marking in an orthography (such tone marking usually consisting of various diacritics). The reasoning goes that since English does not have "those funny marks all over the page," their language should not have them either (Cahill 2001; see also Kutsch Lojenga's paper on tone, this volume).

Both of these examples come from a sense of prestige and perhaps economic advantage of the language being imitated. It is possible that some minority language may want to imitate a neighboring minority language as well.

2.3.2.2 "We do **not** *want the orthography to look like another language"*

Because of rivalry, warfare, or simple pride in their language, some people groups do *not* want their orthography to imitate that of another group they know of. It is a matter of group identity.

For example, in Ghana, the Konkombas [xon] use <ln> word finally to indicate a nasalized lateral (e.g., their autonym Likpakpaln). There is a neighboring group, the Kombas, who are closely related. They also have the nasalized lateral sound, but since many people recognize orthographic <ln> as distinctively Konkomba, the Kombas decided to spell the sound as <nl>. This is purely a matter of indicating independence and a distinct identity through their orthographic choice.

Another example is the K'iche' peoples in Guatemala. SIL workers had proposed and used an orthography for decades that spelled /k/ as <qu, c>, according to the Spanish convention. The idea was that using <qu, c> would more easily enable a transition to Spanish for those who wanted it. In the 1980s, a Mayan resurgence of local identity occurred, and one result was that they wanted <k> to represent /k/, not the pattern of the despised Spanish. Either solution is linguistically defensible; it was the social politics that were the deciding factor.

A final and somewhat extreme example comes from Barbara Hollenbach on Trique (pers. comm.) regarding what she terms "hyperfragmentation." In the state of Oaxaca in Mexico, partly due to the rugged terrain, each town may have its own distinctive pattern of speech. In many of these cases, each town wants to have a different orthography. This is not on the basis of language intelligibility—each town can understand the others—but on the strongly held identity of individual towns. For one Trique language, for example, there were two towns with a single language, totally mutually intelligible. They nevertheless insisted on two separate orthographies.

2.3.3 Orthographies that attach to a certain group

Speakers have attitudes not only toward an orthography used by *another* language; they sometimes have very definite opinions toward orthographies that have become connected with a subgroup of their *own* language. From some places in Latin America, one may hear "You're an *evangelico* and I'm a Catholic, so I support this one." Groups that can be associated with a particular orthography can be religious groups, political groups, clans, etc. Adams (this volume) discusses case histories of this sort.

There are certain implications of this subtype of identity politics for those who wish to propose an orthography that will be used by a wide spectrum of a language group. First, it is necessary to include *all* stakeholders in orthography planning and decisions from the start. If there is an identifiable group, it should have input into the design of the orthography. This entails significant anthropological research if an outsider is involved in the project.

A second implication is that one should closely examine any previous orthographies, and not only for linguistic factors. One should find out who designed the orthography (its history), who currently supports it, and who actually uses it. *Adapting* or *adopting* a neighboring language's orthography entails somewhat different issues, as noted in the previous sections.

2.3.4 Choice of scripts

The choice of entire scripts can be a crucial issue in developing an orthography. This goes beyond the choice of individual symbols. In some areas of the world, there is a choice between a Cyrillic and a Roman script. In another area, the tension may be between Arabic and Roman. Tuareg [ttq] of North Africa uses Arabic, Roman, and Tifinagh scripts (Savage 2008). In signed languages of the world, there is a choice between line drawings vs. photographs vs. a SignWriting-based system, if they choose to represent their language on paper at all rather than totally using video technology (Hopkins 2008). For a collection of thirteen papers exemplifying this in detail, see the recent issue of the *International Journal of the Sociology of Language* which focused on "The Sociolinguistics of Script Choice" (Unseth

2008). Adams (this volume), in particular, discusses the importance and volatility of script choices in southeast Asia. See also Hyslop (this volume) for an in-depth discussion of one such case.

All the sociopolitical factors in this paper also apply to script choice. In especially complex situations, sometimes it has proven desirable to publish with two or even three scripts in the same book.

2.3.5 Summary

An orthography is an expression of a people's *identity*. People accept or reject an orthography based on sociolinguistic factors. If a group doesn't *want* to use an orthography, it doesn't matter how linguistically sound it is—they won't use it. So "what the people want" is not just one more factor; it is the *most critical* factor in *acceptance* of an orthography.

2.4 Educational and psycholinguistic factors

2.4.1 Underrepresentation and overrepresentation

In this paper and for most people developing practical orthographies for unwritten languages, the phoneme is taken to be a real psychological unit (see Dresher 2011). Speakers of a language are generally aware of phonemic differences but not of allophonic variation. It has been said since the days of Pike (1947) that an ideal orthography matches one grapheme (symbol) with each phoneme.[3] However, orthographies around the world often diverge from this, for a variety of reasons, both good and bad, and it is helpful to be aware of the phenomenon itself as well as the factors that lead to these mismatches.

Underrepresentation is using fewer graphemes than phonemes, e.g., when a language uses only five vowel graphemes <a, e, i, o, u> even though there are seven phonemic vowels /a, e, ɛ, i, o, ɔ, u/. Reasons for this could include inadequate linguistic analysis, or perhaps local speakers simply prefer it that way. Often there is influence and even pressure from the national or otherwise dominant language.

---

[3] Actually, the concept goes back much further, though not expressed in modern linguistic terms. Centuries ago, John Hart wrote (1569) that "the writing should haue so many letters as the speach hath voyces, and no more no lesse."

One case is the Ebrié language [ebr] from Côte d'Ivoire (C. Kutsch Lojenga, pers. comm.). The original orthography didn't distinguish fortis and lenis versions of /p, t, c, k/, which were in fact contrastive. Not surprisingly, serious reading problems were the result. More linguistic analysis revealed the fortis/lenis pattern, and Ebrié speakers immediately approved adding <ph, th, ch, kh> to the orthography.

Another case of underrepresentation that is quite common in Africa is not indicating tone in the orthography at all, even if tone is demonstrably contrastive (e.g., Cahill 2001). Most often it seems that a decision to omit tone marking is made on the basis of imitation of a national language, as well as the very real problems of deciding on which phonological level to mark tone (though see Snider, this volume, for a principled approach, and Kutsch Lojenga's paper on tone, this volume, for specific discussion of tone marking). In more cases than I considered in 2001, it does seem that for some languages tone is predictable enough in context that it does not cause significant problems in reading to omit it.

However, in general, underrepresentation is indeed often a problem for reading, where a particular grapheme is ambiguous and represents two or more phonemes. The reader, seeing the grapheme, must guess which phoneme is meant. Sometimes context is enough to disambiguate the word, but there is a significant difference between the abilities of the beginning and the fluent reader in managing such context; the fluent reader has learned to process larger "chunks" of text, so that words before or after the target word can be used to influence the choice of the target word. In contrast, the beginning reader must think through the choices on a more granular level, often sounding out each word, grapheme by grapheme, which slows down fluency. So, underrepresentation affects the beginning reader more than the fluent one. Note that though underrepresentation is a problem for the reader, it is not a problem for someone writing. The writer does not need to make a choice between graphemes but cheerfully uses one grapheme for two or perhaps more phonemes.

Overrepresentation, on the other hand, is using more graphemes than phonemes, often, for example, writing two allophones of a single phoneme. As with underrepresentation, there are a number of reasons why this can happen. It may be that some dialects of a language have a contrast between sounds that are merely allophonic in another dialect. Often, overrepresentation happens because a trade language or official language uses the different graphemes. The example of <d, r> in Ghanaian languages noted in §3.2.1 is again relevant here. In many Ghanaian languages, [d] and [r] are allophones of /d/, and the one-symbol-per-phoneme principle would dictate using only <d>. But because of English and other languages, overrepresentation occurs.

Overrepresentation is less of a problem for reading than it is for writing. When teaching reading, the learner needs to know how to pronounce two different symbols "the same." For writing, however, the writer needs to dig deeper mentally than his ordinary phonemic awareness, to the level of the allophones represented by the graphemes. Thus the writer needs to be phonetically trained to differentiate sounds that he has typically been unaware of up to this point.[4] The alternative to this increased phonetic awareness is rote memorization of which words are spelled with one allophone, and which are spelled with the other. An obvious disadvantage of this rote system is that the writer needs to memorize the spelling of all the words in his language, rather than spell them "as they sound."

2.4.2 Transferability to other languages

A goal of many orthography designers is to aim for an orthography that will have good transferability to other neighboring or national languages, that is, an orthography that resembles these others closely enough so that barriers to learning to read the other languages will be minimized. This can intersect with governmental goals of promoting unity in the country, but it can also be quite a practical benefit for local people who must interact with a larger language.

A previously mentioned example is that in many Latin American contexts the graphemes <qu> and <c> have been used to represent /k/, as Spanish does (see Wise, this volume). The choice of symbols is purely based on transferability. Likewise, the Spanish-style punctuation <¿ ... ?> rather than merely <?> for questions has also been introduced.

A case that I witnessed firsthand in the early 1990s was the national Alphabet Standardisation Committee in Ghana. A group of governmental, university, and NGO representatives were attempting to come up with a common pool of symbols to be used by all Ghanaian languages. One point debated was how to uniformly represent the phoneme /tʃ/ in Ghanaian

---

[4] Such awareness may also be acquired through knowledge of a second language which does contrast the sounds in question.

languages. Different languages had represented it by <ch, c, ts, tʃ, tsch, ky>, and perhaps others. It was "obvious" to some that the symbol chosen for nationwide use should be <ch>, but it was obvious to others that it should be <ky>. What it depended on was the language of transfer (and identity): <ch> for English or <ky> for the very large language group of Akan [aka].

An extreme example of transferability is Karakalpak [kaa], a Turkic language. The orthography developed for Karakalpak used not only the Cyrillic *characters* of Russian but also its *usages* in Russian to represent sounds. The aim was good transferability, but it turns out that the sounds of Russian and Karakalpak are so different that this resulted in a bad representation of Karakalpak sounds (Coulmas 1989:236–237).

2.4.3 Readability

In English, <p, q, d, b> are all the same shape, potentially confusing for a new reader. After all, no matter which way you turn a chair, it is still a chair; why wouldn't the same apply to letters? With English, and with Roman-based orthographic systems in general, you have no practical choice but to use these characters. However, there may be cases where the orthography designer has a choice. In these cases, it is preferable to aim for good visual discrimination. This has at least two dimensions: characters which resemble each other, and characters with too much "cluttering." See the examples below.

(1) Extreme examples (hypothetical):

n n̦ ɲ ɳ ŋ	too many symbols that resemble each other
á ā́ ā̂ ā̋	too many stacking diacritics

Another issue in readability of characters is font selection. A sans serif font is plainer and better for beginners than a font with serifs (see §2.5 below). In more advanced reading materials, other fonts may be used.

2.4.4 Testing

Testing the orthography would seem to be a basic step in orthography development, but it is often not carried out, sometimes due to time pressures, sometimes due to an ignorance of methodology, and perhaps sometimes due to a lack of appreciation for the benefits thereof. But I would suggest that testing an orthography is worth the effort. It will either confirm that an orthography is on the right track or reveal areas of potential improvement.

Testing can reveal weaknesses in linguistic analysis. If people have trouble deciding how to pronounce a word, perhaps a contrastive distinction has been missed, or certain linguistic elements are more psycholinguistically prominent than others. Testing can also reveal personal or group idiosyncratic preferences that may affect acceptability of the orthography. The materials to be tested need not be elaborate; testing can be done with a preliminary vocabulary or elementary dictionary, with trial primers, or with other trial materials.

Testing can be either informal or formal. Informal testing would involve observation as a facilitator teaches someone to read. One can note what symbols readers are having trouble with or observe that certain word breaks are consistently problematic in reading or writing.

More formal testing involves testing specific issues, such as a choice between two symbols. For example, one could ask beginning or more advanced readers to read a passage with one symbol versus another, and the observer would note hesitations and mistakes. The readings could be recorded for later, more detailed, and quantitative analysis if desired. Details of methodology of testing are well beyond the scope of this paper but can be found elsewhere (e.g., Schroeder 2010). Roberts (2008) gives a summary of testing various tone markings in orthographies; references therein include a substantial amount of detail on methodology also. Even more meticulous is Roberts (2011), which details theoretical and practical preparations for a tone orthography experiment.

2.4.5 Note on native speakers' suggestions

Native speaker intuition is a two-edged sword in orthography development. If a local speaker says that there is a problem, this is quite often correct. However, the speaker's *analysis* of the problem may or may not be on target. See Durie (1987) for a case of both the value and limitations of native speaker intuition.

In the early days of Konni orthography, I mimeographed a primitive "ABC" booklet, with single words underneath a drawing of the object indicated. One was <kooŋ> for 'hoe'. One elderly Konni speaker who had been outside Ghana during World War II and had acquired a bit of education told me emphatically that the vowel should not be spelled with <o> but with <u>. I asked him to pronounce the word, and it sounded like [kooŋ]. I asked him to pronounce the word for 'horse', and it was clearly [duuŋ]. The man said, yes, these were the same vowel. Later, after more exposure and analysis, I realized the word for 'hoe' was actually /kʊʊŋ/. Neither one of us was initially correct. To American ears, the [–ATR] vowel /ʊ/ sounded like [o]. But the Konni speaker put /ʊ/ in the same category as its [+ATR] counterpart /u/. Since his education was in English, he had no categories except <a, e, i, o, u>, and he naturally put the /ʊ/ into the closest category in his mind.

2.5 Practical production factors (fonts)

A problem in past decades that was a crucial factor in choosing graphemes for an orthography was physical printing possibilities: what a typewriter had on its keyboard, or what the local printer at a printing establishment had in his literal font box. For example, twenty-eight years ago, shortly before computers became common in field situations, I ordered the "custom keys" *ŋ*, *ɔ*, and *ɛ* to be attached to a new manual typewriter (replacing some keys such as the exclamation point), since it was predictable that a Ghanaian language would need these.

Computers with multiple font and keyboard possibilities have largely ameliorated this issue, but not totally. One must still survey possibilities for local printing and what limitations, if any, are placed on orthographies. There needs to be a stable mode of local production to enable local people to continue with literacy on their own. What that might be will vary with the local situation.

If computers are at all involved, then *Unicode-compliant fonts* are considered "best practice." This will make smooth transitions between computers and different fonts much more likely. A number of free downloadable fonts are available from SIL.[5] A few Latin-based ones are illustrated below. These are all phonetically based and Unicode compliant:

[5] SIL, "The Non-Roman Script Initiative," http://scripts.sil.org and SIL, "SIL Software Catalogue, Fonts," http://www.sil.org/computing/catalog/index.asp (accessed March 5, 2013).

(2) Latin-based fonts:

Doulos SIL	[ðɪs ɪz ə fə'nɛrɪkli beʲst fant]	(like Times New Roman)
Charis SIL	[ðɪs ɪz ə fə'nɛrɪkli beʲst fant]	(designed for readability)
Andika	[ðɪs ɪz ə fə'nɛrɪkli beʲst fɑnt]	(designed for new literacy materials)

Non-Roman, Unicode-compliant scripts are also available, as a few other SIL fonts in example 3 illustrate:

(3) Non-Roman fonts:

Scheherezade (Arabic based)	أنا الألفُ والياءُ
Padauk (Myanmar based)	[illegible]
Abyssinica (Ethiopic)	የዘንዶ ዋሻ በሞኝ ክንድ ይለካል
Tai Heritage Pro (Tai Dam based)	[illegible]

Modern technology has provided not only new opportunities but necessarily new points of decision as well. In a recent alphabet-development workshop for the Ma Mande (a.k.a. Sauk) [skc] people in Papua New Guinea, local speakers of languages were making decisions about how to symbolize certain sounds. Several of them whipped out their cell phones and were counting how many keystrokes would be required for different options. The number of keystrokes would make a significant difference to them. (Ryan Pennington, pers. comm.)

2.6 Further discussion

An obvious implication of all the preceding discussion is the importance of local community involvement. There may be ways in which local speakers can contribute to the linguistic analysis leading to a practical orthography. But certainly for an acceptable orthography, local community involvement is crucial (see Powers 1990 for a discussion of Lakota), though in some communities which have little education or perhaps motivation, it will be minimal.

We must also note that a good orthography—linguistically sound and sociolinguistically acceptable—is only the starting point. Even if a good orthography exists, good teaching materials and instruction are needed for all but the most self-motivated potential readers. The reader is referred to

Waters (1998) and Schroeder (2010) for a more comprehensive look at what is involved in a full literacy effort.

In conclusion, a multitude of factors are involved in devising or adapting an orthography. Linguistic factors are basic, but other issues *will* predictably conflict with these and with each other. All these must be considered and balanced for an orthography to be effective.

> Without literacy, our language was in the process of being exterminated.... He who loses his mother tongue is just a slave to him who is of the lowest class.... But now, even if I die today, I will die happy, because my children have a language which will endure and that they can call their own. (Josué Koné, Miniyanka [myk] speaker, Mali)

References

Cahill, Michael. 2001. Avoiding tone marks: A remnant of English education? *Notes on Literacy* 27(1):13–21.

Cahill, Michael. 2007. *Aspects of the morphology and phonology of Konni.* Publications in Linguistics 141. Dallas: SIL International.

Cahill, Michael, and Elke Karan. 2008. Factors in designing effective orthographies for unwritten languages. *SIL Electronic Working Papers* 2008–001. http://www.sil.org/silewp/2008/silewp2008-001.pdf (accessed November 23, 2012).

Coulmas, Florian. 1989. *The writing systems of the world.* Oxford: Blackwell.

Dresher, B. Elan. 2011. The phoneme. In Marc Van Oostendorp, et al. (eds.), *The Blackwell companion to phonology,* 241–246. 5 vols. Malden, Mass.: Wiley-Blackwell Publishing.

Durie, Mark. 1987. The orthographic representation of nasal vowels in Acehnese. In Philip A. Luelsdorff (ed.), *Orthography and phonology,* 131–150. Amsterdam: John Benjamins Publishing Company.

Eira, Christina. 1998. Authority and discourse: Towards a model of orthography selection. *Written Language and Literacy* 1(2):171–224.

Gudschinsky, Sarah. 1973. *A manual of literacy for preliterate peoples.* Ukarumpa, PNG: Summer Institute of Linguistics.

Hart, John. 1569. An orthographie, conteyning the due order and reason, howe to write or paint thimage of mannes voice, most like to the life or nature. London. Repr. in Danielsson, B., 1955. *John Hart's works on English orthography and pronunciation, 1551, 1569, 1570, Part I: Biographical and biographical introductions, texts and index verborum,* 165–228. Stockholm: Almqvist and Wiksell.

Hopkins, Jason. 2008. Choosing how to write sign language: A sociolinguistic perspective. *International Journal of the Sociology of Language* 192:75–90.

Karan, Elke. 2006. Writing system development and reform: A process. M.A. thesis. University of North Dakota.

Lee, Ernest W. 1982. *Literacy primers: The Gudschinsky method.* Summer Institute of Linguistics Publications in Literacy. Dallas: Summer Institute of Linguistics.

Litteral, Robert. 1999. Four decades of language policy in Papua New Guinea: The move towards the vernacular. *SIL Electronic Working Papers* 1999–2001. First presented to the annual meeting of the Linguistic Society of Papua New Guinea, Madang, 1995. http://www.sil.org/silewp/1999/001/silewp1999-001.html (accessed November 23, 2012).

Pike, Kenneth L. 1947. *Phonemics: A technique for reducing languages to writing.* Ann Arbor: University of Michigan Press.

Powers, William K. 1990. Comment on the politics of orthography. Letter to the editor. *American Anthropology* 92:496–498.

Powlison, Paul S. 1968. Bases for formulating an efficient orthography. *The Bible Translator* 19(2):74–91.

Roberts, David. 2008. Thirty years of orthography testing in West African languages (1977–2007). *Journal of West African Languages* XXXV(1–2):199–242.

Roberts, David. 2011. Autosegmental and pedagogical considerations in preparation for a tone orthography experiment in Kabiye. *Journal of West African Languages* XXXVIII(2):87–106.

Savage, Andrew. 2008. Writing Tuareg: The three script options. *International Journal of the Sociology of Language* 192:5–14.

Schroeder, Leila. 2010. *Bantu orthography manual.* Rev. ed. SIL eBooks 9. Dallas: SIL International. http://www.sil.org/silepubs/Pubs/52716/52716_BantuOrthographyManual.pdf (accessed November 23, 2012).

SIL International. 1965–2001. *Notes on Literacy.* LinguaLinks Library. Version 5.0. Dallas: SIL International. http://www.ethnologue.com/LL_docs/show_contents.asp?bookshelf=Literacy (accessed November 23, 2012).

Simons, Gary F. 1977. Principles of multidialectal orthography design. In R. Loving and Gary Simons (eds.), *Workpapers in Papua New Guinea Languages* 21:325–342. Ukarumpa, Papua New Guinea: Summer Institute of Linguistics.

Smalley, William A. et al. 1963. Orthography studies: Articles on new writing systems. *Helps for Translators* 6. London: United Bible Societies.

Tadadjeu, Maurice, and Etienne Sadembouo. 1984. *General alphabet of Cameroon languages. Bilingual version.* Propelca 1. Yaoundé: University of Yaoundé.

Unseth, Peter (ed.). 2008. The sociolinguistics of script choice. *International Journal of the Sociology of Language* 192.

Waters, Glenys. 1998. *Local literacies: Theory and practice.* Dallas: Summer Institute of Linguistics.

3

Orthography and Phonological Depth

Keith Snider

The debate as to which level of phonological depth should be represented orthographically seems to be locked into phonological theories that predate the 1970s. Typically, only two options receive serious consideration: the classical phoneme (shallow orthography) and the morphophoneme (deep orthography). Consistently representing either form is problematic, however, and this paper demonstrates why neither approach can be recommended as a general strategy. Stratal approaches to phonology, however, with claims that native speakers are more aware of the output of the lexical phonology than of any other phonological level, offer a worthy third alternative. Employing examples of morphophonemic alternations from a number of different languages, this paper demonstrates that regardless of whether the preferred orthographic representation is phonemic or morphophonemic, the level that works best from a practical viewpoint is consistently the output of the lexical phonology.

3.1 Introduction*

It has long been established (e.g., Sapir 1933, 1949; Pike 1947a) that orthographies that represent surface/phonetic forms do not serve their language communities well. Over the years, however, there has been debate in the orthography literature concerning the relative merits of representing morphophonemic/underlying forms (e.g., Chomsky and Halle 1968; Newman 1968; Venezky 1970) as opposed to phonemic forms (e.g., Sapir 1933, 1949; Pike 1947a; Nida 1954; Gudschinsky 1958, 1970, 1973). Although a strong advocate of phonemic orthographies, Gudschinsky nevertheless recognized the need to be practical in these matters. Commenting on this issue, she concludes:

> A useful rule of thumb would seem to be: when morphological distinctions which are important in the language are obscured by limitations on the distribution of phonemes—leading to neutralization of contrasts—the practical orthography should in general symbolize the underlying form of the morphemes rather than the phonemic form that is actually pronounced. (Gudschinsky 1972:22)

While recognizing the need for practical orthographies to represent morphophonemic forms at times, Gudschinsky clearly did not have a principled basis for when it should or should not be done, and instead relied on common sense.

More recently, this same debate has largely continued, albeit under the nomenclature of "deep" versus "shallow" orthographies (e.g., Liberman et al. 1980; Katz and Feldman 1983; Frost, Katz, and Bentin 1987; Katz and Frost 1992), with "deep" corresponding to different modifications of "morphophonemic/underlying" and "shallow" corresponding to different modifications of "phonemic." Although these two approaches are rooted in very different theoretical camps, the proponents of both—and for that matter, the developers of most sound-based orthographies—have a deep desire for orthographies to represent sounds the way native speakers perceive them to sound, i.e., a claim to some degree of "psychological reality." This is reflected in some of the titles of the early works, such as "The psychological

*I am grateful to the following individuals for discussions relating to the topic of this paper and/or comments on it: Larin Adams, Mike Cahill, Elke Karan, Matthew Dryer, Steve Marlett, Keren Rice, Dave Roberts, Jim Roberts, and David Weber. Although the paper has benefited greatly from this help, none of the above can be held responsible for whatever shortcomings remain.

reality of phonemes" (Sapir 1949) and "The reality of morphophonemes" (Newman 1968). However, consistently representing either the underlying form or the phonemic form is problematic, and neither approach can be recommended as a good overall strategy.

One thing I find striking is that few proposals that deal with orthographic depth issues today take advantage of developments in phonological theory more recent than Chomsky and Halle 1968. The theory of Lexical Phonology (Mohanan 1982, 1986), however, together with its evolution into Stratal Optimality Theory (hereafter Stratal OT) (Kiparsky 1998, 2000; Bermúdez-Otero, in preparation), offers a worthy third alternative. Proponents of Lexical Phonology/Stratal OT also claim psychological reality with the notion that native speakers are psychologically more aware of the output of the lexical phonology than of any other phonological level (Mohanan 1982). Close examination of the crucial data in Sapir (1949) and Newman (1968), which respectively support representing phonemes and morphophonemes orthographically, reveals in both cases that they would also be the output of the lexical phonology. Accordingly, §3.2 of this paper examines why native speakers should be more aware of the output of this level.

With respect to overall orthography design strategies, what works in one situation is not necessarily a reliable indicator of good strategy. For example, while most would agree that the English orthography works (actually quite well), most would also agree that many aspects of it are much less than ideal. A similar case can be made with respect to the ancient logographic orthography used in China. On the other hand, what does not work, especially for writers, is often a better indicator of what to avoid.[1] Accordingly, §3.3 focuses on things that don't work and concludes that regardless of whether a given orthographic representation is phonemic or morphophonemic/underlying, what works best from a practical viewpoint is an orthography that consistently represents the output of the lexical level

[1] Given the many irregularities of the English orthography (e.g., /f/ represented by graphemes <f, ph, gh> in *fun, phonology,* and *rough*) and the many characters (over 50,000) of the ancient Chinese orthography, the fact that so many people can read so well in these languages demonstrates rather clearly that motivated readers can probably learn to read well with almost any type of orthography, providing ambiguity between lexemes is kept to a minimum. What is really at stake, therefore, when designing an orthography, is designing one that poses as few problems as possible for writers, especially for societies where the motivation for literacy may not be as high as it is in English and Chinese.

of Lexical Phonology/Stratal OT. We can call this the Lexical Orthography Hypothesis (hereafter LOH).

One may, of course, be critical of Lexical Phonology and Stratal OT as phonological theories,[2] and therefore by extension the LOH, but if so, the question then arises to what extent a different theory might better inform orthography depth issues. As this paper demonstrates, neither the classical phoneme of structuralism nor the morphophoneme of generative phonology, including standard Optimality Theory and other theories rooted in generative theory, is adequate. At this point in time, I do not believe there is a better alternative to the LOH.

3.2 Why native speakers are aware of the output of lexical processes

Postlexical processes, such as the English one that aspirates voiceless stops in different environments, often begin their "lives" as unconscious attempts on the part of native speakers to make the sounds or combinations of sounds in their languages easier to pronounce in different phonological environments. In other words, the processes have phonological conditioning, and native speakers are usually not even aware that they pronounce certain sounds differently. Thus, most English speakers are unaware of the difference between the aspirated and unaspirated *p*'s in English [pʰɪt] 'pit' and [spɪt] 'spit'.

Later, conditioning environments for some of these processes may become lost, or they become obscure due to their interactions with other processes (see Polish Vowel Raising examples below). In some cases, grammatical conditioning partially replaces phonological conditioning (see English Trisyllabic Laxing examples below). In other cases, exceptions to certain postlexical processes begin to creep in for various reasons. Some phonological processes begin to lack complete phonetic motivation, other processes apply only when certain grammatical conditions are met, and still others apply idiosyncratically for undetermined reasons. As a result, contrasts emerge between those lexical forms that undergo the processes and those forms that do not. As native speakers become aware of these

[2] Since the present work is concerned with the application of insights inherent in the Lexical Phonology and Stratal OT theories, I have elected to forego presenting the formal apparatus of these models in the interests of space. The interested reader is instead directed to the relevant references presented above.

contrasts, the forms that undergo the processes become lexicalized in their minds and the processes themselves become lexical processes (see Hyman 1976; Zec 1993; Kiparsky 1995).

Whereas native speakers are relatively unaware of the output of postlexical processes, they are much more aware of the output of lexical ones, and this explains why native speakers often prefer to write words as they are realized after they have undergone lexical processes and before they have undergone postlexical ones (Mohanan 1982, 1986). The output of the lexical phonology, whether that of the rule-based Lexical Phonology or that of the constraint-based Stratal OT, therefore promises to be an excellent level of representation upon which to base an orthography. The following paragraphs describe three kinds of lexicalization processes.

3.2.1 Lexicalization due to loss of phonetic conditioning

Some phonological processes are lexical due to their interaction with one or more other processes. For example, Kenstowicz (1994:75ff., 198) describes a lexical process in Polish whereby /o/ is raised to [u] when it precedes a word-final non-nasal consonant that is underlyingly [+voice]. In other environments, there is phonemic contrast between /u/ and /o/. Example (1) demonstrates the contrast between /u/ and /o/.[3]

(1) Contrast between /u/ and /o/ in Polish

UF	Singular	Plural	Gloss
/u/	šum	šum-i	'noise'
	trup	trup-i	'corpse'
/o/	dom	dom-i	'house'
	sok	sok-i	'juice'

There is also a postlexical process that devoices non-sonorant consonants word finally, as shown in example (2).

[3] The following abbreviations are used in this paper: ATR Advanced Tongue Root; GEN Genitive; N Noun; NOM Nominative; SG Singular; PL Plural; UF Underlying Form.

(2) Non-sonorant consonants devoiced word finally

	UF	Singular	Plural	Gloss
Non-sonorant	/trud/	trut	trud-i	'labor'
	/wug/	wuk	wug-i	'lye'
	/gruz/	grus	gruz-i	'rubble'
Sonorant	/šum/	šum	šum-i	'noise'
	/žur/	žur	žur-i	'soup'

We know that these consonants that are realized as [+voice] intervocalically are not voiceless underlyingly because they contrast in their plural forms with underlyingly voiceless consonants, like those in example (3).

(3) Plural forms with underlyingly voiceless consonants

UF	Singular	Plural	Gloss
/trup/	trup	trup-i	'corpse'
/wuk/	wuk	wuk-i	'bow'

Finally, we see in example (4) that /o/ is raised to [u] when it precedes a word-final non-nasal consonant that is underlyingly [+voice].

(4) Polish vowel raising

UF	Singular	Plural	Gloss
/bor/	bur	bor-i	'forest'
/vow/	vuw	vow-i	'ox'
/lod/	lut	lod-i	'ice'
/voz/	vus	voz-i	'cart'

We know that in order for the raising to occur, the consonant that follows the vowel must be underlyingly [+voice] because in the examples in (5), raising does not occur when the vowel is followed by a consonant that is underlyingly [–voice]. It is evident that the word-final consonants in the singular forms are underlyingly voiceless because they are voiceless in the plural forms.

(5) Vowels not raised before underlyingly voiceless consonants

UF	Singular	Plural	Gloss
/kot/	kot	kot-i	'cat'
/sok/	sok	sok-i	'juice'
/nos/	nos	nos-i	'nose'

We also know that in order for the raising to occur, the consonant that follows the vowel must be non-nasal because in the examples in (6), raising does not occur when the vowel is followed by a nasal consonant.

(6) Vowels not raised before nasal consonants

UF	Singular	Plural	Gloss
/dom/	dom	dom-i	'house'
/dzvon/	dzvon	dzvon-i	'bell'

In example (4), /o/ is raised to [u] in the singular forms for 'ice' and 'cart' because the non-nasal consonant that follows the vowel is underlyingly [+voice] and word final. It can further be seen in these same forms that the underlying /d/ and /z/ of 'ice' and 'cart' are respectively devoiced to [t] and [s] also because they are word final. The result of this interaction is that the output of devoicing obscures the underlying voicing environment that triggers vowel raising. This, in turn, results in surface contrasts between [u] and [o] in words like *lut* 'ice' and *vus* 'cart' in example (4) and *kot* 'cat' and *nos* 'nose' in example (5), even though the underlying vowels in these four words are identical, namely /o/. Contrasts like these cause native Polish speakers to be more aware of the output of vowel raising. In other words, the process is lexicalized.

This is, then, an example of a phonological process in which the conditioning environment has been obscured as a result of its interactions with another process. In this case, word-final non-sonorant consonant devoicing obscures the environment that conditions vowel raising.

3.2.2 Lexicalization due to grammatical conditioning

For some lexical processes, the environment that triggers the process requires that certain grammatical prerequisites be met (Pike 1947b). In many cases, the environment that triggers the process is created by morphemes adjacent to the morpheme that undergoes the process. In other cases, the situation is more complicated. Regardless of how phonological processes acquire grammatical conditioning, sounds that result from such processes often contrast in identical or analogous phonological environments with sounds that have not undergone these processes. Contrasts like these raise awareness in the minds of native speakers of the processes in question.

Consider Trisyllabic Laxing (TSL) in English, which shortens and laxes a long vowel when it is followed by two syllables, the first of which is unaccented. In example (7) one can compare the short, lax vowels of the forms on the right of each example with their long, tense counterparts on the left (examples from Kenstowicz 1994:196, 197).

(7) English Trisyllabic Laxing

a. *-ity* suffix

divīne	[a^j]	divĭn-ity	[ɪ]
serēne	[i^j]	serĕn-ity	[ɛ]
profāne	[e^j]	profăn-ity	[æ]

b. *-ify* suffix

vīle	[a^j]	vĭl-ify	[ɪ]
clēar	[i^j]	clăr-ify	[ɛ]

c. *-ual* suffix

rīte	[a^j]	rĭt-ual	[ɪ]
grāde	[e^j]	grăd-ual	[æ]

d. *-ous* suffix

tȳrant	[a^j]	ty̆rann-ous	[ɪ]
fāble	[e^j]	făbul-ous	[æ]

This purely phonological description is not adequate, however, because the process is conditioned only by the addition of a suffix. Compare the examples in (7) with those in (8), drawn from Kenstowicz 1994:197.

(8) No suffix, no TSL

nīghtingale	[a^j]
stēvedore	[i^j]
īvory	[a^j]

As will be noticed, all of the examples in (7), which undergo TSL, take suffixes, whereas those in (8), which do not undergo TSL, do not take suffixes, even though the latter otherwise satisfy the conditions for TSL. From these examples, one can see that the output of TSL results in surface contrasts between forms that undergo the process and forms that do not, and these contrasts help native speakers of English to be more aware of the TSL outputs. In this case, grammatical conditioning has partially replaced phonological conditioning

3.2.3 Lexicalization due to exceptions

As described in §3.2.1 in connection with Polish vowel raising, occasionally the phonetic environment of a phonological process becomes obscure due to interactions with other phonological processes or due to historical changes. As a result, one occasionally needs to recognize certain processes as not applying to certain morphemes or to certain classes of morphemes. These are idiosyncratic exceptions in the case of the former and categorical exceptions in the case of the latter. For example, with regard to English TSL discussed above, although the process is triggered by the *-ity* suffix, as shown in (9) for no obvious reason it does not apply to *obēse, obēs-ity,* even though this word meets both the phonological and grammatical conditions of the process (cf. *serēne, serĕn-ity* from (7) above).

(9) diosyncratic exception to English TSL

obēse	[i^j]	obēs-ity	[i^j]

Similarly, while, as shown in (7), many suffixes trigger TSL (e.g., *-ity, -ify, -ual*, and *-ous*), there are also several that do not (e.g., *-ery, -ily*, and *-ing*), as shown in (10).

(10) Categorical exceptions to English TSL

brāve	[e^j]	brāv-ery	[e^j]
mīght	[a^j]	mīght-ily	[a^j]
pīrate	[a^j]	pīrat-ing	[a^j]

We can also consider the case of negative prefixes in English. As shown in (11), while the *n* of the *in-* prefix assimilates in different ways to consonants that follow it, the *n* of the *un* -prefix does not.

(11) Categorical exceptions to English Nasal Assimilation

im-potent	un-popular
in-tolerant	un-told
ir-relevant	un-rest
il-logical	un-lock

From these examples, it should be clear that lexical processes are potentially nontransparent and idiosyncratic in nature, with the result that their outputs may contrast with phonologically identical or analogous forms that do not undergo these processes. When this happens, native speakers become more aware of the processes, and the outputs of the processes become lexicalized.

3.3 Orthographic representation of morphophonemic alternations

According to the LOH, if the process or processes responsible for any given morphophonemic alternation are lexical (as the processes discussed in §3.2), one should write the phonemic form, as opposed to the morphophonemic form. However, if the process or processes responsible for the alternation are postlexical, one should write the morphophonemic form. Put another way, according to the LOH, if the process or processes responsible for any given morphophonemic alternation are lexical, orthographies that write the morphophonemic form will be dispreferred. Thus, we write *irrelevant* rather than **inrelevant*. By the same token, as shown below, if the process(es) responsible for the alternation are postlexical, orthographies that write the phonemic form will be dispreferred.

We now examine a number of different morphophonemic alternations, with a view to observing what doesn't work orthographically in different languages.

3.3.1 Failures in consistently representing underlying forms

When the output of a lexical process is phonetically similar to its underlying form, native speakers often don't seem to mind representing the underlying form, even though this goes against the predictions of the LOH. An example of this is Trisyllabic Laxing in English, discussed above. In this case, the output is not drastically different from the underlying form, and mature readers of English don't have a problem with reading the underlying form. The problem, however, with orthographically representing underlying forms that have undergone lexical processes is that underlying forms are often so abstract that native speakers are simply unable to relate them to how they perceive the language to sound.

So, when the output of a lexical process is phonetically quite different from the underlying form, native speakers seem to strongly object to representing the underlying form. A case in point from English is the negative prefix /in/ from example (11). Whereas native speakers tolerate writing forms like *serene* and *sere-nity* with the same vowel, they would undoubtedly be much less tolerant of representing the prefixal consonant of *im-possible, in-tolerant, il-logical,* and *ir-reverent* with the same consonant.

A second case in which writing the underlying form is not acceptable can be made from the Polish vowel data in examples (12) and (13), adapted from examples (1) and (4).

(12) Orthographic representation of /u/ and /o/ in Polish

UF	Phonetic	Orthographic	Gloss
/šum/	šum	szum	‘noise’
/trup/	trup	trup	‘corpse’
/dom/	dom	dom	‘house’
/sok/	sok	sok	‘juice’

In (12), we see that the Polish orthography represents nonraised /u/ and /o/, respectively as <u> and <o>. In (13), one can further see that the raised /o/, which is phonetically realized as [u], is consistently represented orthographically as <ó>.

(13) Orthographic representation of raised /o/ in Polish

UF	Phonetic	Orthographic	Gloss
/bor/	bur	bór	‘forest’
/vow/	vuw	wół	‘ox’
/lod/	lut	lód	‘ice’
/voz/	vus	vóz	‘cart’

From these data, one can see that the raised /o/ in (13) is represented differently from its non-raised counterpart in (12), and this clearly attests to the fact that native speakers of Polish are aware that they are different and that they have not accepted the underlying representation for their orthography. It is equally clear, however, that they have accepted underlying representations of those consonants that have undergone word-final devoicing, choosing to represent the final consonants of words like [lut] ‘ice’ and [vus] ‘cart’ with their underlying [+voice] counterparts. With respect to these consonants, the Polish orthography further conforms to the expectations of the LOH since the LOH predicts that native speakers will prefer underlying forms over surface forms if the process that produces the surface forms is postlexical in nature. We discuss this further below.

Finally, a third case in which representing the underlying form orthographically is not an acceptable alternative can be made from Chumburung [ncu], a Guang language spoken in Ghana (personal data). Like the English and Polish examples above, the processes responsible for the morphophonemic alternations in these Chumburung data are lexical in nature.

In Chumburung, vowel harmony exists between the vowels of stems and prefixes, the latter always harmonizing with the former with respect to the feature Advanced Tongue Root (ATR). In addition, the *-kɪ* noun class prefix harmonizes with the round specification of the stem, as shown in (14).

(14) Vowel harmony between stems and *kɪ* noun class prefix

	[–ATR]		[+ATR]	
[–round]	kɪ̀-sìbɔ́	'ear'	kí-jíʔ	'tree'
	kɪ́-kɛ́ʔ	'head pad'	kì-téʔ	'story'
	kɪ̀-pá	'hat'	kì-jéʔ	'meat'
[+round]	kʊ̀-kʊ̀tɔ̀	'claw'	kù-ɲú	'head'
	kʊ̀-kɔ́	'debt'	kú-d͡ʒó	'yam'

Round harmonization of the prefix is blocked, however, if the first consonant of the stem is labial, as shown in (15), in which case the prefix vowel is realized [–round]. The following examples are illustrative.

(15) Round harmony blocked due to intervening labial consonant

[–ATR]		[+ATR]	
kɪ́-pʊ́	'forest'	kì-bú	'stone'
kɪ̀-pɔ̀rɔ́	'mud'	kì-bòɲìrə́ŋ	'bell'
kɪ́-fʊ́rɪ̂	'rock'	kì-k͡púní	'knot'

When I began my linguistics career, I naïvely believed that a linguistically ideal orthography should represent underlying forms, and so for the Chumburung orthography, I considered the notion of having a single form (perhaps <kɪ->) represent the *kɪ-* noun class prefix. At that time I recall asking a literate but linguistically naïve Chumburung speaker what he thought of having just one form for the *kɪ-* prefix, and therefore spelling words like *kù-kùtí* 'orange' as <kɪkuti>. He was aghast, and assuming that I was having difficulty hearing the word correctly, proceeded to give me a lesson in Chumburung phonetics, explaining that they pronounced this word [kùkùtí]. Our conversation very quickly revealed that this person was totally unaware of any connection between the four different realizations of the prefix and that any deviation from a phonemic representation in the orthography on this point would be totally unacceptable. Further testing of this with other native speakers resulted in the same conclusion, and I quickly abandoned the notion. Accordingly, the Chumburung orthography represents this prefix with four different forms that correspond to /ki-, kɪ-, ku-, kʊ-/,[4] and this has been well accepted now for over thirty years. It is also the case that these representations correspond to the output of the lexical phonology.

In each of these cases, native English, Polish, and Chumburung speakers are very aware of the outputs of the lexical processes and prefer to represent them orthographically.

3.3.2 Failures in consistently representing phonemic forms

As noted above, Pike (1947a) advocates that orthographies should represent the "phonemes" of a language. By phonemes, Pike means phonologically contrastive sounds like the [pʰ] and [b] in English *pit* and *bit*, as opposed to phonologically noncontrastive sounds like the [p] and [pʰ] in *spit* and *pit*. In the case of the former pair, the native speaker is very aware of the difference between these two sounds, while in the case of the latter pair, this awareness is lacking. Since it is generally agreed that orthographies should not represent distinctions of which the native speaker is not aware, orthographies that adhere to the "phonemic principle" in general serve their language communities well, since the principle ensures that noncontrastive sounds, the recognition of which is below the level of native awareness, are not represented in the orthography. However, while all processes that produce noncontrastive sounds are postlexical, the converse is not true. All processes that are postlexical do not necessarily produce noncontrastive sounds; there are many postlexical processes whose outputs have phonemic status. In such cases, an orthography that consists of strictly phonemic representations would not exclude, a priori, representations of postlexical outputs that have phonemic status.

[4] The actual symbols used for these vowels in the orthography are: <i, e̱, u, o̱>, respectively.

I now present examples of three postlexical processes whose outputs have phonemic status. In each case, native speakers have chosen not to represent the classical phonemic forms orthographically.

The well-known German syllable-final devoicing phenomenon, illustrated in (16), is a good example of a postlexical process in which the output of devoicing results in sounds of which the native speaker is not fully aware, but which nevertheless contrast in other environments (data from Wiese 1996:200 and Bettina Wassmer, pers. comm.). In Standard German, voiceless obstruents contrast with their voiced counterparts in all environments except syllable finally. Syllable finally, all obstruents are realized as [–voice]. Compare these examples:

(16) Syllable-final devoicing

a. Underlyingly [+voice]

Syllable final		Syllable initial		Orthographic
lo[p]	'praise (NOM)'	lo.[b]es	'praise (GEN)'	Lob, Lobes
ra[t]	'wheel (NOM)'	ra.[d]es	'wheel (GEN)'	Rad, Rades
sar[k]	'coffin (SG)'	sär.[g]e	'coffin (PL)'	Sarg, Särge
re[k].nen	'to rain'	re.[g]en	'rain (N)'	regnen, Regen
ja[k].den	'hunts (PL)'	ja.[g]en	'to hunt'	Jagden, jagen

b. Underlyingly [–voice]

Syllable final		Syllable initial		Orthographic
ra[t]	'advice (NOM)'	ra.[t]es	'advice (GEN)'	Rat, Rates
fa.bri[k]	'factory (SG)'	fa.bri.[k]en	'factory (PL)'	Fabrik, Fabriken

Despite neutralization of obstruent voicing in syllable-final positions, and despite the fact that the derived voiceless sounds are phonemic in other environments, native speakers of many German dialects have an intuitive feeling that syllable-final voiceless obstruents that are derived from voiced obstruents are different from underlyingly voiceless ones. Accordingly, this difference is reflected in the German orthography, which does not represent those phonemes that result from postlexical devoicing. Instead, the German orthography represents underlying forms in these cases.

Nawuri [naw], a Guang language spoken in Ghana, has a morphophonemic process whereby nasal consonants consistently assimilate to the place of articulation of a following consonant, as shown in (17) (data from Rod Casali, pers. comm., and personal data).

(17) Nasal place assimilation in Nawuri

m̀-bʷɛ́ʲ	ɱ̀-fɔ́	ǹ-dɔ́:ʔ	ɲ̀-jàbì	ŋ̀-kɛ́	ŋ͡m̀-g͡bìní
animals	oil	farms	branches	days	okra (PL)
m̀-pá:ʔ	ɱ̀-fí:ʔ	ń-lí	ɲ̀-t͡ʃú	ŋ̀-kɔ́lɔ́	ŋ͡m̀-k͡pá
bed	here	funerals	water	chests	life

In this case, the output of the process does not always result in a sound that has phonemic status in the language (e.g., the [ɱ] of *ɱ̀fɔ́* 'oil' and the [ŋ͡m] of *ŋ͡m̀-k͡pá* 'life' are not contrastive with the other nasal sounds), which confirms that this process is clearly postlexical. Despite the fact that the other nasal sounds do have phonemic status in the language, native speakers prefer to consistently write the nasal prefix with a single representation, namely <n>.

There is a postlexical process in Chumburung whereby vowels that are [+back/+round] spread this specification leftwards across a word boundary to the last vowel of the preceding word.

(18) Leftward [+back/+round] spreading

kòfí kɔ̀tí Kofi monkey	→	kòfú kɔ́ꜜtí 'Kofi's monkey'
ó-k͡pé kù-ŋú witch nc-head	→	ók͡pó kúꜜŋú 'witch's head'
ɔ̀-ɲárí fʊ́rí man deer	→	ɔ̀ɲárʊ́ fʊ́rí 'man's deer'

In addition, there is a second process whereby vowels that are [+ATR] spread this feature leftwards and rightwards across word boundaries to vowels that are [+high].

(19) Rightward [+ATR] spreading

kòfí kɪ́-lâŋ Kofi hip	→	kòfí kílâŋ 'Kofi's hip'
ò-jú fʊ́rí thief deer	→	òjú fúrí 'thief's deer'

(20) Leftward [+ATR] spreading and leftward [+back/+round] spreading

ɔ̀-ɲárí kɪ́-t͡ʃínî man vein	→	ɔ̀ɲárí kít͡ʃínî 'man's vein'
ɔ̀-ɲárí kʊ̀-ŋú man head	→	ɔ̀ɲárú kú꜌ŋú 'man's head'

A third process in Chumburung deletes the first of two vowels when they are brought into juxtaposition across a word boundary.

(21) Vowel coalescence

à-ɲárí à-sá man three	→	àɲár ꜌ásá 'three men'
à-ní í-dûŋ our heart	→	àn ídûŋ 'our hearts'

In each of these three languages:

1. The different processes result in sounds that have phonemic status in the language. The outputs of these processes would typically be represented in orthographies that strictly adhere to the phonemic principle.
2. Native speakers are not aware of the changes and absolutely reject any thought of representing the changes in the orthography. They prefer instead that each word have a consistent orthographic representation.
3. These processes all occur across word boundaries and are therefore clearly postlexical in nature.

3.4 Conclusion

From the foregoing, it should be clear that for any given language, (1) an orthography that represents surface phonetic forms is not ideal; (2) a strictly morphophonemic orthography will work for some data but not for all; and (3) a strictly phonemic orthography will also work for some data but not for all. By determining which phonological alternations are due to lexical processes and which to postlexical ones, the LOH offers a principled way to distinguish between those outputs that should be represented orthographically and those that should not. The outputs of those that result from lexical processes should be represented, and those that result from postlexical processes should not. A word of caution: the phonological depth issue is only one factor in orthography design that must be weighed against others. And although the LOH does offer a promising beginning point for orthography development, as with everything else in orthography design, the results it suggests must be tested thoroughly before the orthography is fully implemented.

I conclude by presenting a "layman's guide" to distinguishing between lexical and postlexical processes. This is an attempt to summarize the characteristics of these processes with a view to helping those who do not have a grasp of the theories themselves to apply the relevant insights to orthography development. In order to help discover lexical processes, that is processes that produce sounds that the native speaker is fully aware of, ask the following questions:

1. Does a given process apply across the board without exception, or are there lexical exceptions? In other words, in the same grammatical and phonological environment, do some words undergo a particular process while others do not? If there are lexical exceptions to a particular process, then it is important to spell words that undergo that process the way they sound after the process has applied. In the examples above of English TSL, not all suffixes trigger TSL (e.g., *brave/brav-ery, might/might-ily, pirate/pirat-ing*). This means that there are whole classes of lexical exceptions. Then within the class of suffixes that do trigger TSL, there are still idiosyncratic lexical exceptions (e.g., *obese/obes-ity*). This means that the TSL process results in changes that the native speaker perceives.
2. Does a given process lack phonetic motivation? For most processes, there is a phonetic reason why its output sounds the way it does. For example, sounds often assimilate to certain qualities of other sounds. However, if a particular phonological process does not have significant phonetic motivation, native speakers will be more aware of its output,

with the result that one should then spell the word the way it sounds after the process has applied.

3. When a given process applies, does it apply only when a prefix or suffix is added? In other words, does the process have to apply across a morpheme boundary? (Note that we are not talking about a word boundary.) If the process must apply across a morpheme boundary, then the word should be spelled the way it sounds after the process has applied. Again looking at the English TSL example, we see that specification of the environment of the change in purely phonological terms is not adequate. Forms like *nightingale, stevedore,* and *ivory* do not shorten the initial vowel. The change is conditioned only by the addition of a suffix. Since the process is conditioned by a suffix and does not otherwise apply, this tells us that the native speaker will be more aware of the change that the process produces. Hence we should spell these words with the changes.

In order to help discover postlexical processes, that is processes that produce sounds that the native speaker is not fully aware of, ask these questions:

1. When a given process applies, is the new sound it produces one of the contrastive sounds in the language? If the output of the process is not a phoneme, then the word should be spelled the way it sounds before the process has applied. In the Nawuri nasal assimilation process discussed above, the sound [ɱ] is not a phoneme in the language, and so it should not be written with the change because native speakers are not aware of the noncontrastive sounds in their language.
2. When a given process has applied, do native speakers demonstrate a lack of awareness of the output of the process? In other words, do most speakers not realize that anything has changed unless the change is pointed out to them? If native speakers demonstrate unawareness of a process's application, then the word should be spelled the way it sounds before the process has applied.
3. When a given process applies, does it apply across word boundaries? (Note that we are not talking about morpheme boundaries.) If the process applies across word boundaries, then the word should be spelled the way it sounds before the process has applied. A good result of this is

that the word-image does not change even though the word may be pronounced differently when in the context of other words. For examples of this, recall the vocalic processes in Chumburung, discussed above, that occur across word boundaries. Native speakers are not at all aware that they are saying these words differently from how they say them in other contexts. So one should write words the way native speakers perceive them to sound, to the extent that it is possible to determine this, as opposed to the way they actually pronounce them.

Applying these criteria helps to establish the identity of words and, therefore, by extension, where word breaks occur (for more on word boundaries, see Kutsch Lojenga this volume).[5] It eliminates the representation of low-level allophonic variation and also the effect of processes that apply across word boundaries. It further eliminates the effects of phrase-initial and phrase-final phenomena. This allows one to (1) maintain a constant word image and thereby meet the needs of mature readers and (2) write words the way native speakers perceive them to sound and thereby meet the needs of beginning readers.

References

Bermúdez-Otero, Ricardo. In preparation. *Stratal Optimality Theory.* Oxford Studies in Theoretical Linguistics. Oxford: Oxford University Press.

Chomsky, Noam, and Morris Halle. 1968. *The sound pattern of English.* New York: Harper and Row.

Frost, Ram, Leonard Katz, and Shlomo Bentin. 1987. Strategies for visual word recognition and orthographical depth: A multilingual comparison. *Journal of Experimental Psychology: Human Perception and Performance* 13:104–115.

Gudschinsky, Sarah C. 1958. Native reactions to tones and words in Mazatec. *Word* 14:338–345.

Gudschinsky, Sarah C. 1970. More on formulating efficient orthographies. *The Bible Translator* 21(1):21–25.

Gudschinsky, Sarah C. 1972. Notes on neutralization and orthography. *Notes on Literacy* 14:21–22.

[5] Only those criteria which do not make crucial reference to word boundaries are useful in determining where word breaks occur. Otherwise, this is a circular argument.

Gudschinsky, Sarah C. 1973. *A manual of literacy for preliterate peoples.* Ukarumpa, Papua New Guinea: Summer Institute of Linguistics.

Hyman, Larry M. 1976. Phonologization. In A. Juilland (ed.), *Linguistic studies presented to Joseph H. Greenberg,* 407–418. Saratoga: Anma Libri.

Katz, Leonard, and Laurie B. Feldman. 1983. Relation between pronunciation and recognition of printed words in deep and shallow orthographies. *Journal of Experimental Psychology: Learning, Memory, and Cognition* 9:157–166.

Katz, Leonard, and Ram Frost. 1992. The reading process is different for different orthographies: The orthographic depth hypothesis. In Ram Frost and Leonard Katz (eds.), *Orthography, phonology, morphology, and meaning,* 67–84. Amsterdam: Elsevier Science Publishers B.V.

Kenstowicz, Michael. 1994. *Phonology in Generative Grammar.* Oxford: Blackwell Publishers Ltd.

Kiparsky, Paul. 1995. The phonological basis of sound change. In John A. Goldsmith (ed.), *The handbook of phonological theory,* 640–670. Oxford: Blackwell Publishers Ltd.

Kiparsky, Paul. 1998. Paradigm effects and opacity. Ms., Stanford University.

Kiparsky, Paul. 2000. Opacity and cyclicity. *The Linguistic Review* 17:351–367.

Liberman, I. Y., A. M. Liberman, I. G. Mattingly, and D. L. Shankweiler. 1980. Orthography and the beginning reader. In J. F. Kavanagh and R. L. Venezky (eds.), *Orthography, reading and dyslexia,* 137–153. Baltimore: University Park Press.

Lombardi, Linda. 1999. Positional faithfulness and voicing assimilation in Optimality Theory. *Natural Language and Linguistic Theory* 17:267–302.

Mohanan, K. P. 1982. Lexical phonology. Ph. D. dissertation. MIT (Mass.).

Mohanan. K. P. 1986. *The theory of Lexical Phonology.* Dordrecht, the Netherlands: Reidel.

Newman, Paul. 1968. The reality of morphophonemes. *Language* 44(3):507–515.

Nida, Eugene A. 1954. Practical limitations to a phonemic alphabet. *The Bible Translator* 15:35–39, 58–62.

Pike, Kenneth L. 1947a. *Phonemics: A technique for reducing languages to writing.* Ann Arbor: The University of Michigan Press.

Pike, Kenneth L. 1947b. Grammatical prerequisites to phonemic analysis. *Word* 3:155–172.

Sapir, Edward. 1933. La réalité psychologique des phonèmes. *Journal de Psychologie et Pathologique* 30:247–265.

Sapir, Edward. 1949. The psychological reality of phonemes. In David Mandelbaum (ed.), *Selected writings of Edward Sapir,* 46–60. Berkeley: University of California Press.

Venezky, Richard L. 1970. Principles for the design of practical writing systems. *Anthropological Linguistics* 12:256–270.

Wiese, Richard. 1996. *The phonology of German.* Oxford: Clarendon Press. Quoted in Lombardi 1999, 273.

Zec, Draga. 1993. Rule domains and phonological change. In S. Hargus and E. Kaisse (eds.), *Studies in Lexical Phonology,* 365–405. San Diego: Academic Press.

4

Orthography and Tone

A Tone-System Typology with Implications for Orthography Development

Constance Kutsch Lojenga

The majority of the world's languages are tone languages. Words consist of consonants, vowels, and tonal melodies, each of which may serve to indicate minimal distinctions, both in the lexicon and in the grammar. Many existing orthographies of tone languages have no system for marking tone, which may result in serious ambiguities for the reader. This paper describes various ways in which tone can be marked in an orthography. Following that, it focuses on two main types of languages: those with "stable" tone and those in which tones change according to the tonal context. In languages of the first type, tone generally has a heavy functional load, both lexically and grammatically. For these languages, writing tone on every syllable is possible and straightforward. In languages of the second type, that is languages with tonal sandhi rules, it is most important that grammatical distinctions are differentiated by tone marking. Various ways of representing grammatical tone distinctions in an orthography are presented. Each tone-orthography system needs its own specific approach for teaching. The paper is written against the background of African tone languages, where the experience of the author lies. She has published two related articles, one on the topic of tone orthography (Kutsch Lojenga 1986) and one on creating lessons for teaching the reading of tone (Kutsch Lojenga 1993).

4.1 Introduction*

Designing a tone orthography and subsequently creating lessons to teach people to read the tone marking decided upon is not an easy matter. This paper aims to give the background for the first practical decision, namely that of marking the various contrastive tone levels or designing a system in which certain grammatical tone contrasts are marked, based on a major typological subdivision of African tone languages into two main categories.

Following a general introduction on tone languages and tone orthography, I present various ways in which tone can be marked in an orthography. I then introduce a typological division which can be made in African tone languages: those with "stable" tone (where tones are generally not affected by the tones of surrounding syllables) and those with "movable" tone (where tones may move or change according to the tonal context). In languages of the first type, tone generally has a heavy functional load, both lexically and grammatically. In these languages, writing tone on every syllable is possible, straightforward, and important to help the reader disambiguate minimal tone distinctions. In languages of the second type, that is languages with tonal sandhi rules, tone often has a contrastive function particularly in the grammar, so it is most important for the reader that grammatical distinctions are differentiated by tone marking. For this type of languages, a different approach is suggested for representing tone in the orthography. Each tone-orthography system needs its own specific approach for teaching.

4.2 Tone languages

The majority of the world's languages are so-called tone languages. The major concentrations of tone languages are found in Africa, Southeast Asia,

*Unless otherwise indicated, all data presented in this paper is from the author's own fieldwork in Africa.

and Latin America. My own experience lies in Africa where most languages spoken south of the Sahara are tone languages. Words consist of consonants, vowels, and tonal melodies, each of which may serve to indicate minimal distinctions, both in the lexicon and in the grammar of the language.

The language situation in Africa is such that each country has an "official" language, in many cases the language of the former colonial power. In addition, there are many languages of wider communication (LWCs)—e.g., Hausa [hau], Swahili [swa], Lingala [lin], Sango [sag], and Dioula [dgd]—which have had writing systems for many decades. Except for Sango, which officially has some diacritic marking for minimal tone distinctions, tonal LWCs have no tone marking in their orthographies. Many people have learned to read either in the official language or in one of the LWCs.

Writing systems for a number of bigger vernacular languages were developed many years ago. Quite a few of these underrepresent for vowels (vowel quality and/or length) and tone and sometimes also for consonants that are not found in the alphabet of the colonial language or the LWC. Some exceptions are the vowels <ɛ> and <ɔ>, the velar nasal <ŋ>, and sometimes the implosives <ɓ> and <ɗ>. These letters were drawn from the International Phonetic Alphabet and formed part of the Africa Alphabet, introduced by the International African Institute in 1928. No attempts were made to represent tone where it had a contrastive function. In fact there has been much resistance to representing tone in the orthography by literate native speakers and outside linguistic experts alike, for several reasons:

1. It is a feature not found in English, French, Portuguese, and Spanish—the present-day official and former colonial languages of many African countries.
2. It is certainly not an easy matter to analyze the tone system of a language in preparation for developing a tone orthography.
3. Most people, both native speakers involved in language development and outside linguists unfamiliar with the discipline of orthography design, have had a natural supposition that an orthography which *looks* more difficult, such as one with many diacritic signs, is automatically harder to read.

In actual fact, tone is an important feature that is often neglected in orthography design, probably because consonants and vowels appear more "concrete" to many people. Certainly in the past, everything was done to avoid marking tone in a practical orthography, with the justification that "the context will make it clear to the reader." Not marking tone in the orthography of a language in which tone has a heavy functional load has often resulted in serious ambiguities for the reader, in such a way that speakers of tone languages have stumbled when reading texts, often having to go back to the beginning of a sentence in order to try to read with meaning. This has had a discouraging effect, with the result that many have abandoned reading in their native languages. Something that has to be investigated is to what extent readers of a tone language rely on tonal cues compared to consonantal and vocalic cues. In light of the fact that there are quite a few tone languages which also use "talking drums" or "whistled speech" (Cowan 1948:280) to communicate by tonal melodies alone, without the support of consonants and vowels, it may well turn out that the tonal cues are of greater importance than the segmental cues.

With the development of studies in the tonal structure of languages, we are getting more insight in tone systems in general, and in the details of tone systems of particular languages. This knowledge should give a better background for developing adequate tone orthographies. At the same time, experiments and experience in teaching to read and write tone confirm which system works best in which practical circumstances.

Tone orthography, therefore, does not stand by itself. A prerequisite for making decisions for an adequate tone orthography is an analysis of the tone system. At the same time, a tone orthography needs to be accompanied by a well thought-through methodology for awareness raising of tonal contrasts and for teaching people to read with the symbols chosen to mark tone in a language.

Even though the topics of tone analysis and methodology for tone teaching are outside the scope of this paper, I briefly mention here what I consider to be analytical prerequisites for developing an adequate tone orthography. The following areas must be carefully analyzed:

1. the tone system: the number of contrastive level tones of the language, the presence or absence of distinctive rising and/or falling tones, and the tonal melodies belonging to the basic lexical morphemes of nouns and verbs (or their roots);

2. tonal processes: the presence or absence of commonly found tonal processes such as H-spreading, H-shifting, downdrift, downstep, polar tones, and the effects of depressor consonants; and
3. the functional load of tone: a heavier or lighter functional load according to the frequency with which tone is used to make minimal contrasts of meaning in the lexicon and/or in the grammar.

The contrastive function of tone in the *lexicon* is exemplified by the following minimal sets in example (1) from Yaka [axk] and in example (2) Lendu [led]. Yaka is a two-tone language; Lendu is a language with three level tones and a rising tone.

(1) Yaka [axk] (Bantu C.10; Central African Republic)

mbókà	'village'
mbòká	'fields'
mbóká	'civet cat'

(2) Lendu [led] (Nilo-Saharan, Central-Sudanic; D.R.Congo)

ɓú	'canoe'
ɓū	'tribe'
ɓù	'hole'
ɓǔ	'eagle'

The contrastive function of tone in the *grammar* is shown in example (3) from Alur [alz], where every verb (mono-, di-, or trisyllabic) has four inflectional paradigms which contrast by tone alone, using sequences of High, Low, and downstep.

(3) Alur [alz] (Nilo-Saharan, Western Nilotic; D.R.Congo/Uganda)

à-mákʊ̀	'I have taken'
à-máꜜkʊ́	'I habitually take'
á-màkʊ̀	'I will take'
á-ꜜmáꜜkʊ́	'I am taking'

The contrastive function of tone is often visible in the verb system, but there are many other areas in the grammar where tone may display a contrastive function, such as plurality, case, and gender, as well as in locatives and pronouns.

4.3 Tone orthography

Several systems have been used over time and in different parts of the world to represent tone according to the "phonemic principle"—that is, a one-to-one match between the symbol and the toneme—namely:

- accents
- punctuation marks
- numbers
- unused consonant letters.

I will exemplify in §4.3.1 and §4.3.2 the first two of these strategies (namely accents and punctuation marks) as used to represent contrastive lexical tones—that is, the symbols chosen are pitch related. However, any one of these strategies could also be used to mark grammatical contrasts, as will be seen after the discussion about the typology of African tone systems. The difference is, however, of crucial importance for the teaching methodology.

For completeness' sake, I will also describe what has been done in some countries, mostly outside Africa: in §4.3.3, the use of numbers to indicate tone in Mexico, and in §4.3.4, the use of some letters that are not otherwise used in the alphabet to mark tone in some languages of Southeast Asia.

4.3.1 Accents

A frequent way of marking tone is to use accent marks, roughly as used in the IPA. This is shown in example (4).

(4) Tone marked with accents

acute accent	á	é	ɛ́	í	ó	ɔ́	ú	High tone
grave accent	à	è	ɛ̀	ì	ò	ɔ̀	ù	Low tone
wedge	ǎ	ě	ɛ̌	ǐ	ǒ	ɔ̌	ǔ	rising tone
circumflex	â	ê	ɛ̂	î	ô	ɔ̂	û	falling tone

Experience has shown that particularly in francophone countries in Africa, native speakers may suggest using accents when they realize that tone has a distinctive function.

In a two-tone system, either the Low or the High tone can be left without accent. Most frequently, in such languages, the High tone is marked by an accent and the Low is marked by the absence of an accent; however, the opposite is equally possible. In three-tone languages, generally the Mid tone is marked by the absence of an accent.

Occasionally, different accents are used. For example, the circumflex may be used for High tone, as is done in Yaka, where the choice of tone marks had to conform to the system used in the widely known lingua franca Sango. It may not look elegant for a linguist or a teacher, but it works.

In Avokaya [avu] (Central Sudanic, Sudan/D.R.Congo), a three-tone language, the tilde was chosen for Low tone (Kilpatrick 2004:91)—as a mnemonic device to make the people think of a snake crawling on the ground. The tilde is indeed quite different from the acute accent, which is used for High tone—more so than a grave accent would be—which is probably advantageous for reading. The tilde for Low tone (as in <ã>) is also used in several other Central-Sudanic languages in northern Uganda and southern Sudan.

If a language does not have contrastively long vowels, contour tones may be represented by doubling the vowel and marking each part of the contour tone on one vowel, as shown in example (5). Thus, instead of writing <â> or <ǎ>, one could represent these contour tones in the orthography as <áa> or <aá>. The vowel with the contour tone is still short; the writing with two vowels is simply an orthographic device in order to avoid the extra accents.

(5) Contour tones marked by vowel doubling[1]

aá	LH	in a 2-tone language
áa	HL	

This solution has at times been suggested by native speakers of a language, since they hear the two parts of the contour tone and seem to perceive the contour tone as long. It has been successfully implemented in Yaka. Example (6) gives two sentences from a reading booklet in Yaka, which has two tone levels: High, marked by a circumflex, and Low, unmarked. Rising tones are marked by a doubling of the vowel (since the language does not have contrastively long vowels), with a High-tone symbol on the second vowel: <aâ> = /ǎ/; falling tones are similarly written on two-vowel symbols: <âa> = /â/.

(6) Yaka [axk] (Bantu C.10; Central African Republic)

a. dzûlulû dzâkûâ mû dzabuka
spider 3SG-fall in cassava
'The spider falls into the cassava.'

b. Ndzêmbi adzɛ̂ɛ mû ndzaâ ya mbokâ
Ndzembi 3SG-be in road of field
'Ndzembi is on the road to the field.'

The accents are normally placed on the nucleus of the syllable, which in most cases is a vowel. However, there may also be syllabic consonants which need tone marking in the orthography, as is the case in Lyélé [lee], shown in example (7), where the 2SG and 3SG pronouns consist of a syllabic nasal and are differentiated by tone alone, or in Lendu, shown in example (8), which has vowelless syllables whose nuclei orthographically consist of a continuation of the onset consonant or of the last part of the initial consonant cluster.[2]

[1] The following abbreviations are used in this paper: H High tone; L Low tone; M Mid tone; O Object; S Subject; SG singular; V Verb; xH Extra-High tone; xL Extra-Low tone. Note on tone marking: LH (without a period) indicates a Low-High contour tone on one syllable while L.H (with a period) indicates a sequence of Low and High tones on two successive syllables.

[2] For an explanation of these unusual syllable and word structures, see Kutsch Lojenga 1989.

(7) Lyélé [lee] (Niger-Congo, Gur; Burkina Faso)

ń	2sg: 'you, your'
ǹ	3sg: 'he/she, his/her'

(8) Lendu [led] (Nilo-Saharan, Central-Sudanic; D.R.Congo)

zz̀	'stomach' (L)
sśss̀	'bow' (H.L)
ndrr̀	'goat' (L)
tss̀tss	'banana' (L.M)

A system of marking tone by accents can be used for any type of language, for both long and short words. It is somewhat limited in the number of levels it can handle, unless one introduces double acute accents, as in <ő>, and double grave accents, as in <ȍ>, for extra-High and extra-Low tones. As mentioned, using accents for marking tone has been readily accepted in countries where French is the official language, since three of the four basic diacritics are used in the French orthography, albeit with a different function.

4.3.2 Punctuation marks

Punctuation marks preceding and/or following the word may be used for marking tone in the orthography as follows: level tones are indicated by a punctuation mark preceding the syllable, and combinations of these punctuation marks on both sides of a monosyllabic word can be used for contour tones, rising and falling. This system was first introduced by Bolli (1978) and later applied to other languages in Côte d'Ivoire, such as Attié [ati], which has four contrastive tone levels. The system for indicating tone by means of punctuation marks is shown in example (9).

(9) Tone marked by means of punctuation marks

“na	xH	-na'	LH rising
'na	H	na'	MH rising
na	M	“na-	xHL falling
-na	L	'na-	HL falling
= na	xL	na-	ML falling

Even though this system may look a bit unusual, there are several advantages in using punctuation marks to indicate tone:

1. the punctuation marks are more distinctive from each other than the accents, which is easier for the learner;
2. this system is very useful for languages with more than three tone levels (the complete set can handle five levels, which is, in fact, the maximum number of contrastive tones found in African tone languages); and
3. different rising and falling tones can be represented by combinations of the level-tone symbols, one preceding and one following the word.

A disadvantage of using punctuation marks is that this system is really only useful for highly monosyllabic languages, which are, in fact, the languages that tend to have more tone levels. If applied rigidly, this method would break up polysyllabic words. In a language with predominantly monosyllabic words and relatively few polysyllabic words (often compounds), a solution would be to use this system as presented with the monosyllabic words, and to mark only the first syllable of any polysyllabic words. This system is obviously not useful for a language with many polysyllabic roots and for agglutinative languages, since it would not be advisable to break up words into syllables with tone markings in between.

4.3.3 Numbers

Superscript numbers were used following each syllable in Latin-American languages for a time, both for tone analysis and for orthographic purposes, with very limited success. The use of numbers to mark tone in languages in Mexico has not produced good reading results on a wide scale, so much so that in some languages, people have changed to using accents rather than numbers. In Africa, such superscript numbers are sometimes used for tone analysis—but not for tone orthography—particularly for languages with more than three tone levels. Sometimes the superscript number [1] is used for the highest tone and sometimes for the lowest tone.

4.3.4 Unused consonant letters

Unused consonant letters have sometimes been suggested for marking tone, either systematically for one particular tone, or for a particular incidental tone contrast. Any attempt to use letters like <q, x, c, h> at the end of a syllable to mark tone consistently in African languages has, to my knowledge, met with fairly strong opposition and dislike on the part of the native speakers. Since Africa counts many people who have become literate in a LWC such as Swahili, or an official language like French or English, most people already attach a certain sound value to these consonants and find it, therefore, impossible to start relating such symbols to pitch.

In addition, such a system would distort the basic syllable shapes of the language. For example, if a language has only open syllables, writing a <q, x, c, h> at the end of the syllable would make it visually look like a language with closed syllables. It would cause even more complications in languages with closed syllables, creating strange-looking consonant clusters.

4.4 A typology of African tone systems

From my experience with tone languages of all major language families in many countries on the African continent, I propose a broad typological division of African tone languages into two main types, with major repercussions for tone-orthography development, namely:

1. languages with "stable" tone, in which tones are not changed by their tonal environment; and
2. languages with "movable" tone, in which various tonal processes operate, so that tones may change based on the tonal context.

Roberts (2011:94) cites the terminology others have used for these two types of tone systems. Yip (2002) has used the terms "immobile" versus "mobile" tone. Mfonyam (1989) has used the term "dynamic" for the systems with changes based on tonal processes. Bird (1999) has used the binary terminology "shallow" versus "deep" not only for the orthographic depth but also for the tone system, whereby a "shallow" tone system would match my "stable" category and a "deep" system my "movable" category.

4.4.1 Languages with stable tone

The first group consists of languages with stable tone. The tonal melody of words in isolation remains the same in whatever tonal context the word may occur. There are no tonal rules which change tones in context. However, the tonal melody of a word may change for *grammatical* reasons, unrelated to the tonal environment of the word. For example, in some languages, singular and plural nouns are differentiated by tone alone, locative marking may be indicated by tone alone, or various Tense/Aspect paradigms may differ by tone alone. Such tonal changes most often have to be analyzed as tonal replacement or as a floating tone being associated to the tonal melody of the lexical morpheme. In either case, the tones in question are not changed by their tonal environment.

There are quite a few African languages in which the singular-plural contrast for a subset of nouns is made by tone alone. Example (10) is taken from Ndrulo (a Lendu speech variety spoken in Uganda). Singular [+human] nouns may have a Low tone or a Mid tone on the basic root (the first syllable), which is replaced by a High tone in the plural.[3]

(10) Ndrulo [led] (Nilo-Saharan, Central-Sudanic; Uganda)

Singular	Plural	
vìnì	víní	'his sister(s)'
ddùwnì	ddúwní	'his son(s)'
djanì	djání	'his father(s)'
bbuwnì	bbúwní	'his grandfather(s)'

In Fur [fvr], a Nilo-Saharan language spoken in Sudan, one strategy for locative marking on nouns is to add a floating-tone suffix to the relevant noun. The surface result is a tone which is the opposite of the final tone

[3] The examples are written in their orthographic form: <bb> = /ɓ/ and <dd> = /ɗ/. Note that Mid tone is unmarked.

of the tonal melody belonging to the noun. Sometimes, the two tones of a tonal melody are squeezed together onto one syllable. In this case, Low and High are realized together on one tone-bearing unit as a LH contour tone, as in the last two words in example (11), where the High tone on the second syllable has joined with the Low tone on the first syllable to create a rising tone.

(11) Fur [fvr] (Nilo-Saharan; Sudan)

Nouns		Locative Nouns	
bàrù	'country'	bàrú	'in the country'
kɔ̀rɔ̀	'water'	kɔ̀rɔ́	'in the water'
núŋí	'eye'	núŋì	'in the eye'
dɔ́ŋá	'hand'	dɔ́ŋà	'in the hand'
ʊ̀tʊ́	'fire'	ʊ̌tʊ̀	'in the fire'
kìlmá	'heart'	kǐlmà	'in the heart'

4.4.2 Languages with movable tone

The second group of African tone languages consists of languages with movable tone, in which tonal processes operate in various ways. One and the same word may appear with various tonal shapes based on the tonal context. Widespread tonal processes include H-spreading (often with subsequent downstep), H-shifting, and others.

For example, in Ebrié [ebr], a Kwa language spoken in Côte d'Ivoire, the grammatical morpheme 'in' has two realizations, as shown in example (12): *hròmɛ̀n* (L.L) and *hrómɛ̀n* (H.L), depending on the last tone of the underlying tonal melody belonging to the preceding noun. The nouns *ápɔ̂* and *ábɛ̂* have a final Low tone underlyingly: *ápɔ̂* and *ábɛ̀*; thus, *hròmɛ̀n* is realized as L.L in examples (a) and (b). On the other hand, the nouns *áyí* and *ǹtrò* have a final High tone underlyingly: *áyí* and *ǹtrò'*; thus, *hrómɛ̀n* is realized as H.L. in examples (c) and (d).[4]

[4] Note that the orthographic syllable-final *-n* in the postposition *hromɛn* represents nasalization of the vowel; the language has no closed syllables.

(12) Ebrié [ebr] (Niger-Congo, Kwa; Côte d'Ivoire)

a.	ápɔ́	hròmɛ̀n	c.	áyí	hrómɛ̀n
	body	in		thing	in
b.	ábɛ̀	hròmɛ̀n	d.	ǹtrò	hrómɛ̀n
	paddle	in		vegetables	in

4.4.3 Correlation with other phenomena

Having established this major typological division into two types of tone systems, we find some interesting correlations with other typological phenomena, as presented in table 1.

Table 1. Correlations with other phenomena

Languages with "stable" tone	Languages with "movable" tone
• more contrastive tone levels	• fewer contrastive tone levels
• shorter words	• longer words
• heavy functional load of tone in the lexicon as well as in the grammar	• much lighter functional load of tone in the lexicon, but often an equally heavy functional load of tone in the grammar

The first group (the "stable" category) contains some two-tone languages, quite a few three-tone languages, and all four-tone and five-tone languages that I have encountered. Many of these languages are isolating and highly monosyllabic CV or CVC, though some have disyllabic roots VCV or CVCV. Some have no, or hardly any, segmental morphology. These languages generally don't have a system of noun-class affixes. The number of tonal minimal pairs and sets in the lexicon is enormous, and, in addition to Tense/Aspect differences marked by tone alone, there are also lexical verb-tone classes.

The second group (the "movable" category) contains many two-tone languages and a number of three-tone languages (particularly those with H-spreading and downstep). Most often, these languages are agglutinative and have disyllabic roots, often accompanied by a noun-class prefix and/or suffix. Because there are more segmental variables in the word, tone generally does not have a very heavy functional load in the lexicon, though the *grammatical* function of tone can be very heavy. Many Bantu languages fall in this category, but so do many other languages.

4.5 Consequences for tone orthography and teaching methodology

Having established these two major types of tone languages and the link with some other typological phenomena, we can now consider the consequences of this typological distinction for tone orthography and tone-teaching methodology. The principles, procedures, and methodology here described are the same (a) for people who are already literate in one or more languages which are not their mother tongue and who now want to learn to read in their mother tongue and (b) for preliterate people—adults as well as children—learning to read for the first time, in their mother tongue.

4.5.1 Languages with stable tone

Languages in which tone has a heavy functional load benefit from having more tone marked in the orthography than languages with a lighter functional load of tone. This means that in the first category—that is, in languages with stable tone, more contrastive tone levels, and shorter words—it is possible to mark tone on every syllable. With respect to teaching to read tone in such languages, the tone marks—whether accents or punctuation marks—need to be linked to *tone awareness* in the mind of the learner.

Since tone is stable in such languages, marking tone on every syllable will also result in a "constant word image," a concept that is considered important in studies on orthography and reading. Where grammatical tones change as a result of the replacement or addition of a floating tone, such changes will need to be marked the way they surface because that is the point where the grammatical contrast becomes evident.

Lendu is an example of a stable tone language. It has three level tones and one rising tone. Tones are marked by accents, with the Mid tone being marked by the absence of an accent. All verb roots and many noun roots are monosyllabic CV in structure. The following example from Lendu is based on the verb root *ra* 'to go'. The Past, Subjunctive, Present Continuous, and Future are differentiated by tone alone. In addition, the pronominal forms for first and second person are differentiated for number by tone alone. This gives rise to an eight-way tonal contrast, as shown in example (13). This contrast is valid for every verb in the language, though the tonal configurations on the paradigms are not necessarily identical since there are four lexical verb-tone classes, and each class behaves differently in the various Tense/Aspect paradigms.

(13) Lendu [led] (Nilo-Saharan, Central-Sudanic; D.R.Congo)

ma rà rǎ	‘I went’	mà rà rǎ	‘we went’
ma rá rá	‘I should go’	mà rá rá	‘we should go’
má rǎ rǎ	‘I am going’	mǎ rǎ rǎ	‘we are going’
má ra rá	‘I will go’	mǎ ra rá	‘we will go’

As mentioned above in §4.3.2, Attié has four tone levels, as well as a ML fall and a LH rise (the latter is marginal). Tones are marked by punctuation marks; Mid tone is marked by the absence of any punctuation mark and ML is marked by a hyphen at the end of the word. All verb roots and many noun roots are monosyllabic CV.

Verb infinitives in Attié are found on any one of the five main tonal melodies—namely xH, H, M, L, and ML—which means that there are five lexical verb-tone classes. Each verb-tone class has a particular set of three tones which are used in the different Tense/Aspect paradigms. With five lexical verb-tone classes, there are five sets of possibilities. Two of them are presented in example (14), with neutralization of tonal contrasts in certain forms.[5]

(14) Attié [ati] (Niger-Congo, Kwa; Côte d’Ivoire)

ze	‘to go’	'ze	‘to give’
-han -ze	‘we have gone’ (L L)	-han -ze	‘we have given’ (L L)
-han ze	‘we are going’ (L M)	-han 'ze	‘we are giving’ (L H)
'han ze	‘we ought to go’ (H M)	‘han 'ze	‘we ought to give’ (H H)
'han -ze	‘let us go’ (H L)	‘han -ze	‘let us give’ (H L)
-han "ze	‘we didn’t go’ (L xH)	-han "ze	‘we didn’t give’ (L xH)

[5] Note that the orthographic syllable-final *-n* in the pronoun han represents nasalization of the vowel; the language has no closed syllables.

4.5.2 Languages with movable tone

In the second category, languages with movable tone, tone often has a much lighter functional load in the lexicon, although the functional load of tone in the grammar may be extensive. If phonemic tone were written everywhere in such languages, tone could not be written in a consistent way on each word since words are pronounced differently in different contexts. Readers normally link accents to pitch levels and cannot look at a certain written accent such as a Low tone and then pronounce it as a High tone in a certain context. That does not give any orthographic stability.

It would be better to establish a system of tone writing which is linked to the function of tone in the grammar. That way, tone is not marked in places with a light functional load but only in places where tone has a contrastive function in the grammar. In principle, any of the above strategies may be used: accents, punctuation marks (including other special signs such as a slash, a plus sign, or an equal sign), and even numbers or unused consonant letters.

This approach may also be useful when dialects of a language are mutually intelligible but have different tonal rules and realizations in contrastive structures. Representing particular grammatical constructions which are tonally contrastive by one special symbol marking the grammatical construction may have great advantages. The teaching methodology needs to focus on the link between the particular symbol used and the grammatical structure marked.

The following are four examples of marking grammatical tone contrasts which require such a special teaching methodology.

4.5.2.1 Sabaot

In Sabaot [spy], a verb-initial Nilotic language spoken in Kenya, case on nouns may be marked by tone.[6] There are no regular patterns by which "subject tone" is derived from "object tone." (The tone of the word in isolation is normally the same as the tone used for object case.) A nominal subject follows the verb. However, a pronominal subject is incorporated into the verb form, in which case the noun following the verb is not the subject but the object. The contrast surfaces in the tonal melody on the

[6] Sabaot data courtesy of Iver A. Larsen.

noun, as shown in example (15). In the orthography, a nominal subject—on whatever tonal realization—is marked by a colon, as in the first example. The unmarked noun, as in the second example, is the object.

(15) Sabaot [spy] (Nilo-Saharan, Southern Nilotic; Kenya)
kıbakaac (v) :kwaan (s) /kìbakaac kwààn/ 'his father left him'
kıbakaac (v) kwaan (o) /kìbakaac kwáán/ 'he left his father'

Another minimal tone contrast in this language is the difference between 'we' and the indefinite pronoun 'one', popularly also called the "passive." The latter is marked by a slash preceding the word, as shown in example (16).

(16) Sabaot [spy] (Nilo-Saharan, Southern Nilotic; Kenya)
kikiibat (v) mbareet (o) 'we ploughed the field'
/kikiibat (v) mbareet (o) 'one ploughed the field/the field was ploughed'

The slash marks the "indefinite" whatever its surface phonemic tonal realization, which is determined by different factors.

4.5.2.2 Budu

A very interesting solution has been proposed for Budu [buu], a Bantu language spoken in D.R.Congo, which has three Tense/Aspect paradigms that differ by tone alone. Being an agglutinative language, Budu has verb stems which may have two, three, or more syllables. The subject marker is prefixed to the verb. The tonal melodies differ according to the lexical tone class of the verb, the number of syllables in the stem, and the presence or absence of depressor consonants. In addition, there are quite a few tonal differences between the two main dialects.

The following system has been proposed for Budu and is being used to disambiguate these Tense/Aspect paradigms:

1. a colon is inserted between the subject prefix and the verb stem to mark the Past;
2. an equal sign is inserted between the subject prefix and the verb stem to mark the Future; and
3. the Present is marked by the absence of any special symbol.

This is illustrated in example (17).

(17) Budu [buu] (Bantu D.35; D.R.Congo)

a. Past

a:pipo	/ápípò/	'he finished'
a:bhibhiso	/ábhìbhísò/	'he glorified'
a:yokonokiso	/áyòkònòkìsò/	'he taught'

b. Future

a=pipo	/ápípó/	'he will finish'
a=bhibhiso	/ábhìbhísó/	'he will glorify'
a=yokonokiso	/áyókónókísó/	'he will teach'

c. Present

apipo	/ápìpò/	'he is finishing'
abhibhiso	/ábhìbhísò/	'he is glorifying'
ayokonokiso	/áyókónòkìsò/	'he is teaching'

The teaching of tone marked for grammatical contrasts will have to focus on awareness raising of different grammatical concepts—in this case Past, Present, and Future.

4.5.2.3 Western Maninkakan

The third example comes from Western Maninkakan [mlq], a Mande language spoken in Mali and across the border in Senegal.[7] The pronominal system has two sets of two tonally contrastive pronouns: (1) first singular versus first plural and (2) second singular versus third plural. In both sets, the surface tones on the pronouns are identical. The difference is found in the tone on the following syllable (and sometimes tones further along in the utterance), as presented in example (18). This applies to subject pronouns as well as to possessive pronouns in both alienable and inalienable possessive constructions.

[7] Western Maninkakan data courtesy of Fassara Dembele and Carin Boone.

(18) Western Maninkakan [mlq] (Niger-Congo, Mande; Mali)

	form of pronoun	following syllable
1SG	ń	H tone
1PL	ń	L tone
2SG	í	H tone
3PL	í	L tone

Since in each pair, one pronoun represents singular and the other pronoun represents plural, it was suggested that the singular pronouns be written with one letter, <n> and <i>, and the plural pronouns with two letters, <nn> and <ii>. With good teaching, consisting of awareness raising of the grammatical contrast, this should trigger the correct reading of singular or plural, with the High or Low tone following the High-tone pronoun.

The speaker of Malian Western Maninkakan to whom we suggested this possibility was immediately capable of applying it correctly in writing. In fact, this solution was also found in a Scripture portion published several years ago in Senegal (Anon. 2003), though we have no further documentation on this, nor any information on how it was taught.

The examples below in (19) are first written phonemically with their tones, followed by their orthographic representation.

(19) Western Maninkakan [mlq] (Niger-Congo, Mande; Mali)
Subject pronouns

a. Present:

/ń bé tísó xàn/	n be tiso xan	'I am sneezing'
/ń bè tìsó xàn/	nn be tiso xan	'we are sneezing'
/í bé tísó xàn/	i be tiso xan	'you (SG) are sneezing'
/í bè tìsó xàn/	ii be tiso xan	'they are sneezing'

b. Future:

/ń sí tísò/	n si tiso	'I will sneeze'
/ń sì tìsò/	nn si tiso	'we will sneeze'
/í sí tísò/	i si tiso	'you (SG) will sneeze'
/í sì tìsò/	ii si tiso	'they will sneeze'

Possessive pronouns

a. Alienable:

/ń ná tàmò/	n na tamo	'my drum'
/ń nà tàmô/	nn na tamo	'our drum'
/í ná tàmò/	i na tamo	'your (SG) drum'
/í nà tàmô/	ii na tamo	'their drum'

b. Inalienable:

/ń bémbálù/	n bembalu	'my ancestors'
/ń bèmbálù/	nn bembalu	'our ancestors'
/í bémbálù/	i bembalu	'your (SG) ancestors'
/í bèmbálù/	ii bembalu	'their ancestors'

4.5.2.4 Shimakonde

The final example is more complex and comes from Shimakonde [kde], one of the Makonde speech varieties, a Bantu language spoken in northern Mozambique.[8] This language has a two-tone system with many different morphotonological rules determining the phonemic realization of tones on the surface. Solutions have been worked out for each grammatically contrastive pair using accents and an unused consonant letter in syllable-initial position.

According to Leach, who worked on this language for many years, "minimal tone contrasts are the heart and soul of the verbal system" (pers. comm.).[9] Having followed this project for quite a few years, I fully agree.

[8] Low tone is unmarked in the phonemic representations.

[9] Shimakonde data courtesy of M. Benjamin Leach.

Shimakonde has two main aspectual prefixes *-ndi-* 'Perfective' and *-nda-* 'Imperfective.' Each of these has two paradigms differentiated by tone alone: (1) Past versus Anterior in the Perfective; and (2) Present versus Future in the Imperfective.

In the orthography, tone is marked on only one form of a minimal pair. Example (20) is drawn from Leach 2010:182. The phonemic realizations and the orthographic marking are presented side by side.

(20) Shimakonde [kde] (Bantu P.23; Mozambique)

a.	/vándítukúúta/	vandítukuta	'they ran'
	/vanditúkuúta/	vanditukuta	'they have run'
b.	/vándátukúúta/	vandátukuta	'they run'
	/vandatúkuúta/	vandatukuta	'they will run'

High tone is marked by an acute accent on the essential syllable, precisely where the contrast is located. Once this syllable is read with the correct tone, the tones of the subsequent syllables in the word will automatically be read correctly.

The second issue in Shimakonde concerns the use of a "silent" <h> syllable initially in independent negative verbs. This orthographic <h> is added preceding the Low-tone negative prefix *a-*, which is optionally realized in speech, though most commonly, it is not pronounced. It is shown in example (21). The important part of the prefix is its Low tone, which is marked here by orthographic <h>. This is an example, then, of the use of a letter as a tonal marker.

(21) Shimakonde [kde] (Bantu P.23; Mozambique)[10]

/vápáali/	vapali	'they are present'
/(a)vapaáli/	havapali	'they are not present'

[10] Vowel length in penultimate position is predictable and, therefore, not indicated in the orthography.

4.6 Conclusion

In this paper, I have presented an overall tone-system typology of African tone languages with practical repercussions for representing tone in their orthographies. Many existing orthographies of African languages as well as those that are in the process of being developed could benefit from a certain amount of tone marking. Coupled with a good methodology of teaching tone, readers would benefit with quicker understanding without constantly having to reread sentences.

I propose that a tone analysis of an African language be accompanied with a thorough documentation of the functional load of tone in the language concerned, both lexically and grammatically.

In languages with stable tone and a heavy functional load of tone, both lexically and grammatically, a system could be devised to represent tone exhaustively in the orthography, and experiments could be conducted with a good teaching methodology.

In languages with movable tone, solutions should be sought along the lines of the languages cited above, in order to disambiguate grammatical contrasts. This is an approach which is still very much in its infancy. It is likely that some solutions, like the Western Maninkakan example, are easy to write and teach while others, like the Shimakonde example, are more complex.

In addition, several issues need to be thought through and further tested. First of all, in three of the examples cited, one of the tonally contrastive forms is left unmarked. Experience has shown that "absence of symbol" is the hardest to teach, whether the symbol is linked to a particular pitch level or to a grammatical structure. Most likely, this is also the case in these sets in which all but one are marked for their grammatical feature. An experiment could be conducted in which both or all three categories are explicitly marked for writing the language and for teaching people to read.

Second, developing a methodology for teaching these two radically differing types of systems (one in which the tone orthography chosen relates to the spoken pitch levels, and one in which the symbolization refers to different tone patterns marking grammatical contrasts) is yet another challenge. Different approaches have to be worked out for people who are already literate in a language of wider communication and for those who are in the preliterate stage. Each approach needs to include awareness raising of tone by lexical tone contrasts, and/or focusing on the grammatical tone contrast.

References

Anonymous. 2003. *Korentingoolu 1* [1 Corinthians in Senegalese Western Maninkakan]. Dakar, Sénégal: La Mission Evangélique.

Bird, Steven. 1999. Strategies for representing tone in African writing systems. *Written Language and Literacy* 2(1):1–44.

Bolli, Margaret. 1978. Writing tone with punctuation marks. *Notes on Literacy* 23:16–18.

Cowan, George M. 1948. Mazateco whistled speech. *Language* 24:280–286. Repr. in D. Hymes (ed.). 1964. *Language in culture and society: A reader in linguistics and anthropology.* New York: Harper and Row. Page reference is to the 1948 edition.

Kilpatrick, Eileen. 2004. Orthographies of Moru-Ma'di languages. *Occasional Papers in the Study of Sudanese Languages* 9:85–91.

Kutsch Lojenga, Constance. 1986. Some experiences in writing and teaching tone in Africa. Special issue, *Notes on Literacy* 1:59–65.

Kutsch Lojenga, Constance. 1989. The secret behind vowelless syllables in Lendu. *Journal of African Languages and Linguistics* 11:115–126.

Kutsch Lojenga, Constance. 1993. The writing and reading of tone in Bantu languages. *Notes on Literacy* 19(1):1–19.

Leach, Michael Benjamin. 2010. Things hold together: Foundations for a systemic treatment of verbal and nominal tone in Plateau Shimakonde. PhD. dissertation. Utrecht: LOT (Landelijke Onderzoekschool Taalwetenschap/Netherlands Graduate School of Linguistics).

Mfonyam, Joseph Ngwa. 1989. Tone in orthography: The case of Bafut and related languages. Ph.D. dissertation. Yaoundé, Cameroon: University of Yaoundé.

Roberts, David A. 2011. A typology for tone orthography. *Written Language & Literacy* 14(1):82–108.

Yip, Moira. 2002. *Tone.* Cambridge Textbooks in Linguistics. Cambridge: Cambridge University Press.

5

Basic Principles for Establishing Word Boundaries

Constance Kutsch Lojenga

Orthography development involves more than establishing an alphabet for a language. The more challenging aspect consists of deciding on the boundaries of "orthographic words." This paper considers the topic of establishing word boundaries—a process in which phonological, syntactic, and semantic criteria play a role. The principles discussed are illustrated with examples from languages spoken in various parts of Africa.

5.1 Introduction

5.1.1 Language development

A good number of the world's languages have had a written tradition for many years. Their written code was decided on a long time ago—in quite a few cases even centuries ago. Speakers of such languages may hardly be aware of the fact that there are still many languages in the world which have as yet no orthographic standard. To them, the system they learned in school for writing their own language may seem so natural that they have difficulty conceiving of the problems in designing an orthography for a yet unwritten language.

However, looking around the globe, there are still many so-called minority languages without a written form. Some of these "minority" languages are not even extremely small in population, though others may be. Since language forms part of the identity of people, all ethnic groups have the right to develop a written form of their language as an expression for their cultural heritage, and for their spiritual development or personal enjoyment.

When we talk about developing a written form for a language, what comes to mind most readily is creating an alphabet—choosing the set of symbols with which the words of the language will be written. In fact, most of the attention of people involved in orthography design—and most of the documentation on the subject—has been focused on creating the alphabet, because this is definitely the first and most concrete aspect of language development.

However, there is more to orthography development than creating an alphabet. Even though in speech, a complete clause or sentence may come out in one uninterrupted flow, the clause or sentence will need to be "cut up" into words when written on paper. The establishment of the boundaries of orthographic words has often intuitively followed the system of a language with which the people involved in the orthography design were already familiar—sometimes leading to results that are not ideal. Very little has been written on the topic of establishing word boundaries,[1] except here and there in orthography manuals for specific languages.

Orthography development is inextricably linked to linguistics. A linguistic study of an unwritten language is essential for developing an accurate orthography. First, a thorough study of the sound system of a language should reveal the inventory of contrastive vowels and consonants, which is a prerequisite for choosing the alphabet letters. Then, morphology and syntax are necessary for establishing word boundaries. Morphophonology is important because one needs to represent the results of the sound processes between roots/stems and affixes. Finally, higher-level syntax (complex

[1] I choose to use the term "word boundaries" where others use the term "word breaks" or "word division" (cf. Van Dyken and Kutsch Lojenga 1993). All these terms essentially refer to the same thing.

clauses, etc.) and discourse are important for punctuation. All of these factors—the symbols, word boundaries, and punctuation—need to be decided upon and then applied systematically and consistently in the written language so as to facilitate the reading of texts in that language.

This paper addresses the topic of word boundaries. Its aim is to give practical advice on this topic to those who are in the process of developing a written form for a particular language as well as to those who need to revise certain word-boundary decisions in languages which have received an orthography at an earlier time. This practical advice is useful only if based on knowledge of the grammatical structures of the language for which decisions need to be made. Since the experience of the author in the domain of language development and orthography design lies exclusively in Africa, the perspective of thinking on this issue as well as the examples come from that background.

In the two decades that have passed since I co-authored a general article on word boundaries (Van Dyken and Kutsch Lojenga 1993), I have continued to consult on orthography design in numerous languages in Africa. With each new language, new issues have emerged that needed to be dealt with, so my experience in all aspects of orthography design has grown immensely. In this paper, therefore, I will touch on principles laid out in the previous article, while at the same time looking at the bigger picture of establishing word boundaries from a different and very practical angle, and somewhat rearranging the priorities of the earlier principles.

Since languages vary widely in their structures, it is impossible to provide readers of this paper with solutions to every type of problem they may encounter. Rather, developing a system of word boundaries for a newly to-be-written language will involve weighing various criteria against each other, making a first decision, testing it out in terms of how people can read and write as a result of that decision, and, in some cases, returning to the basis and making a different decision to be tested out—until finally settling on what hopefully will turn out to be the best solution for the readers and writers of the language. (Related to this, see Karan's paper, this volume, about the importance of not rushing standardization.)

The 1993 article focused on the criteria for defining word boundaries and gave some examples illustrating each of these criteria. This time, I will reiterate these criteria briefly, and then move on to a more practical approach, namely treating various linguistic structures found in most languages which need to be considered for writing morphemes conjunctively or disjunctively.

5.1.2 Orthography design

Orthography design includes two major domains: the alphabet, and all other conventions. A preliminary choice of letters for the alphabet can be made as soon as the basic inventory of contrastive sounds has been established. As a basic principle, each contrastive vowel needs to have its own representation. A grapheme should be chosen for each vowel, preferably a monograph, other than doubling the vowel symbol for long vowels when the language has short and long vowels contrastively. If the number of contrastive vowel qualities exceeds five, as is the case in many languages, additional symbols have to be chosen to represent the extra vowels.

Those choices of vowel symbols are extremely important from a psycholinguistic and a sociolinguistic perspective. The psycholinguistic intuition of the speakers of a particular language is normally very much influenced by the sound values that were attached to the vowel symbols when they learned to read in an official language or a language of wider communication. Thus, choices for vowel letters need to correspond as much as possible to the speakers' prior learning experience in order to ensure a smooth transition into acquiring reading skills in the mother tongue. Sociolinguistically, these choices are important for gaining acceptability of the writing system in the community. Diacritics above or below vowel symbols marking different vowel qualities are less ideal, since that space may be needed for marking prosodic features, particularly tone. (For various ways of marking tone, see my paper on tone, this volume.)

Consonants are often a bit more "concrete" than vowels, and a set of symbols—monographs, digraphs, and sometimes even trigraphs—can be established fairly easily to represent each contrastive consonant. In languages with geminate consonants, it is best to use monographs as much as possible, since they can be "doubled" more easily than digraphs.

With a basic decision on the alphabet in place, the speakers of the language can start writing words, which can be collected in a lexicon or dictionary. In the process, one can discover if the system as proposed holds for both reading and writing.

In addition to these "basics" of deciding on the alphabet, there are other matters that need to be dealt with. The most important issue beyond the alphabet decisions is cutting up the sentence into chunks on the page, that is, establishing the boundaries between words, thereby creating "orthographic words" in such a way as to facilitate fluent reading of text in the language. Other issues include punctuation and decisions on capitalization.

Establishing word boundaries is something that takes place over a period of several years and requires research and analysis in the domains of morphology (including, of course, morphophonology) and clause syntax, so that word boundaries can be established which follow the natural linguistic patterns of the language.

Relatively little has been written about the topic of word boundaries. However, many people involved in developing or improving writing systems have expressed their need for more information and guidance on this topic. Pike and Pike (1982) have devoted a chapter in their book *Grammatical Analysis* to this topic, and similarly Elson and Pickett (1988) in their book *Beginning Morphology and Syntax.*[2] Furthermore, Guthrie (1948) wrote a monograph entitled "Bantu Word Division," treating issues specifically related to a subgroup of the Niger-Congo language phylum, covering about one-quarter of Africa's languages. All of these have mentioned various principles which are also treated in the present paper in a new context and with examples from a wide range of African languages.[3]

5.2 Word boundaries

5.2.1 Introduction

An uninterrupted flow of speech needs to be divided into distinct "orthographic words" on the page. How does one cut up speech into words on the page in such a way that it helps both a beginning and a fluent reader to read with ease? On what basis does one establish language-specific rules? Or are there general principles? Then there is the question of how and where to use hyphens and apostrophes—which can be used for "intermediate" solutions.

[2] See Pike and Pike 1982:98–116, chapter 6, "Criteria for Word Division"; and Elson and Pickett 1988:157–161, chapter 17, "Word Boundaries."

[3] After writing this paper, I became aware of an appendix in Van Otterloo 2011 about word-boundary issues in the Bantu language Kifuliiru [flr]. Most, but not all, of the decisions that were made for that language apply very similar principles to the ones discussed in this paper.

The issue of establishing word boundaries for a newly to-be-written language is of crucial importance for the future of its written form; it is an important factor in the success of a literacy program. There are some general principles, but on top of that, each language needs tailor-made solutions because each language has its own specific grammatical structures. A thorough knowledge of these structures will help in formulating the language-specific rules that are necessary in addition to the general principles for establishing word boundaries.

When it comes to word-boundary decisions, the following possibilities exist:

1. conjunctive writing (joining morphemes);
2. disjunctive writing (separating morphemes); and
3. intermediate solutions, such as using hyphens or apostrophes.

Both hyphens and apostrophes can be used to mark a connection between two morphemes which is not so close that one would write the two together but still close enough that one would not want to separate them altogether. Apostrophes can also be used for cases of elision, particularly in grammatical morphemes.

If the people involved in the decision-making process—be they native speakers of the language or linguists from another language background—do not give this topic special thought, they may blindly follow word-boundary conventions from another language they are familiar with, such as English or French, the main international languages in Africa, or a language of wider communication such as Swahili, Hausa, or Sango [sag].

An example of a resulting "mismatch" between a word boundary in French or English on the one hand and an African language on the other hand is sometimes found in Bantu languages which have augments in addition to the regular noun-class prefixes. Native speakers of these Bantu languages have at times interpreted these augments as the equivalent of the French or English "article." And just as *the house* or *la maison* are written as two orthographic words, people would initially separate the augment from the rest of the word and write it as a separate orthographic word. However, this morpheme is phonologically and tonally dependent on what follows and should, therefore, be joined to the prefix and the lexical root (and it is not even the equivalent of the English "article"). This is illustrated for the Bantu language Havu [hav] in example (1).

(1) Havu [hav] (Bantu D/J.52[4]; D.R.Congo)[5]

a. <olulimi> 'tongue' *<o lulimi>
o-lu-limi
AUG-CL11-tongue

b. <abahiizi> 'hunters' *<a bahiizi>
a-ba-hiizi
AUG-CL2-hunter

c. <egikere> 'toad' *<e gikere>
e-gi-kere
AUG-CL7-toad

So, where should one look for guidelines to help make decisions on word boundaries? The basic "recipe" is the following. First, apply general principles for word-boundary decisions to the language under study, taking into consideration the specific morphological and syntactic structures of the language. To this, add the following with care, verifying any conclusions each time against the general principles mentioned above: consult native-speaker intuition (be aware of influence from other, unrelated languages), and follow conventions used in languages with common linguistic patterns.

Practical advice here suggests looking at what closely related languages with similar structures have done, and considering whether some of their specific word-boundary conventions would fit the language concerned or perhaps create problems. This can provide arguments for or against proposed word boundaries in a particular language.

It is not a good principle to make decisions about word boundaries by trying to create solutions for isolated cases. Rather, one should look at the issues in a larger syntactic context or in their paradigms. In this way, one can immediately oversee the repercussions of a choice in terms of how it affects similar structures or other items in the same paradigm.

In the following sections, we will look at various issues which have a bearing on word-boundary decisions. In §5.2.2 we will see that the basic

[4] Bantu languages are identified by their Guthrie classification number (see Guthrie 1971).

[5] The following abbreviations are used in this paper: AUG Augment; AUX Auxiliary; CL Classifier; FUT Future; IPF Imperfective; NEG Negative; PF Perfective; PL Plural; PR Present; SG Singular; SP Species.

syllable structures of a language have repercussions for the syllable structures of orthographic words. Following that, we will look in §5.2.3 at different types of morphemes and the implications of the categorization of morphemes for word-boundary decisions. In §5.2.4 we will consider the topic of morphophonological processes and how to use this information in decisions on writing certain morphemes conjunctively or disjunctively. In §5.2.5 we will discuss the issues of morphophonemic spelling and constant word image. Finally, in §5.2.6 we will consider the topic of fast and slow speech and the repercussions for cases of elision.

5.2.2 Syllable structures

Each language has its own particular syllable structures. Some languages have only open syllables; others have both open and closed syllables. Some languages with closed syllables have heavy constraints on which consonants may occur syllable finally. When a language contrasts short and long vowels, there may be constraints on the occurrence of long vowels in certain syllable positions of the word. A detailed analysis of the syllable structures of a language will serve as input for word-boundary decisions, since, as a principle, word-boundary decisions should never leave orthographic words with impossible syllable structures. Specifically:

1. if the language has no closed syllables, no word on the page should appear with a closed syllable, even if a final vowel is elided in fast speech;
2. if a language has closed syllables, only those consonants which can occur syllable finally in pre-pausal position should appear at the end of an orthographic word; and
3. if the language does have long vowels, but never in a word-final syllable (as is often the case in Lacustrine Bantu languages), then no orthographic word should have a long vowel in a word-final syllable.

Malila [mgq] is a Bantu language with both prefixes and augments. Nouns and adjectives always appear with their augment, which consists of a vowel. In addition, like many Bantu languages, the language has only open syllables. When a vowel-initial morpheme (e.g., an adjective or a demonstrative) follows a noun, the last vowel of the noun is elided in speech. If the elided vowel is not represented in the written form, the result will be a closed syllable on the page, which does not reflect the syllable structures of this particular language. In addition, there is no evidence of this second word being a suffix or an enclitic, because vowel harmony doesn't play a role, nor does vowel shortening (a strategy relevant in this language to show a measure of "unity" between a lexical and a grammatical morpheme—cf. Kutsch Lojenga 2010). Therefore, the noun and following word should be written as separate and complete orthographic words; the elision takes place automatically across word boundaries. This is illustrated in example (2).

(2) Malila [mgq] (Bantu M.24; Tanzania)

a.	abaana	<abaana abiinji>	*<abaan abiinji>
	'children'	'many children'	
b.	ishipeeni	<ishipeeni ɨshɨkʉʉlʉ>	*<ishipeen ɨshɨkʉʉlʉ>
	'knife'	'old knife'	
c.	imifupa	<imifupa imibiibi>	*<imifup imibiibi>
	'bones'	'bad bones'	
d.	amajeembe	<amajeembe iɨga>	*<amajeemb iɨga>
	'hoes'	'these hoes'	

5.2.3 Grammatical morphemes

Just as a phonological analysis is a prerequisite for establishing the alphabet of a language, so a grammatical analysis—particularly of the morphology and the clause-level syntax—is a prerequisite for establishing word boundaries. Such an analysis is important because there is much variety in language structures, so what in one language is expressed morphologically may be expressed syntactically in another language.

Speech can be seen as a concatenation of morphemes. The most important thing, therefore, is to know the status of the morphemes in the language. Every language has lexical morphemes—specifically noun roots and verb roots, and often at least some adjective and adverb roots. In addition, every language also has grammatical morphemes—such as nominal classifiers, postpositions, pronominal morphemes, associative markers, and negative markers. However, it is important to know what status these morphemes have in the grammatical structure of the language. Are they affixes, clitics, or independent morphemes?

In every language, there are clear-cut cases, and there are also situations in which it is not so easy to determine whether a grammatical morpheme is an affix, clitic, or free morpheme. In fact, the analysis of the grammatical morphemes into these three categories will be tremendously helpful in deciding whether they should be written attached to another word or as independent orthographic words. Affixes are grammatically and phonologically bound to a lexical morpheme while clitics are grammatically independent but often phonologically bound. Free, or independent morphemes, are neither grammatically nor phonologically bound.

Lexical morphemes can never be broken up orthographically—they must be written as one unit (including any obligatory affixes). In the case of grammatical morphemes, one needs to decide for *every* grammatical morpheme whether it is an affix, a clitic, or an independent morpheme, and consequently whether or not it should be joined to a morpheme next to which it occurs in a sentence. In most cases, these decisions are fairly straightforward. However, in every language there are always several instances of morphemes for which it is difficult to decide whether they are affixes or clitics. This may have repercussions for the decision on whether they should be fully joined or whether they should be half joined to the neighboring morpheme by using a hyphen or an apostrophe.

In the following paragraphs, we will look at each of these morpheme categories in turn and follow each discussion with some advice on word-boundary decisions. The methodological question on how to discover which grammatical morphemes are affixes, clitics, or independent morphemes already involves principles which will immediately be helpful in making decisions with respect to word boundaries.

Most independent grammatical morphemes can be established on the basis of the grammatical criteria cited in §5.3.1 below, namely their (a) mobility, (b) separability, and (c) substitutability, as well as the phonological criterion discussed in §5.3.2.1 of whether or not they can be cited in isolation. If they fulfill any of these criteria, there is no doubt that they should be written as independent orthographic words.

Affixes are on the opposite end of the scale from independent morphemes: they show a strong "belonging" to another morpheme, often a lexical morpheme—although they may also occur next to a grammatical morpheme, especially in agglutinative languages which may have orthographic words containing strings of affixes.

For practical purposes, I divide affixes into those that are obligatory in the citation form of nouns and verbs (e.g., noun-class affixes), and those that are non-obligatory, i.e., that do not form part of the citation form of words. The obligatory affixes cannot even be separated from the noun or verb in the citation form—even if they can be replaced by other affixes—so the practical consequence is that they must be written together with the lexical morpheme to which they belong. As for the non-obligatory affixes (e.g., locative affixes and verbal derivational affixes), once their affix status is established, they should also be written together with the root/stem to which they belong. In most languages, there are two kinds of affixes: derivational and inflectional. The former are often placed closer to the lexical root, whereas the latter are more often on the "outside" of the word.

Very often, affixes are clearly phonologically bound to the (lexical) morpheme to which they belong, whether by tone, stress, vowel harmony, or another categorical morphophonological process. This fact, as well as the fact that no other lexical morphemes can intervene between a lexical root and an affix, indicates that they should be written conjunctively with the lexical or grammatical morpheme with which they occur. The same is true for strings of affixes that must occur in a fixed order around a lexical root: they should be written as one long orthographic word.

Clitics are morphemes which are in a way between affixes and independent forms. They are grammatically independent, but they are often phonologically bound. It is not always easy, therefore, to distinguish analytically between the non-obligatory affixes and clitics. In fact, there may not always be a clear dividing line. In principle, an affix is attached only to words from one particular grammatical category whereas a clitic may attach to words of various grammatical categories and often functions more at the phrase or clause level (e.g., plural markers in some languages, case markers, or subordinate-clause markers).

Affixes—and very often also clitics—are phonologically dependent on their "host," i.e., the word to which they belong in the sentence. This dependence may be shown prosodically by stress or tone, or, for example, by vowel harmony or another vocalic or consonantal morphophonological process. As mentioned above, all affixes need to be written together with the root or stem to which they belong. In the case of clitics, if they are phonologically bound to their host, they should not be written totally separately either. One could show the close phonological connection by choosing an intermediate solution—joining them to their host morpheme and at the same time keeping them a bit separate by using a hyphen or an apostrophe.

Only if there is no immediate phonological relationship between word and clitic can one consider writing the clitic separately. One such situation would be if the clitic contains the vowel /a/, which does not undergo vowel-harmony processes in many languages. However, in many cases, clitics are clearly phonologically dependent on their host. If word and clitic show such a relationship, even though the clitic can also join words of other grammatical categories, it would be good to show that there is this close-knit relationship, and a hyphen or an apostrophe could be used to mark that relationship, rather than separating the word and clitic altogether.

The other point which should be mentioned here is that it is possible to differentiate in word-boundary decisions between *proclitics* and *enclitics*. Proclitics precede a word while enclitics follow a word. When it comes to word recognition in the reading process, it is easier to learn to recognize a word that has a constant visual image, especially at the beginning of the word. Proclitics would "disturb" this visual image and immediate recognition of at least the beginning of the word. If a proclitic, therefore, does not have a clear and strong phonological dependence on its host, one may decide to write it separately. If it does undergo a morphophonological process, it would be better to write a hyphen or an apostrophe, depending on the particular phonological structure. In this way the beginning of the lexical morpheme is partly separated and can still be easily recognized.

This issue is much less relevant for enclitics, which *follow* a word. In that position, at the end of the word, it would be good to show the link between the clitic and its host either by writing them conjunctively or by inserting a hyphen or an apostrophe, without separating them entirely, since a clitic at the end of a word will not interfere with the global recognition of the root.

5.2.4 Morphophonology

Every language that has affixes will most likely also have some morphophonological processes.[6] These processes take place at morpheme boundaries between vowels, consonants, or consonants and vowels.

[6] Here and there, a language can be found which does not have segmental affixation, hence no morphophonology. Such languages may have tonal modifications, a topic which is not relevant in the present discussion.

Before working on the details of the morphophonological processes and the repercussions of these processes for the orthography, it is necessary to analyze the grammatical morphemes, including affixes, clitics, and independent forms. For each category, one needs to know the underlying form and, in the case of affixes and clitics, the allomorphs, and the rules by which these are produced.

The next step is to decide as far as possible which grammatical morphemes should be written conjunctively with a neighboring lexical root or stem, and which ones should be written disjunctively. All affixes need to be written conjunctively. The problem arises with clitics, and particularly proclitics: they may or may not be written conjunctively.

Morphophonology concerns the changes that take place when two morphemes come in contact with each other. In the theory of Lexical Phonology (Mohanan 1986), a distinction is made between two types of processes, with practical repercussions for the orthography: (a) lexical processes, those that take place within a polymorphemic word and (b) postlexical processes, those that take place across word boundaries.

Postlexical processes—changes that take place between words in a sentence—are automatic processes, generally the result of chaining the words together in (fast) speech. These processes are irrelevant for the orthography, since every orthographic word needs to be written the way it is cited in isolation. However, the results of the morphophonological processes at the lexical level—that is, within word boundaries—must be represented in the written form. This issue of lexical processes, therefore, is relevant in the case of affixes as well as in the case of those clitics which are written either conjunctively or with a hyphen or apostrophe. (For further discussion on this topic, see Snider, this volume.)

The study of affixes and clitics, therefore, must establish the underlying forms, the forms of the different allomorphs which appear on the surface, and the rules which produce them, including the environments. Rather than making a list of morphophonological rules and processes which take place throughout the language, it is more practical for the sake of making decisions about the orthography to take each affix and study what changes it undergoes and/or causes and provide examples of each form in every possible environment.

Morphophonological processes are mostly assimilatory in nature, but sometimes one comes across cases of dissimilation. Such processes may operate progressively (from left to right) or regressively (from right to left), or both directions may be involved simultaneously when certain features are assimilated or dissimilated.

There are different types of morphophonological processes. Some frequent processes which take place between vowels are glide formation, diphthongization, coalescence, and elision (see also Casali 1998). Rules differ from one language to another. Even the outcome of coalescence rules may differ between languages.

Many languages have vowel harmony such as vowel-height harmony, rounding harmony, front harmony, and [ATR] harmony. Vowel-harmony processes which take place across morpheme boundaries involve assimilation of some feature. Such processes may also differ from one language to another. Especially in languages with an [ATR] vowel-harmony system, in which the feature [ATR] is dominant, the affix vowel may change if the root has dominant vowels, or the root vowels may change if the affix has a dominant vowel. Vowel-harmony processes show phonological unity, and this must be represented in the orthography—in the case of affixes, by joining them to the root/stem, and in the case of clitics, by joining them to the root/stem or half-joining them with a hyphen or apostrophe. If the vowel-harmony process produces allomorphs which contain existing phonemes, then these should be written as pronounced, for the sake of readability, writability, and teachability.

5.2.5 Morphophonemic spelling

At this point, I will make a brief excursion to two frequently mentioned topics, namely the concept of morphophonemic spelling and, related to that, the concept of a constant word image. Often, these concepts are understood in such a way that a root or a grammatical morpheme should be written in its underlying form so that it has a constant form in writing, irrespective of morphophonological changes. This is then said to be advantageous for easy and quick word/morpheme recognition, especially for fluent readers. Indeed, one ought to do everything possible to encourage easy recognition of words on the page. However, when it concerns word-internal categorical morphophonological changes from one phoneme to another, one should really aim to write the resultant form of the word, representing the outcome of the morphophonological changes.

5.2.5.1 Malila

We can illustrate this with an example from Malila, the Bantu language referred to earlier, in which every noun-class prefix with a high vowel has two realizations. Underlyingly, prefixes with a high front vowel contain the [–ATR] sound /ɪ/, orthographically represented by <ɨ>; those with a high back vowel are underlyingly /ʊ/, orthographically <ʉ>. When the noun root/stem contains [+ATR] vowels, the prefix vowel changes to /i/ and /u/ respectively, written as <i> and <u>. These vowels, /ɪ/ and /i/ as well as /ʊ/ and /u/, are contrastive vowel qualities in the phonological system of Malila. Some people might suggest that it is just as easy to read if, in the prefixes, the two vowels /ɪ/ and /i/ are represented the same way, perhaps as <i>, in order to keep the symbolization as simple as possible. Similarly, they might suggest that both /ʊ/ and /u/ be written as <u> in prefixes. However, there are a number of serious drawbacks with this kind of "morphophonemic" spelling, which make it unadvisable.

In such a system, the orthographic vowel symbols <ɨ> and <i> on the one hand, and <ʉ> and <u> on the other, stand first of all for contrastive vowel qualities. Those learning to read will establish a separate symbol-sound relationship for each of these. If then, in certain affixes, that orthographic distinction is neutralized, and only one of them is written, learners might still be able to read but their symbol-sound awareness will be disturbed, since, from time to time, especially in affixes, they will have to read the "opposite" sound from the one that they have originally learned for that symbol. This will confuse their awareness of these contrastive sounds with the result that they can no longer write the two correctly in any position.

The teaching, too, will be impossible, since first, each vowel symbol will have to be taught with its own sound value and second, one vowel symbol of each pair will have two sound values. For orthography development, readability is not the only consideration; writability and teachability are equally important factors, and these become particularly relevant when it concerns the establishment of orthographic words and the writing of word-internal morphophonological sound changes. The concept of a constant word image, therefore, does not take precedence over writing the output of morphophonological sound changes within the boundaries of an orthographic word.

Malila has seven contrastive vowels, /i, ɪ, ɛ [~e], a, ɔ [~o], ʊ, u/, which correspond orthographically to <i, ɨ, e, a, o, ʉ, u>.[7] The examples below contain the augment-plus-prefix combinations /ʊmʊ-/ ~ /umu-/ for noun class 1 and noun class 3, and /ɪʃɪ/ ~ /iʃi-/ for noun class 7. The [–ATR] forms are the underlying forms. They change to become [+ATR] next to a root with [+ATR] vowels.

Writing only five vowels in the affixes would underdifferentiate in the grammatical morphemes, whereas in the lexical morphemes, the seven vowels are distinctively written. If both /ʊ/ and /u/ were written as <u>, and /ɪ/ and /i/ were written as <i>, some very confusing situations would emerge.[8]

This first set of nouns in example (3) concerns the high back vowels <ʉ> and <u>. If the prefixes were to be written morphophonemically, they should all be written with the vowel <ʉ>, which is the underlying vowel in the morpheme but most likely one would choose the other vowel, <u>, to keep it simple. The starred forms are clearly an unacceptable solution.

(3) Malila [mgq] (Bantu M.24; Tanzania)

a.	/umu-tiinho/	<umu-tiinho>		‘ladle’
b.	/ʊmʊ-lyaangɔ/	<ʉmʉ-lyaango>	*<umu-lyaango>	‘door’
c.	/ʊmʊ-lʊme/	<ʉmʉ-lʉme>	*<umu-lʉme>	‘husband’

Example (a) is written exactly as it should be. In example (b), the second orthographic representation is not ideal because readers receive wrong information right from the beginning of the word. Most likely, however, they will have no difficulty reading the word. In example (c), the second representation would be very strange: while all three back round vowels are identical in pronunciation, the third one is represented differently in writing, which would be very confusing for readers.

The second set of nouns in example (4) contains the high front vowels <ɨ> and <i>. The same issue is illustrated here.

---

[7] Note that [e] and [o] are allophones of /ɛ/ and /ɔ/ when followed or preceded by a high [+ATR] vowel in the root.

[8] In the examples, hyphens for the morpheme boundaries are inserted for the sake of clarity; they are not part of the Malila orthographic system.

(4) Malila [mgq] (Bantu M.24; Tanzania)

a. /iʃi-jiiji/ <ishi-jiiji> 'village'

b. /ɪʃɪ-nama/ <ɨshɨ-nama> *<ishi-nama> 'food'

c. /ɪʃɪ-lɪlɪ/ <ɨshɨ-lɨlɨ> *<ishi-lɨlɨ> 'mat'

For examples (3) and (4) from Malila, the two sounds neutralized in the orthography are, in fact, very close. The question is where the limit of such decisions would be, if in other instances, the phonetic difference were much bigger—as is the case in the following example.

5.2.5.2 *Lika*

The second example is taken from Lika [lik], a Bantu language spoken in D.R.Congo (data from Kutsch Lojenga 2009). Lika has [ATR] vowel harmony, in which both affixes and roots may be affected. The quality of affix vowels may be changed by a "dominant" root morpheme, and the quality of the root vowels may be changed by a "dominant" suffix. In addition, the [+ATR] counterpart of the vowel /a/ is /o/. It will be clear from example (5) that it would be impossible, even for fluent readers, to write the underlying form of the roots with /a/ and then read them with /o/. Rather, the output of the lexical process needs to be the input for the orthographic choices.

(5) Lika [lik] (Bantu D.201; D.R.Congo)[9]

a. Causative:

ká-gab-á	'to sell'	kó-gob-ís-ó	'to cause to sell'

b. Imperative:

ká-kpakyán-á	'to walk'	kpakyán-á	'walk! (SG)'
tó-kpokyón-ín-i	'let us walk!'	kpokyón-ón-í	'walk! (PL)'

5.2.6 Fast and slow speech

In fast speech, all words are chained together. However, in writing, nouns and verbs definitely need to be written in their complete form (including any affixes they may have). They should not be written together with other independent words or morphemes in the sentence (see §5.3.2.3), nor should

[9] Lika does not appear in Guthrie's classification. The number comes from Maho's online New Updated Guthrie's List (NUGL, Maho 2009).

cases of postlexical elision in speech change the orthographic shape of lexical morphemes or of complete orthographic words (see the Malila data in example (2) in §5.2.2).

The issue of fast and slow speech needs to be taken into consideration in every possible case of elision. The elided vowel in a grammatical morpheme may be "replaced" by an apostrophe. However, before deciding to do so, it is important to verify if the vowel is deleted both in fast speech and in slow speech, i.e., if there is no way of pronouncing the "lost" vowel, even in slow speech. If, however, in slow speech, the vowel can be pronounced, it should be written consistently in the particular construction. If, on the other hand, the elided vowel cannot ever be pronounced, the result of the elision process must be written (as with the vowel of the articles *le* and *la* in French preceding vowel-initial nouns: *l'arbre* or *l'association*).

Generally, the result of the elision process is indicated by replacing the elided vowel with an apostrophe (and leaving no space between the morphemes), as in example (6) of the associative construction in Lugwere [gwr], a Bantu language of Uganda.[10] The associative marker could be considered a proclitic to N2, the possessor. This proclitic is a monosyllabic form, ending in a vowel. When the noun begins with a vocalic augment, elision takes place between the associative marker and the augment, whereby the original vowel /a/ of the associative marker is elided. In writing, it can be replaced by an apostrophe, as follows:

(6) Lugwere [gwr] (Bantu E.17; Uganda)

a.	omwoyo	gwa	omusaiza	>	<omwoyo gw'omusaiza>
	heart	of	man		'the heart of the man'
b.	ensaka	ya	amata	>	<ensaka y'amata>
	pot	of	milk		'a pot of milk'
c.	emiyembe	gya	abaana	>	<emiyembe gy'abaana>
	mangoes	of	children		'the mangoes of the children'
d.	elyengi	lya	eitooke	>	<elyengi ly'eitooke>
	ripe.one	of	banana		'the ripe (one of the) banana'

In fact, there is another possible way to represent this elision in spelling, namely by writing the non-elided vowel (the augment) before the

[10] All Lugwere data in this paper courtesy of Richard Nzogi.

apostrophe, in that way preserving the syllable patterns of the language in the written form. The form in its totality must be one orthographic word on the page. (Note that it is not acceptable to separate the augment entirely from the noun to which it belongs and write the associative marker containing the augment vowel separately.) This solution has been applied in Kifuliiru (Van Otterloo 2011) but has been applied here in example (7) to the Lugwere data for the sake of comparision with example (6).

(7) Lugwere [gwr] (Bantu E.17; Uganda)

<omwoyo gwo'musaiza>	*<omwoyo gwo musaiza>
<ensaka ya'mata>	*<ensaka ya mata>
<emiyembe gya'baana>	*<emiyembe gya baana>
<elyengi lye'itooke>	*<elyengi lye itooke>

Whichever solution is chosen, the important issue is that people choose the one they feel most comfortable with, and that they learn to apply it consistently when they write their language.

5.3 Criteria for writing grammatical morphemes

In this section, I will review the various criteria for writing morphemes conjunctively or disjunctively that were discussed in Van Dyken and Kutsch Lojenga (1993). It has become clear that some of these criteria relate specifically to certain grammatical constructions found in languages. These will be mentioned in §5.3.3 when the different constructions are discussed with respect to word-boundary decisions.

Languages vary tremendously with respect to their structures. Some are isolating; others are agglutinative. Some have SVO clause structures; others, SOV or VSO; and yet others have more than one possibility, determined either by Tense/Aspect considerations or by discourse-pragmatic factors. Some languages have prepositions; others have postpositions. Because of the wide variety in grammatical structures, it is impossible to come up with a uniform system for establishing word boundaries. Therefore, linguistic criteria have been established which can be applied in individual languages, in order to help determine the status of morphemes and subsequently make choices for word boundaries.

The linguistic criteria may be divided into three main domains: grammatical, phonological, and semantic. In Van Dyken and Kutsch Lojenga

(1993), the semantic criterion was presented first, followed by the grammatical and phonological. However, many situations have convinced me that for word boundaries, the grammatical criteria should be used first, in order to determine the linguistic status of the morphemes—i.e., as affixes, clitics, or independent grammatical morphemes. This is the first information needed to make decisions on word boundaries. After that, the phonological criteria are important for decisions about writing affixes and clitics. Finally, the semantic criteria can be used particularly for various types of compound constructions. I will present the previously established criteria here in this new order: grammatical, phonological, and semantic.

5.3.1 Grammatical criteria

The grammatical criteria include:

- mobility;
- separability; and
- substitutability.

5.3.1.1 Mobility

Mobility refers to a situation in which a morpheme can take different places in a sentence, sometimes with different shades of meaning. These are often short grammatical morphemes or particles, such as locatives, demonstratives, and negative markers. The fact that such morphemes can take different places in a sentence is a clear signal that they are independent morphemes and should thus be written separately from other words.

In Lendu [led], a Nilo-Saharan language spoken in D.R.Congo, the negative particles <nzá> (used when the verb is inflected in the Perfective aspect) and <nzɨ̌> (used in the Imperfective aspect) can be placed in one of two slots in the clause, with different discourse functions. The two slots are: (1) clause-final position and (2) following the subject, with a particle <rɨ> in clause-final position. This is illustrated in example (8). Since these negative markers are mobile, they are considered independent grammatical morphemes and must therefore be written as separate orthographic words.

(8) Lendu [led] (Nilo-Saharan, Central-Sudanic; D.R.Congo)

a. ma jʉ̀ ddà **nzá**
1SG drink-PF water neg
ma **nzá** jʉ̀ ddà rɨ
1SG NEG drink water NEG
'I have not drunk water'

b. ké ɓí ɓǐ **nzɨ̌**
3SG walk-IPF walk neg
ke **nzɨ̌** ɓí ɓǐ rɨ
3SG NEG walk-IPF walk NEG
'he is not walking'

5.3.1.2 Separability

Separability refers to a situation in which a grammatical morpheme can be separated from a neighboring lexical morpheme by the insertion of another lexical morpheme. In this case, the grammatical morpheme is most likely an independent morpheme and should therefore be written as a separate word. Note, however, that there are languages with strings of affixes, whereby the insertion of another affix should not be taken for a signal to break up the orthographic word.

Lendu has two word-order possibilities: SVO (in the Perfective aspect) and SOV (in the Imperfective aspect). In the Perfective aspect, the subject pronoun and the verb are adjacent to each other, but in the Imperfective paradigms, the object separates the (nominal or pronominal) subject from the verb, as shown in example (9).[11] This is a clear reason to consider the subject pronouns as independent morphemes and thus independent orthographic words.

[11] In this example, the focus is on the switch in word order between Verb and Object. However, the Imperfective aspect also contains a tonal auxiliary element which is associated to the pronoun to its left.

(9) Lendu [led] (Nilo-Saharan, Central-Sudanic; D.R.Congo)

a.	**ma**	dzi	rù	b.	**má**	rù	dzǐ
	1SG	buy-PF	clothes		1SG.AUX	clothes	buy-IPF
	'I have bought clothes'				'I am buying clothes'		

5.3.1.3 *Substitutability*

Substitutability refers to a situation in which a lexeme can be substituted by a grammatical morpheme in the same syntactic slot—i.e., paradigmatic substitution. In this case, too, the morpheme will most likely have to be written separately. This is often the case with true pronouns, as shown in example (10), also from Lendu (cf. §4.1).

(10) Lendu [led] (Nilo-Saharan, Central-Sudanic; D.R.Congo)

a.	**ngba**	ddà	ndrɨ̀	b.	**ndrǔ**	chɨ	dza	chɨ́
	child	pull	goat		people	build-PF	house	build
	'the child has pulled the goat'				'the people have built a house'			
	ke	ddà	ndrɨ̀		**kpa**	chɨ	dza	chɨ́
	3SG	pull	goat		3PL	build-PF	house	build
	'he has pulled the goat'				'they have built a house'			

In Lendu, the subject pronominals are true pronouns since they can be substituted by a nominal subject. They never occur together with the subject noun. Hence they are independent morphemes and need to be written disjunctively. All other pronouns in the same paradigm need to be written as separate orthographic words as well.

This is contrary to most Bantu languages, which have subject morphemes that do not replace a nominal subject but remain with the verb whether or not a nominal subject is present. One such language is Swahili, shown in example (11).

(11) Swahili [swh] (Bantu G.42; Tanzania/Kenya)

a.	a-na-lala <analala>	b.	m-toto	a-na-lala <mtoto analala>
	3SG-PR-sleep		CL1-child	3SG-PR-sleep
	'he is sleeping'		'the child is sleeping'	

In such cases, these morphemes are considered subject prefixes of the verb and need to be written conjunctively. They may also fall within the scope of vowel harmony and/or be tonally dependent on the verb. In addition to these subject prefixes, most Bantu languages have independent subject pronouns as well—true, independent morphemes—which may be used for extra emphasis but are not obligatory in the sentence.

5.3.2 Phonological criteria

The phonological criteria include:

- pronounceability in isolation;
- phonological unity; and
- phonological bridging.

5.3.2.1 Pronounceability in isolation

Pronounceability in isolation refers first of all to those grammatical morphemes which *can* be pronounced in isolation. If so, they are most likely independent morphemes.

Ngiti [niy], a Nilo-Saharan, Central-Sudanic language, has affirmative and negative markers. Both can, on their own, be used as the answer to a question, as shown in example (12). Since they can be used with meaning in isolation, they are independent morphemes and should therefore be written as independent words.

(12) Ngiti [niy] (Nilo-Saharan, Central-Sudanic; D.R.Congo)

Have you come from the fields?	<ɨwà>	'yes'
Did you see the children?	<ɨnzá>	'no'

Second, this criterion applies to those grammatical morphemes which cannot be pronounced in isolation and which must therefore automatically be written together with the main lexical morpheme. This is further supported by the criterion of phonological unity described below.

5.3.2.2 Phonological unity

Phonological unity relates to influence from the lexical morpheme to grammatical morphemes and/or vice versa by phonological processes. This shows that the morphemes belong together and should therefore be written as one word in the orthography. This often concerns prosodic features like tone, nasalization, or any type of vowel harmony. A feature such as vowel harmony normally spreads throughout the word, including its affixes. As for tone, often certain affixes are covered under the tonal melody of the whole word. These are indications that the vowel or tone of a certain grammatical morpheme is not independent of the elements of the lexical morpheme.

Komo [kmw], a Bantu language spoken in D.R.Congo, like Swahili discussed in §5.3.1.3, has subject prefixes which must be written conjunctively with the verb (data from Van Dyken and Kutsch Lojenga 1993:12). Example (13) shows some instances of subject prefixes which have two forms, according to the vowel-harmony system operating in the language. This phonological unity is an extra criterion to show that these subject morphemes have to be written attached to the verb.

(13) Komo [kmw] (Bantu D.23; D.R.Congo)

a.	ne-bangi	'I have feared'	b.	bo-bangi	'you (pl) have feared'
	nɛ-yɔngi	'I have spoken'		bɔ-yɔngi	'you (pl) have spoken'

In Lyélé [lee], a Niger-Congo, Gur language of Burkina Faso, the morpheme meaning 'in' follows the noun and forms a phonological unit with it because of the vowel harmony (and tone). For this reason, it should be written attached to the noun, as shown in example (14). Its underlying form is *-wa*; when it follows a [+ATR] noun, it surfaces as *-wə*.

(14) Lyélé [lee] (Niger-Congo, Gur; Burkina Faso)

a. <kɛ̀lɛ́**wa**> *<kɛ̀lɛ́ wa>
courtyard-in

b. <gɔ**wa**> *<gɔ wa>
bush-in

c. <yólówə> *<yóló wə>
bag-in

d. <mǐn**wə**> *<mǐn wə>
fire-in

Mvuba [mxh], a Central-Sudanic language of D.R.Congo, has a system of case marking by clitics following the last element of a particular syntactic constituent. While subject noun phrases are unmarked, object noun phrases are marked by a clitic consisting of a vowel which is underlyingly /-e/, but which has various allomorphs conditioned by the final vowel of the noun phrase. The vowel of the clitic immediately follows the last vowel of the word to which it is attached, without an intervening break or glottal stop. For these reasons, the clitic is attached to the final element of the noun phrase by a hyphen.

(15) Mvuba [mxh] (Nilo-Saharan, Central-Sudanic; D.R.Congo)

Subject	Object	
<habo>	<habo-o>	'chicken'
<habo dehu>	<habo dehu-e>	'other chicken'
<evhe>	<evhe-e>	'pygmee'
<ɨna>	<ɨna-a>	'him'
<bʉkʉ vhɨvhɨ>	<bʉkʉ vhɨvhɨ-e>	'small banana'

5.3.2.3 Phonological bridging

Phonological bridging refers to the question of how to divide words in a phrase or sentence when in speech everything is blended together. Should the "bridging" be written as pronounced—in which case words will change shape according to the various environments in which they occur—or should each orthographic word remain stable? Linguistically, this refers to postlexical rules, which are an automatic consequence of chaining or blending words together in speech. Such postlexical, mostly gradient (rather than categorical) morphophonological phenomena should not be represented in the written form of the language, where each orthographic word should present a "constant visual image" in every environment in which it occurs. The blending, together with the sound processes, comes automatically as people read. In this situation, each word should retain its constant image in the written form (cf. the discussion of fast and slow speech in §2.6 and the Malila data in example (2) in §5.2.2).

5.3.3 Semantic criteria

The semantic criteria include:

- referential independence;
- conceptual unity; and
- minimal ambiguities.

5.3.3.1 Referential independence

Referential independence refers to the fact that each orthographic word must communicate meaning in isolation. Here, it becomes clear that (noun-class) affixes, which are obligatory when a word is pronounced in its citation form, must definitely be attached to the root/stem, since neither the root by itself nor the affix is a referentially independent form. The concepts of referential independence and pronounceability in isolation are close and are often applicable together. The first notion refers more to the semantic aspect and the second more to the phonological aspect.

Swahili and most other Bantu languages have singular and plural noun-class markers. The prefixes themselves have no referential independence, nor do the noun roots without their prefixes. Hence the fact that the noun-class markers are indeed prefixes which need to be written conjunctively with the roots. In addition, no element can ever be inserted between the noun-class marker and the root, which is another criterion for writing them together. This is illustrated in example (16). Separating the prefix from the root (as shown in the starred forms) would be unthinkable.

(16) Swahili [swh] (Bantu G.42; Tanzania/Kenya)

a.	<watoto>	‘children’	*<wa toto>
	CL2-child		
b.	<mayai>	‘eggs’	*<ma yai>
	CL6-egg		

c. <mizizi> 'roots' *<mi zizi>
CL3-root

5.3.3.2 Conceptual unity

Conceptual unity is a criterion that needs to be considered in the case of compound words. If two independent words acquire a new meaning when put together, they are conceptually a unit and there should be a closer link on the page than if they were two independent units.

In Ngiti, *atɔakpà* 'type of cooking pot' is made up of *atɔ* 'year' and *akpà* 'something long'. Probably, this was originally a type of cooking pot which would last for a long time, but now it is one conceptual unit.[12] Compound nouns are dealt with in more detail in §5.4.3.

5.3.3.3 Minimal ambiguities

Minimal ambiguities relates to two (near-)homophonous expressions that are segmentally the same but with a slightly different tone or stress pattern, and which have somewhat different meanings. There is the possibility of writing the morphemes in the expression conjunctively in one of the meanings and disjunctively in the other meaning. In English we find that *lighthouse* and *blackbird* are compounds which form one conceptual unit comprising the meanings of both elements, and which have a different stress pattern from *light house* and *black bird*, which are nouns phrases in which each element represents its primary meaning. Generally, a language is not expected to have many such examples.

5.4 Morphosyntactic topics

5.4.1 Subject pronouns or prefixes?

In some languages, subject pronominal forms are written conjunctively with the verb (or another grammatical morpheme preceding the verb), whereas in others, they are written disjunctively. What is behind

[12] In Ngiti, this compound noun is written with a hyphen as <*atɔ-akpà*>. The language has no long vowels or diphthongs, so whenever there are two vowels in succession (only in compound words), it was decided to write a hyphen in order to help readability of the individual components of the word.

those differences? And on what basis should one make a choice for a newly to-be-written language? When is a pronominal form an independent word, and when does it have to be considered a prefix?

The crucial test is to look at the third-person forms—he/she, they—and provide a nominal subject instead. If the pronominal form disappears and is replaced by the nominal subject, it is a pronoun indeed, and it will need to be written separately from the verb by the criterion of substitutability. If, on the other hand, the 3SG or 3PL pronominal form is not omitted when a nominal subject is introduced, then it is most likely a subject prefix which needs to be written attached to the verb since it is not a substitutable morpheme. In many languages, there may be phonological reasons like tone or vowel harmony which will give extra backing for writing the subject prefix together with the rest of the verbal elements. If this is so, then at the same time, the morphemes for all other persons will have to be considered prefixes as well and written attached to the verb root/stem (cf. also the discussion about substitutability in §5.3.1.3).

The following examples from Attié [ati] of Côte d'Ivoire and Lugwere [gwr] of Uganda parallel examples (10) and (11) from Lendu and Swahili in §5.3.1.3.

(17) Attié [ati] (Niger-Congo, Kwa; Côte d'Ivoire)[13]

a. < **ba** -fe wu >
3PL buy-PF couscous
'they have bought couscous (local dish)'

b. < **tsabiɛ** -fe wu >
people buy-PF couscous
'the people have bought couscous'

(18) Lugwere [gwr] (Bantu E.17; Uganda)

a. <bayemba>
ba-yemba
3SG-sing-FUT
'they will sing'

b. <abaana bayemba>
abaana **ba-**yemba
children 3SG-sing-FUT
'the children will sing'

[13] In Attié, punctuation marks are used to mark tone: the hyphen represents Low tone.

5.4.2 Nouns and pronouns with adpositions

The term "adpositions" covers both prepositions and postpositions. Some languages have prepositions, others have postpositions, in line with other word-order configurations in the language. In prepositional languages, a noun (phrase) or a pronoun is preceded by a preposition; in postpositional languages, a noun (phrase) or a pronoun is followed by a postposition. In many languages, prepositions and postpositions are independent morphemes and thus written as separate orthographic words; in others, some adpositions may be bound morphemes (cf. example (14) from Lyélé).

However, it is acceptable to make one orthographic decision for prepositions or postpositions accompanied by a noun (phrase) and another decision for prepositions or postpositions accompanied by a pronoun. Since pronouns are often short words, it is not uncommon to find languages in which they are written conjunctively with an adposition. Such a decision is systematic and can be learned for both reading and writing.

In Swahili, as shown in example (19), the preposition *na* 'with' is written separately when found with a noun (phrase) or with the independent pronouns, but it is written together with the shortened, monosyllabic forms of the independent pronouns.

(19) Swahili [swh] (Bantu G.42; Tanzania/Kenya)

<na mtoto>	'with the child'
<na mimi>	'with me'
<naye>	'with him'
<nami>	'with me'

5.4.3 Compound nouns

Compound nouns are a frequent phenomenon in many languages. They consist of at least two roots, which can be two noun roots or, for example, a noun root and an adjective root or a verb root. In addition, grammatical morphemes could be included as well, such as obligatory class markers or derivational morphemes.

Some compound nouns are transparent, that is, the meaning of the whole equals the sum of the meanings of the constituent parts, as in example (20) from Ngiti.

(20) Ngiti [niy] (Nilo-Saharan, Central-Sudanic; D.R.Congo)

odu-mbǐ	'slingshot'	< *odu* 'stone' + *imbi* 'vine, rope'
àbǐ-dhɔ̀	'date'	< *àbǐ* 'moon' + *ɨdhɔ* 'day'

In others, only one part of a compound noun is transparent and the other part may never occur independently, so it is impossible to discover its basic meaning. These are well known as "cranberry morphemes," after the word *cranberry*, where *cran* has no apparent independent meaning. This is the case with the Ngiti word in example (21).

(21) Ngiti [niy] (Nilo-Saharan, Central-Sudanic; D.R.Congo)

kìlì-ku	'midnight'	< *kìlì* '?' + *iku* 'night'

In yet others, the phonology of the language may indicate that it is a compound (e.g., a break in vowel harmony or some tonal reason), but neither part exists on its own. For example, the word *bɨ̌-hòlǒ* 'inedible mushroom, SP' in Ngiti mixes [–ATR] <ɨ> with [+ATR] <o>.

Finally, there are compounds in which both parts may be transparent but the meaning represents a totally new concept, not directly (though maybe historically) derivable from the individual meanings of the constituent parts, as in the Ngiti words in example (22).

(22) Ngiti [niy] (Nilo-Saharan, Central-Sudanic; D.R.Congo)

àlɔ̌-àyi	'weaver bird'	< *àlɔ̌* 'axe' + *àyi* 'female'
atɔ-akpa	'type of cooking pot'	< *atɔ* 'year' + *akpà* 'something long'

What approach should one take with these various kinds of compound nouns? It is here that we may apply semantic considerations, in particular the criterion of conceptual unity.

First of all, in the case of those compounds that are semi-transparent or non-transparent—where one or both parts have no independent meaning—the compound represents one concept. For these compounds, there really is no choice but to write them as one word, even if, phonologically, it is clear that they consist of more than one part.

As for the transparent compounds, one should first ascertain if there is a clear distinction between these compounds and inalienable possessive constructions in the language, and if so, how that difference is marked. If there is no clear difference, one will have to agree on one way of writing both of them; otherwise writers will be confused as to when to write the parts together or separately. If there is a clear distinction between inalienable possessive constructions and transparent compounds, the latter may be written conjunctively like the other categories of compound words, but another solution should then be found for inalienable possessive constructions.

5.4.4 Reduplication

Conceptual unity is also an important criterion in word-boundary decisions relating to reduplication. Many languages make use of reduplication or even triplication. As with compounds, one can distinguish between transparent reduplication and non-transparent reduplication. If a language has instances of non-transparent reduplication—where the single form has no meaning on its own—there is no reason to use a hyphen between the two parts, because they represent one concept. After all, it is not sure if such forms are really cases of reduplication or if they just accidentally contain two identical syllables. The Ngiti nouns and modifiers in example (23) have no non-reduplicated counterpart, so there is no reason to write the two parts separately or even with a hyphen.

(23) Ngiti [niy] (Nilo-Saharan, Central-Sudanic; D.R.Congo)

ndùmùndúmú	'blind person'	* <ndùmù-ndúmú>
mbìrìmbìrì	'spider'	* <mbìrì-mbìrì>
dhèdhè	'some'	* <dhè-dhè>
tsɛ́tsɛ́	'greasy'	* <tsɛ́-tsɛ́>

If the non-reduplicated part also exists on its own and reduplication takes place to intensify the meaning, then one could decide to write the two parts separately. However, if there are any morphophonological processes, like vowel deletion in example (24) or tonal changes, the best solution would be to write those also as one orthographic word. In the Ngiti words in example (24), some reduplicated and triplicated modifiers also have a simple form, but because of the fact that vowels are elided in the process, these are written as one word.

(24) Ngiti [niy] (Nilo-Saharan, Central-Sudanic; D.R.Congo)

ádzǐ	'long, SG'	ádzàdzǐ	'long, PL'	<	adzi + adzi
odú	'heavy, SG'	odódú	'heavy, PL'	<	odu + odu
ɨsɔ́	'lightweight'	ɨsɨ́sɔ́	'lightweight, easy'	<	ɨsɔ + ɨsɔ
		sɔ́sɔ́sɔ́	'very lightweight'	<	ɨsɔ + ɨsɔ + ɨsɔ

If reduplication is used in verbs—e.g., as an intensifier, or to express iterativity—then this reduplication forms a new stem, in which case it should be written as one word, so that it can subsequently be inflected as a unit. This is the case with the Lugwere words in example (25).

(25) Lugwere [gwr] (Bantu E.17; Uganda)

a.	kuluka	'to weave'	
	kulukaluka	'to weave fast and continuously'	*<kuluka-luka>
b.	kutema	'to cut'	
	kutematema	'to cut fast and continuously'	*<kutema-tema>

In case two different strategies are adopted for the broad topic of reduplication—writing non-transparent reduplicatives as one orthographic word and transparent ones as two orthographic words—it is very important to test if writers can put this rule into practice in a consistent way.

5.5 Steps in establishing word boundaries: a summary

In conclusion, the following steps summarize the procedure for establishing word boundaries:

1. Study the phonology, morphology, and basic syntax of the language to determine the status of the grammatical morphemes as affixes, clitics, or free morphemes. Study the morphophonology to determine the sound processes that take place between root/stem and affixes as well as clitics.
2. Make a first decision to write affixes conjunctively and free morphemes disjunctively. Then check if this agrees with native-speaker intuition and if native speakers can put it into practice when writing the language.

3. Look at the morphophonological processes between root/stem and affixes, and write the phonemes resulting from the processes. Pay particular attention to cases of elision.
4. Subsequently, study every other grammatical morpheme to find out if it could possibly be a clitic, and if it is phonologically dependent on a neighboring morpheme. For each morpheme, check if it exercises or undergoes a morphophonological process. If so, explain the dependence of the relevant morpheme and see if people are in favor of writing it together with the other morpheme or with a hyphen or apostrophe. Make a decision for each morpheme (or set of morphemes) individually.
5. Make it clear that all "decisions" are tentative until everybody sees that it works for reading (check if people stumble), writing (check if they can follow the rule with ease), and teaching. Small books can be published at this point, exactly in order to find out if the word-boundary rules work.
6. Reconsider! If people seem to live well with the particular choice, then continue with it, and they will gradually get used to it. Check to make sure the topic has been studied thoroughly. If it appears to cause difficulties, then weigh the criteria and arguments again and make a different decision. It may take a few years for every detail to be settled.
7. Document each decision (with examples) in an orthography statement or guide, both for the present and the future generation, so that everybody now and in the future can attempt to follow the same set of word-boundary conventions.

References

Casali, Roderic F. 1998. *Resolving hiatus.* New York: Garland Publishing.

Dyken, Julia R. van, and C. Kutsch Lojenga. 1993. Word boundaries: Key factors in orthography development/Les frontières du mot: facteurs-clés dans le développement d'une orthographe. In Rhonda Hartell (ed.), *Alphabets of Africa,* 3–20/*Alphabets de langues africaines,* 3–22. Dakar, Senegal: UNESCO and Summer Institute of Linguistics.

Elson, Benjamin F., and Velma B. Pickett. 1988. *Beginning morphology and syntax.* Third edition. Dallas: Summer Institute of Linguistics.

Guthrie, Malcolm. 1948. *Bantu word division: A new study of an old problem.* London: Oxford University Press.

Guthrie, Malcolm. 1971. *Bantu prehistory, inventory and indexes.* Vol. 2 of *Comparative Bantu: An introduction to the comparative linguistics and prehistory of the Bantu languages.* Farnborough, UK: Gregg International Publishers.

Kutsch Lojenga, Constance. 1994. *Ngiti: A Central-Sudanic language of Zaire.* Köln: Rüdiger Köppe Verlag.

Kutsch Lojenga, Constance. 2009. [+ATR] affixes in Bantu languages. Paper presented at the Third International Conference on Bantu Languages, Tervuren, Belgium. 25–27 March 2009.

Kutsch Lojenga, Constance. 2010. Vowel shortening in the noun phrase in Malila. In Karsten Legère and Christina Thornell (eds.), *Bantu languages: Analyses, description and theory,* 131–142. Köln: Rüdiger Köppe Verlag.

Maho, Jouni Filip. 2009. NUGL online: The online version of the New Updated Guthrie List, a referential classification of the Bantu languages. June 4, 2009 version. http://goto.glocalnet.net/mahopapers/nuglonline.pdf (accessed November 29, 2012).

Mohanan, K.P. 1986. *The theory of Lexical Phonology.* Dordrecht, the Netherlands: D. Reidel Publishing Company.

Otterloo, Karen van. 2011. *The Kifuliiru language.* Volume 1: *Phonology, tone, and morphological derivation.* SIL International Publications in Linguistics 146. Dallas: SIL International.

Pike, Kenneth L., and E. Pike. 1982. Rev. ed. *Grammatical analysis.* Summer Institute of Linguistics and the University of Texas at Arlington Publications in Linguistics 53. Dallas: Summer Institute of Linguistics. http://www.sil.org/acpub/repository/41339.pdf (accessed November 29, 2012). First published 1977. Page reference is to the 1982 edition.

6

Standardization: What's the Hurry?

Elke Karan

Using case studies and citations from a variety of literature, this chapter presents arguments against rushing the writing system design and standardization process for newly written languages. It highlights a variety of conditions under which best practices may call for "slowing down" and allowing a standard to evolve through practice rather than prescription. The peaceable coexistence of more than one standard for some languages illustrates that there can be more than one "correct" way to write. Granting more freedom in writing might be more motivational for a language community to actively engage in literacy practices than a single prescriptive standard.

6.1 Introduction

Coulmas (1996:379–380) defines *orthography* as "a normative selection of the possibilities of a script for writing a particular language in *a uniform and standardized way*" (emphasis mine). But who does the selecting? How long might the process toward standardization take? Is standardization of the writing system a requirement for literacy to take root in a speech community?

It is unlikely that from the outset everyone will write a newly written language in "a uniform and standardized way" or that a proposed writing system will meet with across-the-board acceptance. Stebbins (2001) discusses *multiple* existing orthographies for an endangered language in Canada, Sm'algyax (a.k.a. Coast Tsimshian) [tsi], spoken by about four hundred adult speakers and refers to *standardization* as a "thorny" issue. Mason and Allen (2002), working with Haitian Creole [hat], a language with more than seven million speakers, note that standardization of the written form can be a struggle for non-dominant languages and that it is not always attained.

Implementing a single norm for a language, regardless of location, number of speakers, literary tradition or lack thereof can be a challenge indeed. This may explain the more recent trend of disassociating the concept of standardization from the term *orthography.* Sebba (2009:36) states, "An orthography for a particular language may be standardized, but it does not have to be, and even if there is a standard orthography for a language, variation may be present, either officially legitimated or not."

The term *working orthography* is at times used in language development situations to refer to orthographies used in early vernacular publications but not yet standardized (Bauernschmidt 1980; SIL 1999). Modifications can easily be introduced to improve upon the yet flexible and experimental system as inadequacies or objections are uncovered.

Working orthography is also used in the context of language documentation. It refers to a system designed for notation purposes, such as for wordlists (Mosel 2006; also see documentation project reports posted online by the Language Documentation Training Center, such as for Betawi [bew], Dayak Ngaju [nij], and Javanese [jav][1]). Such systems are not necessarily expected to be adopted by the community for their functional purposes. Mosel (2006:79) states:

> [F]or the data base of the project, especially for the lexicon, a consistent working orthography that distinguishes between norms and variants is a prerequisite, but this does not necessarily imply that the local transcribers have to learn and use it. Later, when the

[1] http://www.ling.hawaii.edu/ldtc/languages.html (accessed October 31, 2012).

> speech community decides on their own norms, the working orthography can be adjusted to their standard orthography.

Various factors are alluded to in this quotation: intended function of a system; stages in the writing system development process; whether or not the speech community's desires have been given expression and taken into consideration; and speech varieties. Other factors also come into play, but these will not be discussed here. They have been covered at length in the literature (Pike 1947; Smalley 1959; Berry 1968; Powlison 1968; Eira 1998; Malone 2004; Seifart 2006; Cahill and Karan 2008).

What might seem like a novel idea to some is that writing systems need to be tested and that the expectation should be that they are not fixed once for all (Baker 1997) but are subject to change. Symbolization choices made amongst various options should not be held too tightly or presented prematurely as the standard. Snider (2001:323) urges language development workers to expect criticism of early efforts and recognize that a writing system will "undergo change for years to come." He presents this as a "natural and healthy process" which "should not be discouraged."

Writing system development should indeed be viewed as a process (Karan 2006), one that should not be rushed. It is important to articulate what the objective of developing a writing system is. Is it simply (a) to provide a standard to enable documentation and/or publication, or is it also (b) to develop positive attitudes in the speech community toward the written form of their language and to motivate individuals to read and to write their language? If it is the latter, the question needs to be posed: Is it necessary for a writing system to be standardized for this to take place? Developing positive attitudes may take more time than developing a code.

On the basis of various case studies, I propose that it could be beneficial to slow down the writing system development process and that under certain conditions, which I shall enumerate, it may be best to allow a standard to evolve naturally instead of prescribing right from the start how a given language should be written. It may even be beneficial to allow two (or several) standards to co-exist.

6.2 The "normative" expectation

In general, the expectation is that a written language would have one writing system, and that the system would be taught uniformly to speakers and learners of that language, i.e., that there would be a standard, against which practices could potentially be compared and judged as "right" or "wrong." This is, however, an editor's and school teacher's mindset. In a society where dictation plays a key role in the education of the young and books are viewed as authoritative, creative spelling and deviations from the standard are usually not welcome.

Governments understandably favor standardization (Bergman 1989). It makes language development more feasible and may reduce the cost of education. Often a government agency, such as an applied linguistics institute for instance, may handle matters related to language planning. Proactive corpus planning usually involves these components: linguistic analysis, the publishing of linguistic descriptions, the designing of a written code, the development of new terminology for use in additional domains, and the production of a variety of literature and reference works—ideally including a dictionary. These activities and products are expected to lead to a unified standard.

Allowing for alternate spellings for a limited set of words within a single standard might be allowed. This is usually the result of historical factors or dialectal issues. A dictionary, if one exists, would include the permissible spelling variations.

However, freedom of spelling within a society is not usually looked upon with favor. After all, that is not scientific and does not fit in with current understandings of what language development is. Having a language written in a variety of ways would be viewed as an obstacle to language development and to the implementation of a mother tongue-based education program, for instance.

There is also the question of relative status. Jaffe (2000:505–506) comments that "orthography is one of the key symbols of language unity and status itself" and further that "it is not only important to 'have' an orthography, but it is also critical for that orthography to have prescriptive power—to be standardized and authoritative, like the orthographies of dominant languages."

Stebbins (2001) also makes a strong case for orthography standardization for endangered languages. When there are only about four hundred adult speakers of a language left, most over fifty years old—as is the case in Sm'algyax of British Columbia, Canada—it seems counterproductive to have four or five competing writing systems while trying to teach the language to the younger generation. Yet, logic is not what rules. Even though a Sm'algyax practical orthography has been in use for over twenty years, the wider community is not necessarily embracing it.

Trudgill (1983:161) seems less convinced of the necessity of standardization of the written code. Referring to spelling, he states that "it is argued" that language standardization is necessary, but also that it is "an open question as to how much, if any, standardization is really required." He points out an *undesirable* side effect: that "deviations from the standard are interpreted as incontrovertible evidence of ignorance."

I agree that standardization is desirable. But these questions remain: How soon should a standard be proclaimed? Who decides what it should be? And what should happen if there are divergent opinions and practices? There are no clear-cut answers. Each situation is different and requires discretion and sensitivity to the sociopolitical situation at hand. Whether a standard develops naturally or by deliberate intervention, it may require more time to establish than expected.

6.3 Conditions which justify slowing down or delaying standardization

There seem to be some legitimate reasons for non-standardization of a language's writing system or non-application of an existing standard. In some cases, all that may be needed is additional time for linguistic analysis, community involvement, training efforts, testing, and diffusion in the move toward standardization. Other situations, discussed in §6.3.3–6.3.6, may be more complicated, and it may actually be prudent to embrace non-standardization or freedom in writing, at least for the time being.

6.3.1 Need for adequate time for analysis and community involvement

Careful linguistic analysis takes time. An initial analysis may need to be modified as additional data is gathered. The implementation of a writing system is a lengthy process, requiring training of potential users and the production of a variety of literature. Mother tongue speakers need to be given the opportunity to have input. A writing system needs to be tested with a broad representation of the language community. Several revisions may be needed. This was the case for Southeastern Nochixtlan Mixtec

[mxy] of Mexico. SIL consultant Inga McKendry (Karan 2006) reported that experimentation with various tone marking systems finally led to a workable system. Five different options were found to be unsatisfactory, before the sixth option was tried and had good results. Promoting one of the earlier solutions as the standard could have been detrimental to popular literacy.

Even if a writing system is backed by an official decree, it may be rejected if it does not find favor with the general population or various influential groups or agencies. Wedekind and Wedekind identify four factors which help promote a writing system: community participation, the contribution of local authors, the production of literature, and support through the school system. They state that these "can make the difference between a fruitless literacy campaign and a living literature" (1997:26). A community has to like the look of their writing system. It should not look strange to them. It should meet with their approval and make them proud.

It is sad indeed when good intentions combined with years of work and financial investment do not bring about the desired language development results. For instance, in Micronesia in the 1970s, language development and education goals failed to come to fruition when outside linguists did not realize the importance of community involvement in the decision-making process. They developed standard orthographies and prepared reference books such as grammars, dictionaries, and school materials, but did not test for community acceptance or effectiveness. Speech communities did not embrace the standards in some cases. The orthographies actually worked against, rather than promoted, vernacular language literacy (Yunick 2000; Rehg 2004).

6.3.2 Planning for adequate diffusion and testing

A language may be written inconsistently simply because writers, editors, and educators have not been adequately trained. This will result in inconsistent spelling between publications and even within a single publication. There is a positive side to this: at least there are pioneers interested in writing the language. Motivation to write in a non-dominant language cannot be taken for granted and anyone with such motivation needs to be encouraged. Such individuals need to be involved in orthography discussions and in the testing and implementation of the proposed standard—or of an agreed-upon revised standard. Writers' actual, uninhibited writing before being "trained" needs to be analyzed. Deviations from the proposed standard might reveal mother-tongue-speaker intuitions possibly indicating a point of linguistic misanalysis or highlight certain symbolization preferences. For example, various Sm'algyax conventions changed over time. Thus a new dictionary was produced, based on writers' preferences and practices that came to light through usage of the practical orthography between 1978 and 2001 (Stebbins 2001).

6.3.3 Accommodating those already literate in another orthographic tradition

Several standards may have evolved for a single language, each with its own loyal following. Baker (1997), for instance, refers to competing orthographies as well as to languages written in more than one script.[2] Or else, a writing system reform may have been introduced. Insisting that everyone submit to another standard than the one they are used to is risky business. Orthography design and orthography reform are seen as political acts and can trigger very strong reactions. When certain sectors of the population are already used to an existing system, it is best to accommodate them. Diplomacy will go further than dictating adherence to an imposed standard. Introducing a new standard slowly, in new domains and to the younger generation, will take time but will also pay great dividends in terms of avoiding conflict and stress for those already literate.

An accommodating approach, for instance, was taken in Germany when Fraktur and Kurrent scripts were replaced with Latin script (Karan 2006). In the Central African Republic, the 1984 decreed standard for Sango [sag] met with resistance. The language had been written with a French-based orthography for several generations and much of the corpus had been written in that tradition. The government did not insist on adherence to the official standard in new publications and in reprinted materials but rather adopted a permissive stance, which Fasold (1997:260) refers to as a "laissez-faire policy." In a more positive light, this could be interpreted as an act of diplomacy and conflict avoidance. Despite this lax stance on the part of the government, and although Sango is not used in primary or secondary schools, the new

[2] The use of more than one script for a language is usually referred to as digraphia (Dale 1980, DeFrancis 1984). Karan (2006:62–63) briefly lists causes for digraphia with examples. See Berlanda (2006) for a literature review and detailed discussions of digraphia situations from around the world.

orthography is slowly making inroads. Spelling continues to be inconsistent, but a closer look at recently published materials and environmental print reveals that resistance seems to be weakening in that the new standard is, in many cases, increasingly applied in writing Sango consonants and vowels. Writing tone has met with stronger resistance and continues to be discussed. In the meantime, thanks to an accommodating approach, publication and literacy efforts are able to continue (Karan 2006).

6.3.4 Uniformity not highly valued

At times, orthographic variation, whatever the cause, is not seen as problematic by the local population. They appreciate freedom in writing and see the imposition of a standard as interference. If the community is not likely to embrace and promote a single standard, it makes no sense to insist on one. This seemed to be the case with Jamaican Creole English [jam]. Cassidy (1993:136) notes that the use of his writing system for the language is limited to academic circles "because there is no demand among readers for a consistent system."

Brody (2002, 2004), as well, reporting on Yucatec Maya [yua] notes that the lack of uniformity in writing the language does not cause readers and writers distress. In fact, graphic and word level variation is accepted and expected. That the name of a town is written in six different ways is not viewed as a problem. In fact, what became a "source of conflict and mistrust" was an effort to adopt a unified alphabet at a 1984 meeting, where only speakers from the state of Yucatan were represented. Brody's report can serve as a warning: "There was a popular perception that the 1984 alphabet was established by and for linguists, who sought minimal popular input" (2004:15). The expectation of writers and educators interviewed by Brody was that "if left to evolve organically, suitable norms and conventions would emerge and variation would diminish on its own" (ibid., 17).

6.3.5 Language variation

Language variation is a challenge for orthography design. This has always been the case. Concerning Dutch in the nineteenth century, Geerts, Van den Broeck, and Verdoodt (1977:185) note that "uniform spelling proved to be impossible since there was no generally acknowledged standard language."

Designing an orthography for a language with variation increases the potential for conflict. Social influence may not be equitably distributed between speakers of various dialects. Jaffe (2000:500) makes a startling strong comment: "Non-standard speakers are those whose speech does not have its own orthography; those who do not have the social power to standardize and prescribe linguistic form.... Orthography is a potent and often contested focus for issues of social and symbolic control." Because orthography design can create an arena for political struggles to be played out, it is especially important not to be hasty in declaring a written standard in situations where there are a number of dialects. Additional research, public-relations work, discussions, and testing will be required.

Stebbins (2001:167), reporting on Sm'algyax, comments that "people tend not to want a prestige norm to be based on any dialect but their own." Speakers' perceptions of similarity or differences between their way of speaking and that of others may not necessarily correlate with linguistic distance between dialects. Therefore, attitudes and inter-group relationships, not linguistic factors, will determine if one standard will be acceptable to all. The desire for affiliation versus separate identity will play a major role in such a decision. There are five basic approaches to writing system design in a dialect situation:

6.3.5.1 *The dialectal approach*

In a dialectal approach, different orthographies and separate sets of literatures would be developed for each dialect. This approach emphasizes linguistic differences and sociocultural distance between groups, resulting in linguistic and social fragmentation, and is therefore not encouraged (Bergman 1989; Robbins 1992). To force harmonization between varieties, when separate identity is what is desired by the speech community, is also not desirable. It could be interpreted as denying them their linguistic rights. If dialect differences are minor, one option would be for the dialects to share a body of literature but allowing alternate spellings for a specific list of words.

6.3.5.2 *The reference dialect approach (unilectal)*

If common identity and desired affiliation outweigh other factors, it may work to base the writing system on one of the dialects. This would be a unilectal approach using a reference dialect. Which dialect is chosen may be influenced by (a) the relative location (a central location may have fostered a widespread regional comprehension due to bilectalism); (b) the number of speakers; and/or (c) an elevated level of prestige. Robbins (1992:612) comments that prestige is usually tied to "centers of power, trade, and learning." Designing a writing system based on a reference dialect and using these criteria has been the status quo in practice and has been upheld as a good option for years (Nida 1947; Pike 1947; Sjoberg 1966; Wiesemann, Sadembouo, and Tadadjeu 1983). But, caution is in order: privileging one sector of the population by choosing its speech variety as the reference dialect could be misinterpreted as deliberate favoritism and offend speakers of other dialects.

On the other hand, if speakers of all varieties are part of the discussions and process, and respect and concern is shown for all varieties so that speakers do not feel that their language rights are threatened, much can be gained. It is important that all are able to learn the system well—that it not be exceedingly opaque for some of the dialects, making it difficult for speakers of those dialects to learn it. It must be made clear to all that adherence to a written standard allows text to be read with various dialect pronunciations. It is not an attempt to regulate speech. (See the Lisu and Lahu case study in Adams, this volume, for an example where this approach was successfully applied.)

Languages with speakers on different sides of international boundaries present an additional challenge for standardization since harmonization across borders is more difficult to orchestrate.[3] In addition, the regional and international languages, which influence what the speech communities expect and want, are likely to be different. If there is an interest in sharing reading materials or publishing common school materials, there needs to be support and commitment at the national level.[4]

6.3.5.3 *The differentiated approach*

Another approach is the differentiated approach. To provide extra support for those wanting to learn to read, materials intended for reading and

[3] The standardization of Hausa [hau] in Niger and Nigeria (Wolff 1991, 2000) and the harmonization between Indonesian [ind] and Standard Malay [zsm] (Asmah Haji Omar 1989) are two sample success stories.

[4] See Funnell 2004 for a literature review and case study for cross-border language issues.

writing instruction, as well as easy-to-read materials, would be produced in a "teaching orthography" based on the various dialects (i.e., a pedography using a dialectal approach). However, since experienced readers are able to deal with much more orthographic abstraction than beginners, a single body of literature would serve across dialects (unilectal or multidialectal approach, discussed in 6.3.5.2 and 6.3.5.4, respectively). This approach, suggested by respected individuals (Pike 1947; Nida 1954; Gudschinsky 1973; Robbins 1992), is a perfectly viable option but has not proven popular.

6.3.5.4 *The multidialectal approach*

Berry (1968:741) contrasts situations where there is a "linguistic center"—i.e., where there is a dialect that merits its "choice as a standard"—with a situation where it may be necessary to employ a "composite orthography on sociolinguistic grounds." Simons (1977:325) defines such an orthography as "one in which the phonologies of many dialects of a language are compared and accounted for in designing the orthography." It would not represent one specific dialect, but, through careful choices in symbolization, would be specifically designed to extend to all of the dialects. By taking the linguistic realities of all the varieties into consideration, it would, hopefully, avoid the stigmatizing of some. This approach, known as the multidialectal approach, is not to be confused with the fifth approach described below, i.e., it is not a writing system based on an artificial speech variety.

Because the multidialectal approach usually involves less-conventional measures and less-than-ideal practices such as over- or underrepresentation, it would be prudent to plan for an extended time of testing with a variety of learners: those already literate in another language (needing transfer skills), those who are not yet literate in any language, and individuals from every dialect region. Since reading would be easier than writing with a more abstract system, it is especially important to also test how well people can write original compositions using the system.

6.3.5.5 *The unilectal approach based on an artificial dialect*

A final approach is the unilectal approach based on an artificial dialect. Developing a writing system based on artificial language or on a historical reconstruction is not recommended. Reading and writing such a system would require learning a system foreign to everyone and result in low motivation. Nida warns against it (1954), as does SIL's *LinguaLinks* (SIL 2002) in this statement: "Be aware of the danger of arriving at an orthography not appreciated or owned by any of the dialects." Stebbins (2001:188) reports that some community members consider the "hybrid" practical orthography used to teach Sm'algyax in schools "inauthentic because it does not accurately represent any one of the Sm'algyax dialects associated with particular villages."

6.3.6 Conflicting views

Conflicts over orthography are not uncommon. Some of the causes are local politics, differing script preferences, competing writing traditions, disagreements over symbolization, among others. When people do not see eye to eye on orthography issues, when the process gets messy and factions seem to be having a tug-of-war, it may be wise to take standardization off the agenda for a while. Coulmas (2000:47) warns: "As the most tangible subsystem of language, writing lends itself easily to political instrumentalization." Where there is already open contention and rivalry, forcing an issue as political as a writing system will likely fan the flames of a power struggle. (See the first case study in Adams, this volume.) Berry (1968:737) states, "Where systems of writing become identified (as often happens) with unreasoning and unreasonable political, national or religious passions there is little that the linguist can or should do."

Although I recognize the potential for tension and intense emotions surrounding the orthography development and standardization process, I think that there are some things a linguist *can* do. The role of peacemaker is always appropriate. Sacrificing one's personally held ideal solutions may be the first step. Helping the various groups reach *their* literacy and education goals is also appropriate. Publication need not come to a halt if an agreement is not reached. Baker (1997:120), writing about competing orthographies for French-lexicon creoles, reports that either "in spite of" or "because of" these competing systems, "there has been a substantial increase in the number of texts published in these languages."

Offering to test various symbolization options and presenting test results may provide helpful, eye-opening information. Time, new insights, and increased understanding may, in time, smooth things over. The next generation of leaders may take a different view on matters and be more ready to negotiate.

6.4 Standardization and the implementation of a reform take time

Marlett (2010:185) notes two elements which must be in place for the widespread use of a written language: "an adequate writing system" and "a broad-based acceptance of that writing system." These two elements also figure prominently in Smalley's list of maxims (Smalley 1959; discussed in more detail in Hinton, this volume) and Malone's list of criteria for an ideal writing system (Malone 2004).

In cultures where reading or writing in the local language is of little consequence, speakers may take little interest in how it might be written. In such a situation, it may take decades to work toward an accepted standard. For example, "paper and books were of no tangible importance" among the Seri [sei] in Mexico when Edward and Mary Moser designed a practical alphabet for the language in the mid-1950s (Marlett 2010:185). Due to the irrelevance of written materials in the Seri culture, it would have been quite difficult to check on the acceptance and adequacy of the writing system. The Seri language never played any significant role in formal education. Yet, decades later, some self-taught Seri writers began taking an interest in documenting Seri culture and scientific knowledge. These gifted individuals are currently producing literature in Seri sought after by the community. Thus Seri is moving from mostly oral use to the written domain as well. Through usage, the need for some changes in the writing system became evident. It was not the alphabet that needed changing—the Seri appreciated symbols which indicated Seri distinctiveness. Rather, writers suggested changes for word breaks and punctuation conventions. A Seri committee, not expatriates, is taking responsibility for determining norms for their writing system—this approximately fifty years after linguists began analyzing the language. Fifty years is actually a relatively short time span compared to how long it took to standardize some European languages.[5]

[5] Note: implementing a reform can also take years. A cross-border Dutch spelling reform project launched in 1864 resulted in spelling debates and conflict that lasted ninety years (see Geerts, Van den Broeck, and Verdoodt 1977). A more recent German spelling reform turned into a ten-year national conflict (see Coulmas 2000; Giersberg 2007).

6.4.1 Standardization of European languages

The idea that there should be a single writing standard for languages is based on precedents set by majority languages. It is easy to forget that standardization for these languages often involved a very long process. It was not necessarily linguists or government departments or pedagogues who had the most influence on how languages were written. Norms developed over time, based on individual, local, then regional decisions.

Jaffré and Fayol challenge our preconceptions by this statement (1997:41, translated and cited in Coulmas 2003:94): "None of the European alphabetic orthographies is the fruit of deliberate linguistic calculation. They are all natural children of tinkering and groping in the dark, which nonetheless have reached a quasi-functional balance." It appears that there had been freedom to experiment.

Charpentier (1997:233) points out that the standardization of Western languages has only been accomplished in the eighteenth and nineteenth centuries and that prior to that, "for the vernaculars each scribe and each publishing house had their own conventions in Europe until printing had been established for at least two centuries." He suggests that, possibly, norms may not be as important as we think.

Johnson (2005:18–27), discussing the history of the German orthography specifically, comments that by the end of the fourteenth century, there was already "a substantial body of written German in existence, the norms for which had evolved without any genuinely systematic, that is, overtly prescriptive, intervention." In fact, there were various writing traditions being practiced in different parts of the country. Authors usually wrote in their local dialect.

Keller (1978:361–362) indicates that lack of uniformity in written German did not seem to be a major concern to readers or publishers:

> Spelling in German was allowed to remain irregular and often arbitrary.... The reader of manuscripts was used to a multiplicity of dialectal forms and irregularity of spelling. The reader of printed books expected nothing else and accepted the same orthographic abundance.... Although printers and booksellers were no doubt interested in nationwide sales, linguistic uniformity was not a precondition.

School districts in Germany eventually had their own orthographic guidelines, but these were only drawn up in the nineteenth century. Efforts at reform and standardization at an orthography conference in 1876 failed, but a second effort in 1901 was more successful. It mostly consisted of affirming the already widely used Prussian school guidelines as the norm to be employed. Early dictionaries by Konrad Duden allowed for quite a few spelling variations. Pedagogical considerations did not play a big role in the 1901 German orthography conference. The agreed-upon standard was viewed as less than perfect. Reforms were anticipated. However, what key players did not recognize at the time was how very difficult it would be to introduce changes, i.e., to modify a standard. This needs to be kept in mind when developing a writing system for non-dominant languages.

The English orthography was also not imposed top-down. Scragg (1974) contrasts the evolution of the English standard through usage and decision making over time by scribes and printers with the top-down implementation of the French spelling standard by specific decision makers who had been given such authority:

> English spelling seems to have been particularly resistant to the interference of linguistic philosophers. The situation was quite different in France, where the Académie Française, founded in 1635, had the specific duty of prescribing on linguistic matters. (Scragg 1974:81)

But even the influence of the Académie remained limited for quite some time: their first two editions of dictionaries were not prescriptive but rather simply reflected writing practices of the day.

Promotion of a written standard through the education system, popular access to dictionaries, and widespread usage of religious materials have been key factors for successful standardization of many languages. But this does not mean that standardization took hold quickly.

As already implied, one main reason for allowing adequate time before establishing a standard is that it is difficult to implement necessary changes later. Quite a few authors have commented on the difficulty of implementing orthography reforms. Here are just three:

> The greater and grander the tradition of literacy, literature, and liturgy in an orthographic community, the less likely that even minor systematic orthographic change will be freely accepted and the less likely that any orthographic change will be considered minor. (Fishman 1977:xvi)

> There would, of course, be opposition from people who do not want to relearn. A pattern once learned takes on a sacredness which becomes sacrilege to violate. (Smalley 1954:176)

> The status quo of the orthography may be regarded as sacred, i.e. as something in which change is perceivable only as degradation. (Eira 1998:180)

6.4.2 The standardization process for newly written languages

Developing and promoting a writing system is a complex process. It involves all kinds of levels of cooperation and infrastructures. Those involved in the process may feel pressured to get the job done quickly. Mason and Allen (2002) make this very point:

> Whereas many of the world's major languages underwent the standardization and normalization stages of their written form over a period of several centuries, today's modern less-prevalent languages are forced to undergo rapid standardization processes within a period of less than one or two decades.

Sometimes linguistic analysis is not given enough care. I personally know of situations where literature had to be destroyed later because the phonological analysis was done in a hurry.

Linguistic training may suggest that orthography design is straightforward and can be accomplished fairly quickly in a "scientific laboratory." We read of the following procedure followed by the Central Institute of Indian Languages:

> First, a linguistic description is obtained or made. Secondly, the phonemic inventory is mapped onto the alphabet of the standard script of the language used at the state level; thirdly a trilingual dictionary of about 2,000 words is prepared. Rules for the spelling system are evolved, and primers written. The primer and dictionary are handed over to the State Education Department for use in primary schools. The basic purpose is to provide initial literacy to the child in his own tribal language and to ensure a gradual transfer to the state's standard language and its writing system. (Gerbault 1997:178–179)

Using local languages in the school system is praiseworthy. This will help children from minority language groups succeed instead of suffer educational discrimination. However, the clear-cut procedure used for coming up with the writing system is worrisome. The process does not mention community involvement in the decision-making process nor testing the new writing system before it is promoted through the school system.

Eira (1998:176) recognizes that what linguists may consider an ideal solution may not find popular acceptance, stating "whether or not one can propose principles for a linguistically optimal writing system, it does not at all follow that linguistic efficacy is the only or the most significant factor in the creation of orthography, defined as the accepted standard for writer/readers of the language." (See Hinton, this volume, for further discussion of this issue.)

It is therefore important to consider which factors contribute to the acceptance or rejection of a written standard. Apart from the linguistic system of the language and national level policies, sociolinguistic issues such as ethnic and religious identity and tradition need to be considered. One of the biggest hurdles for a single standard's implementation is that of language variety within the larger speech community. Although these factors are less tangible than linguistic structure, they are influential.

Robinson and Gadelii (2003:§5.6) highlight a language's role as "a symbol of identity." Their experience has shown that seeing a language being put into writing for the first time can evoke "many different kinds of feelings" which need to be expressed. It is important for the community to be involved in the development of the written standard and to participate in the debate.

Other publications also express the importance of community involvement (Kutsch Lojenga 1996; Eira 1998; Malone 2004). Clearly, decision making by a community requires more time than it would take an intellectual making independent decisions at a desk. Script choice, dialect issues, attitudes toward other languages, symbol choices, the promotion of the written standard, literature production, who should be responsible for what, all need to be considered. Robinson and Gadelii (2003:§5.6) warn that this approach can be very complex:

> These questions cannot be dealt with quickly or easily. Some may be settled by a deliberate process of consultation and decision-making, others may evolve slowly with a consensus gradually developing. Language issues may form part of a broader cultural or political agenda.

Malone concurs: "Writing systems are not developed quickly. They take time and patience, dialogue and compromise." She considers the language committee the main decision-making body and urges such community leaders to encourage mother tongue speakers to write in their language as much as possible, as this will bring to light the strengths and weaknesses of the "tentative" writing system. Concerning community involvement, she states: "And it is through participating in decision making, that people make the writing system their own" (Malone 2004:45).

Community acceptance and ownership are thus recognized as key in promoting a written standard. These cannot be rushed. Brody (2004:19), discussing lack of uniformity in spelling Yucatec Maya, states, "I concur... that variation is neither static or *[sic]* immutable; it may be better viewed as a transitory condition, as a series of *unhurried* steps along a meandering path" (emphasis mine). The process of standardization should clearly not be approached as a race against time.

6.5 Additional case studies

Case studies are particularly instructive. I have liberally interwoven them in the previous sections. I now present a few more. Some challenge the preconception that standardization is a must. Others alert us to factors that indicate that it may be wise not to rush the standardization process and instead to allow a natural evolution to take place over time, maybe even several generations. And others show that a series of changes are simply part of the natural process of working toward standardization. Some indicate that it's OK to backtrack and reverse bad decisions.

6.5.1 Colloquial Arabic in Lebanon and Yucatec Maya: Something in common

Mosel (2006:79) anticipates that local language workers in a documentation project may be afraid of making "spelling mistakes" and offers solace in this: "As long as the orthography has not been standardized, there is no such thing as a right or wrong spelling." Surprisingly, fear of spelling mistakes can discourage literacy engagement. This is backed up by experience.

For instance, Thonhauser (2003) reports on interviews he conducted with individuals in Lebanon concerning their attitudes toward writing. Three international languages are taught in Lebanese schools: English, French, and Standard Arabic. Opportunities to use these languages outside of school were limited. Adults who had gone to school and were interviewed did not feel confident or motivated to write in any of them. Each has an opaque orthography, causing students consternation and frustration. The traditional education system focused on rules and correct form, suggesting that writing activities in a language presume mastery. Aware that they had not attained this requisite level of skill, students did not actively pursue writing in these languages. Their motivation had been squelched.

At the other end of the scale was the colloquial form of Arabic which did not have an established standard and rules. Because of this lack of a standard it was not perceived as suitable for "real" writing. However, this is the language pressed into service for communication in chat rooms and e-mails. Individuals are not concerned about making errors. They write freely using their intuitions for spelling and expect their readers to be able to decipher the message.

This case study illustrates that a standard may be perceived as a schoolmaster looking over one's shoulder and that freedom from spelling rules can be quite liberating for writers. Therefore, in language communities where formal schooling may have created negative attitudes toward writing or had a negative effect on self-esteem, it may be better to allow a standard to develop naturally through usage over time.

Brody (2002, 2004:18–19) also expresses this. She reports that some Yucatec Maya speakers who learned to read and write in Spanish and had difficulties with orthographic rules claimed that they could not write in Maya. They simply lacked confidence and doubted they could. Brody suggested that "a widespread tolerance for graphic and orthographic variation could go a long way toward eliminating the mystique of written language" and "help make writing and reading more appealing activities to a wider variety of speakers, thus ultimately promoting and assisting the development of the written language" (Brody 2004:18–19).

6.5.2 Biatah Bidayuh

The next case study illustrates the fine line between desired affiliation and separate identity.[6] When opinions concerning what an orthography should

[6] This report is based on Grace O. Tan and James Arritt (pers. comm.) as well as Noeb and Ridu 2006.

look like diverge, should freedom to be different reign or uniformity be held as the ideal?

The Bidayuh of Malaysia are closely related culturally and have a common sense of identity. However, they speak languages which, despite having similar phonemic inventories, are not mutually intelligible. Missionary efforts using the Bidayuh languages in the region (from about 1850 on) resulted in various spelling traditions. An amazing amount of print materials was produced and is in use in local churches, contributing to the preservation of these languages (Noeb and Ridu 2006). However, there was a sense among the local population that these "disparate spelling systems are inconsistent with Bidayuh unity, and they should be rectified" (ibid., 11). In 1955 the Bidayuh National Association[7] was formed, and its purpose was specified as "to assert the Bidayuh identity and to reaffirm its ethnicity" (ibid., 8). In more recent years (from 2000 on), discussions on how to unify the various orthographies took place, but diverse practices continued. The Bidayuh asked for assistance, and, under the umbrella of a newly formed Bidayuh Language Development Project and with the help of some consultants it was hoped that a unified alphabet could be worked out. Indeed, a trial Bidayuh unified alphabet was proposed in November 2001. Three months later it was presented and discussed at a two-day orthography promotion workshop attended by a hundred participants from the various regions. Reactions varied. Some were positive, but some people from the Biatah [bth] language group objected. They liked their own writing traditions. The trial alphabet was tested, some revisions were made, and two follow-up workshops were held to work toward a consensus. August 10, 2003 seemed like a momentous day: an agreement was reached, and thus a unified orthography was established for the Bidayuh languages.

However, it turned out that apparent yielding in public did not in fact indicate consensus. One language group in particular was unhappy with decisions made and reverted to writing with a system close to the original one they had been using. A second group improved upon the "unified" alphabet to suit their needs. The Biatah also struggled—not with spelling rules, it seems, but with aesthetic issues. The glottal stop, to be written with an apostrophe, occurred in high-frequency words. They did not like

[7] This association was later renamed the Dayak Bidayuh National Association to express affiliation with other associations interested in representation, economic development, and nation building.

the way the apostrophe looked at the end of so many words. They also preferred underrepresentation for length of penultimate vowels and were unwilling to accept one other symbolization proposed. By 2006, efforts at language development in Biatah had stalled. Yet, language development efforts in other Bidayuh languages were going forward thanks to the Bidayuh Language Development Project, which had begun work in 2000 (ibid., 23). Dictionary workshops, writers' workshops, and a curriculum development seminar had already taken place. There was a good chance that each of the Bidayuh language varieties would be introduced as a subject in schools.

The need for an agreed-upon, improved way of writing Biatah thus resurfaced with the hope of using Biatah in schools. So, in 2008, the Biatah, aware of inadequacies of their traditional way of writing the language, returned to the drawing board: twenty Biatah speakers and an outside consultant met for an "orthography consultation" with the goal of coming up with a consensus on how to write Biatah. The starting point for the discussion was a well-known story text written in four different ways. One of the versions employed the "agreed-upon" unified writing system of 2003. Another version employed a system presented as the most "phonemically accurate," but not a single attendee wanted to adopt that one. Instead, the committee came up with a compromise between two of the four versions. This fifth option was agreed upon for future use, but it was not seen as the *final* solution. Instead it was acknowledged as a work in progress, and the committee voted for its adoption with the stipulation that future improvements could be incorporated. This 2008 agreed-upon Biatah orthography was then used in the development of kindergarten materials.

This case study confirms how much impact existing writing traditions have and that it is not easy to diverge from them. Aesthetics is surprisingly important, and linguistic accuracy does not necessarily rank very high in the decision-making process. Although affiliation between groups may be important, harmonization between languages may be an elusive goal. There has to be acceptance from the community, or there will be no motivation to use the system. The idea of using a writing system with the expectation that it may change, is the way to go where there is reluctance to firmly commit to something.

6.5.3 Lawa of Thailand: Two standards

Should groups that share a common linguistic and cultural heritage be urged to work toward a unified orthography? Shouldn't linguistic unification and a common writing system be held up as an ideal? This next case study illustrates how literacy rates in a dominant language and differing objectives may influence speech communities to opt for different symbolizations from those of neighboring communities.[8]

Lawa has two main speech varieties: Western Lawa [lcp] (or Mae Hong Son), which has had a writing system based on an adapted Thai script for about forty years, and Eastern Lawa [lwl] (or Bo Luang), which has been used mainly for oral communication until recent years. The two varieties have a very low level of inter-comprehension.

In 2006, school teachers in the Eastern Lawa region asked for help with designing an orthography for their "dialect" for use in village schools. Based on comparative linguistic analyses of the two varieties, SIL consultant Mark Holt expected that harmonization would be fairly straightforward since the phonologies were nearly identical, differing only in diphthongs. It seemed that three of the eight Western Lawa diphthongs were not needed for Eastern Lawa, but two different diphthongs occur which Western Lawa does not have. The expectation, therefore, was that five diphthongs would be written as in the Eastern dialect, and provision would be made for the two that are unique to the Eastern dialect. However, the speech community's motivations went in a different direction. Harmonization with the Western Lawa writing system was not a priority for them.

The Eastern Lawa speech community was mostly motivated to have their writing system stay as close to the standard Thai system as possible. Speakers of the language accepted carrying over the Thai diphthongs but refused graphic representations for the other diphthongs which were not part of the Thai writing system. They found it perfectly acceptable that a sound could be represented in more than one way since that is how the Thai system works. However, having one symbol represent more than one sound and having the other diphthongs underrepresented was a concern. They came up with a compromise: the Thai diphthong representations were to do double duty. Diphthong symbols would primarily represent Thai pronunciations, but secondary pronunciations for Lawa diphthongs

[8] Information for this case study was provided by Mark Holt (pers. comm.).

could be signaled by a small dot, meeting the remaining symbolization needs. Holt comments that this is actually a very workable solution since oral Eastern Lawa is being influenced by Thai and there appears to be free variation for some of the non-Thai diphthongs, i.e., they are at times pronounced as in standard Thai. It is thus likely that the dot will not be written consistently.

There was an important difference between the writing system design process for Eastern Lawa and that of Western Lawa. Western Lawa speakers were for the most part non-literate when the orthography design process and literature production began. They were mostly concerned with learning to read and write their own language, not with skill transfer to Thai. Two generations later, amongst the Eastern Lawa, basic literacy in Thai had been achieved by the majority in the community. Thus they are much more active in the orthography design process for their own language. They have their expectations and ideas. They view Lawa literacy as a stepping stone to Thai literacy and vice versa.

Cross-dialect harmonization and standardization was not feasible in this situation, but the two standards serve their speakers well as they engage in diverse literacy activities. What is important is that the communities are motivated to use the systems, that they see them as theirs, and are willing to pass them on to the next generation.

6.5.4 Reversing bad decisions: The case of Kalagan Tagakaulu and Shona

Kalagan Tagakaulu [klg] is a minority language of the Philippines with 83,000 speakers. Shona [sna] is a dominant language in Zimbabwe and enjoys special status as national language. It is spoken as a first language by 10.7 million speakers in three African nations and by an additional 1.8 million speakers who use it for communication purposes.[9] What did the orthography development processes for these two very different languages have in common? They illustrate that, indeed, orthography design can at times be like "tinkering and groping in the dark."[10]

[9] Data for both languages is based on Lewis 2009. Information on Kalagan Tagakaulu was provided by Bus and Jean Dawson (pers. comm.).

[10] Jaffré and Fayol's phrase (1997:41), as translated into English and cited by Coulmas (2003:94).

6.5.4.1 Kalagan Tagakaulu

In Kalagan Tagakaulu, first publications—an alphabet book and a primer—were printed in a tentative orthography in the 1950s. The orthography used was well accepted. Although linguistically it had not adequately taken stress and length into account, readability was not greatly impeded. Some orthography changes were implemented in the late 1960s. These were not motivated by shortcomings inherent to the system or by popular request. Instead, they were based on a consultant's conviction that it would be better to conform to the spelling patterns of other languages used in the region. The orthography changes introduced were thus based on the standard of Visayan (a.k.a. Cebuano) [ceb], a regional language of communication. Two main changes were introduced.

First, since in Visayan <y> never follows consonants, it was decided to write Kalagan Tagakaulu palatalization with an <i> instead. But the two languages are structurally different. Since Kalagan Tagakaulu syllable structures allow for consonants to be followed by two consecutive vowels (CVV), writing palatalization with an <i> caused confusion between palatalization and true /i/ vowels as the first in a vowel series.

Second, since Visayan never noted glottal stops at the end of words, this practice was carried over into Kalagan Tagakaulu. But the glottal stop is a high-frequency phoneme in Kalagan Tagakaulu. Not to write it in one of its commonly occurring positions undermined the accuracy and efficiency of the orthography.

Both of the changes posed serious problems. Readability of texts was severely affected. Decisions to introduce the changes were quickly reversed. In addition, a solution for noting vowel length was found, improving the original orthography. Contrary to expectation, bridging to Visayan, the dominant language of the region, or to Filipino, the national language, did not pose a problem for readers of Kalagan Tagakaulu despite the orthographic differences.

6.5.4.2 Shona

Fortune (1972) reports that until about 1920 Shona had been written in a variety of ways based on the various dialects. It was discovered that the dialects were quite similar; thus a unified orthography was proposed by

South African linguist Clement Doke. This orthography, based on a central group of dialects which had a larger number of speakers and also a larger phonemic inventory, was to be implemented in 1932. His proposed system, which included eight phonetic symbols based on the Africa Alphabet, which Africanists were promoting at the time, was not welcomed. There were two main reasons. First, there were just too many unfamiliar letters. Second, people feared that publishing with this alphabet would require special equipment and thus be more costly. In response, Doke replaced two of the special symbols with digraphs. The Ministry of Education prescribed this revised version as the one to be used, but it too was never accepted. Materials continued to be printed using older orthographies.

In 1955, a committee reviewed Doke's system and proposed a new orthography. It avoided special symbols altogether, using digraphs instead. There was underrepresentation: eight distinctive sounds were represented by four symbols. This resulted in too many ambiguities in texts. In the process of preparing a dictionary, it was decided that each of these sounds needed to be represented. Thus in 1967, the Shona Language Committee reconvened and recommended that all sounds be distinguished as in Doke's alphabet, but without the use of special symbols. The proposed alphabet was approved by the Ministry of Education and has been in use ever since. Some, however, critique this orthography (Magwa 2002; Zivenge, Mheta, and Kadenge 2010) and would like to see remaining shortcomings addressed.

These two case studies illustrate that the ideas of a linguist, a consultant, a committee, or a government do not necessarily line up with the desires of the people, and that sometimes bad decisions are made. These should be reversed so that they do not impede language development efforts. This too is part of the experimental process in the move toward standardization. Clearly, readability should not be sacrificed for the sake of cross-language harmonization, nor for economy in symbolization. Time is *not* of the essence; acceptance and efficiency are.

6.6 Conclusion

As seen above, several authors in recent publications have alerted those involved in language development that developing an orthography takes time and that a push for quick standardization of newly written languages may be inappropriate. There are indications that standardization may not even be a requirement for literacy to take hold in communities. Research has shown that excessive focus on the code can actually be demotivating for people who wish to write but dare not do so for fear of making mistakes. This suggests that more freedom in spelling could be advantageous.

There is no denying that standardization has clear advantages when it comes to training writers or teachers and preparing textbooks for use in the formal school system. However, it could be detrimental to rush the standardization process or to declare a writing system as *the* standard when a population objects to its script, symbol choices, certain conventions, or hasn't been given a chance to express their preferences as to how their language ought to be written. It takes time to do careful linguistic analysis, to involve the population in the decision-making process, and to test a system or symbolization options adequately.

I have illustrated that the orthography design process can be likened to a sequence of stages proceeding by trial and error. If an orthography is presented as a work in progress rather than a finished work, introducing necessary changes will likely be easier. Official endorsement does not necessarily promote popular acceptance, so it seems logical to seek endorsement *after* there is popular acceptance.

Testing an orthography is essential. It will reveal effectiveness, acceptability, degree of potential extendability across dialects, and, possibly, needs for revision. Time should not be seen as an *expenditure* but rather as an *investment* which will yield good returns. Uniformity in writing cannot be expected when awareness raising and training have been neglected. Publishing need not be halted when there is variation in writing. During the early experimental and testing stages, it may be prudent to print in smaller numbers. Readability of texts should not be sacrificed in the name of harmonization.

Avoiding conflict is of the utmost importance. Given time, divergence in writing practices may lessen and a standard may evolve naturally. Insisting on a single standard which the language community does not support, will likely work against good language development goals. The passage of time may help people gradually overcome their initial emotional reactions. Smalley's criterion (Smalley 1959) of "maximum motivation"—a community's positive attitude toward a writing system and their wanting to use it—is still key as much now as it ever was. Linguists and consultants need to recognize that their role is not to persuade or convince but to inform, facilitate, and assist the community to work toward what will be motivational for them.

References

Asmah Haji Omar. 1989. The Malay spelling reform. *Journal of the Simplified Spelling Society* 2:9–13 (J11). http://www.spellingsociety.org/journals/j11/malay.php (accessed November 22, 2012).

Baker, Philip. 1997. Developing ways of writing vernaculars: Problems and solutions in a historical perspective. In Tabouret-Keller et al., 93–141.

Bauernschmidt, Amy. 1980. The ideal orthography. *Notes on Literacy* 32:12–21.

Bergman, T.G., ed. 1989. *Proceedings of the Round Table on Assuring the Feasibility of Standardization within Dialect Chains.* Noordwijkerhout, the Netherlands, September 1988. Nairobi: Summer Institute of Linguistics.

Berlanda, Elena. 2006. New perspectives on digraphia: A framework for the sociolinguistics of writing systems. Major Research Paper for the Graduate Programme in Theoretical and Applied Linguistics. Toronto: York University. http://www.omniglot.com/language/articles/digraphia/digraphia_EBerlanda.pdf (accessed November 22, 2012).

Berry, Jack. 1968. The making of alphabets. In Joshua A. Fishman (ed.), *Readings in the Sociology of Language,* 737–753. First presented at the 8th International Congress of Linguistics (August 5–9, 1957). The Hague: Mouton.

Brody, Michal. 2002. To the letter: A microanalysis of currently contested graphemes in the Maya of Yucatan. In R. McKenna Brown (ed.), *Endangered languages and their literatures.* Proceedings of the Sixth FEL Conference in Antigua, Guatemala, 8–10 August 2002. Bath, England: Foundation for Endangered Languages.

Brody, Michal. 2004. Variación gráfica y ortográfica – ¿obstáculo o camino viable?: El caso de maya yucateco. [Graphic and orthographic variation: Obstacles or viable options? The case of Yucatec Maya.] Paper presented at the 2004 Meeting of the Latin American Studies Association, Las Vegas, Nevada, October 7–9, 2004. English version at http://lasa.international.pitt.edu/members/congress-papers/lasa2004/files/BrodyMichael.pdf (accessed November 22, 2012).

Cahill, Michael, and Elke Karan. 2008. Factors in designing effective orthographies for unwritten languages. *SIL Electronic Working Papers* 2008-001. SIL International http://www.sil.org/silewp/abstract.asp?ref=2008-001 (accessed November 22, 2012).

Cassidy, Frederic G. 1993. Short note on Creole orthography. *Journal of Pidgin and Creole Languages* 8:135–137. Quoted in Baker 1997, 120.

Charpentier, Jean-Michel. 1997. Literacy in a pidgin vernacular. In Tabouret-Keller et al., 222–245.

Coulmas, Florian. 1996. *The Blackwell encyclopedia of writing systems.* Oxford: Blackwell.

Coulmas, Florian. 2000. The nationalization of writing. *Studies in the Linguistic Sciences* 30(1):47–59.

Coulmas, Florian. 2003. *Writing systems: An introduction to their linguistic analysis.* Cambridge: Cambridge University Press.

Dale, I. R. H. 1980. Digraphia. *International Journal of the Sociology of Language* 26:5–13.

DeFrancis, J. 1984. Digraphia. *Word* 35(1):59–66.

Eira, Christina. 1998. Authority and discourse: Towards a model of orthography selection. *Written Language and Literacy* 1(2):171–224.

Fasold, Ralph W. 1997. Motivations and attitudes influencing vernacular literacy: Four African assessments. In Tabouret-Keller et al., 246–270.

Fishman, Joshua A., ed. 1977. *Advances in the creation and revision of writing systems.* The Hague: Mouton.

Fortune, George. 1972. *A guide to Shona spelling.* Salisbury, Rhodesia: Longman Rhodesia.

Funnell, Barry John. 2004. A contrastive analysis of two standardized varieties of Sena. M.A. dissertation. University of South Africa.

Geerts, G., J. van den Broeck, and A. Verdoodt. 1977. Successes and failures in Dutch spelling reform. In Fishman (ed.), 179–245.

Gerbault, Jeannine. 1997. Pedagogical aspects of vernacular literacy. In Tabouret-Keller et al., 142–185.

Giersberg, Dagmar. 2007. *Chronicle of a long debate: The spelling reform.* Goethe-Institut, Online-Redaktion. http://www.goethe.de/ges/spa/siw/en630493.htm (accessed November 22, 2012).

Gippert, Jost, Nikolaus P. Himmelmann, and Ulrike Mosel, eds. 2006. *Essentials of language documentation.* Trends in Linguistics. Walter de Gruyter.

Gudschinsky, Sarah. 1973. *A manual of literacy for preliterate peoples.* Ukarumpa, PNG: Summer Institute on Linguistics.

Jaffe, Alexandra. 2000. Introduction: Non-standard orthography and non-standard speech. *Journal of Sociolinguistics.* 4(4):497–513.

Jaffré, J.-P., and M. Fayol. 1997. *Orthographes: Des systèmes aux usages* [Orthographies: From systems to their use]. Paris: Flammarion.

Johnson, Sally. 2005. *Spelling trouble? Language, ideology and the reform of German orthography.* Clevedon: Multilingal Matters.

Karan, Elke. 2006. Writing system development and reform: A process. M.A. thesis. University of North Dakota. http://artssciences.und.edu/summer-institute-of-linguistics/theses/_files/docs/2006-karan-elke.pdf (accessed November 26, 2012).

Keller, R. E. 1978. *The German language.* Atlantic Highlands, N.J.: Humanities Press. Quoted in Weber 2005, 86.

Kutsch Lojenga, Constance. 1996. Participatory research in linguistics. *Notes on Linguistics* 73:13–27.

Language Documentation Training Center. 2004–2012. *Language documentation projects.* University of Hawaii at Manoa. http://www.ling.hawaii.edu/ldtc/ (accessed November 22, 2012).

Lewis, M. Paul, ed. 2009. *Ethnologue: Languages of the world.* Sixteenth edition. Dallas: SIL International. http://www.ethnologue.com (accessed November 22, 2012).

Magwa, Wiseman. 2002. The Shona writing system: An analysis of its problems and possible solutions. *Zambezia* 29(1). http://archive.lib.msu.edu/DMC/African%20Journals/pdfs/Journal%20of%20the%20University%20of%20Zimbabwe/vol29n1/juz029001002.pdf (accessed November 22, 2012).

Malone, Susan, ed. 2004. *Manual for developing literacy and adult education programs in minority language communities.* Bangkok: UNESCO.

Marlett, Stephen A. 2010. A place for writing: Language cultivation and literacy in the Seri community. *Revue Roumaine de Linguistique* 55(2):183–194.

Mason, Marilyn, and Jeffrey Allen. 2002. Intra-textual inconsistency: Risks of implementing orthographies for lessprevalent languages. *LISA Newsletter* XI/1.3.

Mosel, Ulrike. 2006. Fieldwork and community language work. In Jost Gippert, Nikolaus P. Himmelmann, and Ulrike Mosel (eds.), *Essentials of language documentation,* 67–85. Trends in Linguistics. Walter de Gruyter.

Nida, Eugene. 1947. *Bible translating.* London: United Bible Societies.

Nida, Eugene. 1954. Practical limitations to a phonemic alphabet. *The Bible Translator* 05(1):35–39. Reprinted in Smalley et al., 22–30.

Noeb, Jonas, and Robert Sulis Ridu. 2006. Language development in Bidayuh: Past, present and future. In Calvin R. Rensch et al. (eds.), *The Bidayuh language: Yesterday, today and tomorrow,* Part I, 3–30. Kuching, Sarawak, Malaysia: Dayak Bidayuh National Association.

Pike, Kenneth L. 1947. *Phonemics: A technique for reducing languages to writing.* Ann Arbor: The University of Michigan Press

Powlison, Paul S. 1968. Bases for formulating an efficient orthography. *The Bible Translator* 19(2):74–91.

Rehg, Kenneth L. 2004. Linguistics, literacy, and the law of unintended consequences. *Oceanic Linguistics* 43(2):498–518.

Robbins, Frank E. 1992. Standardization of unwritten vernaculars. In Shin Ja J. Hwang and William R. Merrifield (eds.), *Language in context: Essays for Robert E. Longacre,* 605–616. Summer Institute of Linguistics and the University of Texas at Arlington Publications in Linguistics 107. Dallas: Summer Institute of Linguistics and the University of Texas at Arlington.

Robinson, Clinton, and Karl Gadelii. 2003. *Writing unwritten languages: A guide to the process.* UNESCO. http://portal.unesco.org/education/en/ev.php-URL_ID = 28300&URL_DO = DO_TOPIC&URL_SECTION = 201.html (accessed November 22, 2012).

Scragg, D. G. 1974. *A history of English spelling.* Manchester: Manchester University Press.

Sebba, Mark. 2009. Sociolinguistic approaches to writing systems research. *Writing Systems Research* 1(1):35–39.

Seifart, Frank. 2006. Orthography development. In Jost Gippert, Nikolaus P. Himmelmann, and Ulrike Mosel (eds.), *Essentials of language documentation,* 275–299. Trends in Linguistics. Walter de Gruyter.

SIL. 1999. What is a working orthography? *LinguaLinks Library,* Version 4.0 CDROM. http://www.sil.org/lingualinks/literacy/referencematerials/glossaryofliteracyterms/whatisaworkingorthography.htm (accessed November 22, 2012).

SIL. 2002. Developing an orthography for related dialects. LinguaLinks Library, version 5. at: Develop an orthography/Developing an orthography/Developing a tentative orthography/Assessing factors affecting orthography decisions/Assessing sociolinguistic factors affecting orthography decisions. Dallas: SIL International.

Simons, Gary F. 1977. Principles of multidialectal orthography design. In R. Loving and Gary Simons (eds.), *Workpapers in Papua New Guinea Languages* 21, 325–342. Ukarumpa, Papua New Guinea: Summer Institute of Linguistics.

Sjoberg, Andrée F. 1966. Socio-cultural and linguistic factors in the development of writing systems for preliterate peoples. In William Bright (ed.), *Sociolinguistics,* 260–276. Proceedings of the UCLA Sociolinguistics Conference 1964 (Janua Linguarum XX). The Hague: Mouton.

Smalley, William A. 1954. A problem in orthography preparation. *The Bible Translator* 05(4:)170–176. Reprinted in Smalley et al., 53–59.

Smalley, William A. 1959. How shall I write this language? *The Bible Translator* 10(2):49–69. Reprinted in Smalley et al., 31–52.

Smalley, William A., et al. 1963. Orthography studies: Articles on new writing systems. *Helps for Translators* 6. London: United Bible Societies.

Snider, Keith. 2001. Linguistic factors in orthography design. In Ngessimo M. Mutaka and Sammy B. Chumbow (eds.), *Research mate in African linguistics: Focus on Cameroon,* 323–332. Köln: Rüdiger Köppe Verlag.

Stebbins, Tonya. 2001. Emergent spelling patterns in Sm'algyax (Tsimshian, British Columbia). *Written Language & Literacy* 4(2):163–193.

Tabouret-Keller, Andrée, et al., eds. 1997. *Vernacular literacy: A reevaluation.* Oxford: Clarendon Press

Thonhauser, Ingo. 2003. "Written language but easily to use!" Perceptions of continuity and discontinuity between written/oral modes in the Lebanese context of biliteracy and diglossia. *Written Language and Literacy* 6(1):93–110.

Trudgill, Peter. 1983. *Sociolinguistics: An introduction to language and society.* Harmondsworth: Penguin.

Weber, David John. 2005. Writing Quechua: The case for a Hispanic orthography. *UCLA Latin American Studies* 87. Los Angeles: UCLA Latin American Center Publications, University of California.

Wedekind, Klaus, and Charlotte Wedekind. 1997. *The development of writing systems: A guide.* Adaptation and translation of other works for use at the Workshop on Orthography Design, November 10–December 19, 1997.

Asmara: Curriculum Department, The Ministry of Education.

Wiesemann, Ursula, Etienne Sadembouo, and Maurice Tadadjeu. 1983. Guide pour le développement des systèmes d'écriture des langues africaines [Manual for the development of writing systems for African languages]. *Collection PROPELCA* No. 2. Yaoundé: Société Internationale de Linguistique and University of Yaoundé.

Wolff, Ekkehard H. 1991. Standardization and varieties of written Hausa. In Utta von Gleich and Ekkehard Wolff (eds.), *Standardization of national languages*, 21–32. Symposium on Language Standardization, February 2–3, 1991. Hamburg: University of Hamburg and the Unesco Institute for Education. http://www.unesco.org/education/pdf/35_57.pdf (accessed November 22, 2012).

Wolff, Ekkehard H. 2000. Language and society. In Bernd Heine and Derek Nurse (eds.), *African languages: An introduction,* 298–347. Cambridge: Cambridge University Press.

Yunick, Stanley. 2000. Linguistics, TESL, and language planning in Micronesia. *Studies in the Linguistic Sciences* 30(1):183–200.

Zivenge, William, Gift Mheta, and Maxwell Kadenge. 2010. The effects of Shona language change on monolingual lexicography: The need for a revised alphabet. *Lexicos* 20:708–715. http://lexikos.journals.ac.za/pub/article/view/164 (accessed November 22, 2012).

7

Orthography Wars

Leanne Hinton

There are an increasing number of Native American communities and individuals who are developing writing systems based on English spelling, often rejecting practical writing systems developed by linguists in order to do so. This paper examines some of these writing systems and looks at "code-external" considerations that have overridden the "code-internal" design factors that linguists hold dear. Since orthographic issues evoke a great deal of passion, the mutual trust between communities and linguists can be affected if linguists do not take into account the reasons for the preference of English-based Practical Orthographies (EPOs) over Linguistic Practical Orthographies (LPOs). LPOs in communities without means for ongoing community education in literacy in the local language will ultimately and repeatedly be abandoned in favor of systems using the spelling rules of English.

7.1 Orthography and politics*

Orthography—the conventions chosen for the visual representation of a language—can be a lightning rod for all the personal, social, and political issues that wrack speech communities. As Sebba (2007:14) writes, orthography is not just a systematized set of letters and spelling rules but also something "fundamentally ideological." In the case of languages developing new writing systems, orthographic design can become a divisive issue within a community and can also create problems between the members of a community and the linguists who are working with them. Although the problems are usually argued as "code-internal" issues—that one kind of symbol or spelling principle is superior to another—there is really a whole spectrum of "code-external" considerations that drive such debates, both among community members and linguists. Linguists who cannot accept the primacy of the community's code-external considerations may find that trust between them and the community they work with could be damaged.

As linguists, we tend to approach orthographic design with strongly held views coming from our profession. Our own experience with phonetic transcription and linguistic analysis leads us to a very decided preference for writing systems based on phonetic, phonological, and morphological principles. There are excellent reasons for preferring such writing systems, many of them based on theories of native-speaker language processing and other important and reasoned considerations (see Snider, this volume). From the beginning of our linguistic education, we have learned to recognize the failings and illogic of English spelling rules and to have deep pride in the descriptive adequacy of the writing systems used in our field.

As part of our service as linguists to the communities whose languages we study, we have often had the pleasure of assisting in the development

* I would like to thank Barbara McQuillen, Carole Lewis, and Kay Inong for the Yuroks, Tim Ramos, James BlueWolf and DeeAnna Chavez for Big Valley, and Sam Brown and Roy Cook for the Kumeyaays for many discussions about orthography, and for allowing me to include their writing systems in this paper. Thanks to Jeanette King and Lois Meyer for bibliographical assistance. Thanks to Mike Cahill, Keren Rice, and the various anonymous reviewers of previous versions of this paper for their insightful criticisms, which definitely helped improve it. And thanks to Juliette Blevins, Andrew Garrett, and Pam Munro for more discussions about orthography from the linguists' point of view—and especially to Margaret Langdon, now deceased, who devised the first practical writing system for Kumeyaay and was a formative influence on me in the beginning of my own orthographic adventures.

of writing systems for practical use. Happy with the opportunity to help design orthographies that lack the illogical flaws of English, we have made it a common practice to develop a phonemic orthography that corresponds to what we believe are the intuitions of a native speaker about the sound system of the language, following most of the pronunciation principles of the International Phonetic Alphabet (IPA) or the Americanist system, modified for practical purposes to avoid hard-to-reproduce special symbols. These Linguistic Practical Orthographies (henceforth LPOs) are successfully utilized by many communities.[1]

But there are also many code-external considerations that impinge on the ultimate design that will be found to be acceptable by the members of the speech community for whom the writing system is intended—and many of these considerations will be at odds with the linguists' principles. As Joshua Fishman (1977:xi) wrote:

> The very sophistication of the linguist's professional skills in code description and code creation merely intensified the separation trauma when it became increasingly obvious that it was necessary to go outside the code and to confront the real world if writing systems were not only to be devised but employed.

Writing several decades later, Frank Seifert makes a similar observation, which suggests that Fishman's observations have not been well listened to:

> The idea persists that a good orthography is simply one that represents all phonological contrasts. However, orthography development is in fact a highly complex issue, which involves not only phonological, prosodic, grammatical and semantic aspects of the language to be written, but also a wide variety of non-linguistic issues, among them pedagogical and psycholinguistic aspects of reading and writing and the sociolinguistic situation. (Siefert 2006:275)

In the past few decades, we have witnessed a new wave of establishing writing systems for American Indian languages, fueled by the development of language revitalization programs. Since for a large proportion of communities the languages are sadly moribund, the responsibility for revitalization is falling increasingly on the shoulders

[1] Alternatively for languages with complex morphophonemic processes, a "deep" orthography may be developed, representing underlying form (Jones 1995, Seifert 2006). For more on this topic, see Snider, this volume.

of semi-speakers and second-language learners. In a growing number of cases, the community leaders of the language programs thus developed are dominant in English, and being highly literate in English, they may insist on utilizing English spelling rules in the writing systems for their heritage languages. These English-based Practical Orthographies (henceforth EPOs) are becoming more common and are sometimes even replacing already-established LPOs.

Furthermore, since the people who are dominant in English may base their intuitions about their heritage language on something closer to the English phonemic inventory, they may not agree to a writing system that represents all and only those distinctions made by native speakers. This is anathema to all that linguists have been trained to believe in, especially since often the resulting system may fail to take into account phonemic distinctions extant in the spoken language or else may overdifferentiate beyond the distinctive sounds present in the language. Linguists may also be disappointed at the lack of economy of a spelling system that has more than one way of representing a given sound or spells a sound differently depending on its orthographic environment. And if a writing system does not reflect a native-speaker model, linguists can feel that their entire effort to document an endangered language is undermined.

Nevertheless, linguists are often forced to come to terms with the code-external issues that affect the opinions of speech communities concerning orthographic choice and to recognize that these considerations may outweigh the orthographic principles that linguists hold dear. Examples of such code-external issues abound.

The phonetically based Hangul system of Korean, considered by many linguists to be one of the very finest writing systems ever developed (Kim-Cho 2002; Kim-Renaud 1997), nevertheless took more than four hundred years after its invention to gain such prestige, its very simplicity and efficiency being thought of as inferior to the difficult but artistic and learned Chinese-based system that it was competing with. In this case the two systems were part of a class struggle, so that mass literacy itself—which was part of the motivation for the development of Hangul—was a very political issue.

An illustration of the emotion engendered by orthographic considerations can be found in this discussion of the Māori [mri] macron to represent vowel length:

> One reform which got Bruce into hot water was his double vowel orthography for Maori. Maori has phonemically long (or geminate) vowels which in writing were sometimes distinguished from short vowels by carrying a macron or, more often, were not distinguished at all (it is easy to leave out a diacritic). On practical as well as theoretical grounds Bruce advocated writing a long vowel as a double vowel (as in Maaori), and he and his immediate colleagues followed this practice in their publications and teaching. Nothing stirs up the public more than an attempt to reform spelling. A nationwide controversy erupted in the late 1950s and went on for years. There were public debates; friends fell out; the same book would be printed in rival editions by the opposing camps, one with double vowels, one without. Under sustained heavy fire Bruce stuck to his guns, and eventually won tolerance of the double vowel orthography, and, more importantly, general acceptance among teachers and scholars of Maori of the principle that long vowels should be orthographically marked, either by macron or doubling. (Hollyman and Pawley 1981:21)

Note that Bruce Riggs did not win his argument that length should be marked by doubling. In the long run, it is the macron that has prevailed.

The debate between differentiation and unification in the representation of dialects is a common one. Dialect differences rarely become problematic until people try to write them down. Dialect diversity of languages presents practical problems for the development of materials and the training of teachers (with the added problem that not every village with its own variety of speech will have its own local teachers). Thus, from the point of view of the government, and also of some language activists, it is strongly desirable to have a standard variety of a given language which will be used for materials and teacher training. Yet speakers may insist that their own dialect should be written as spoken. (See Hernandez 2004; Luyx 2003; Hinton and Hale 2001:248–249; and Karan, this volume.)

On the whole, then, complete and consistent representation of the distinctive sounds (or morphemes) of a language, which might be seen as the linguists' motto, has both advantages and flaws with regard to the code-external needs of a community and the larger social and political processes that impact them.

7.2 Five criteria for an adequate new writing system

One important issue in the movement toward indigenous-language revitalization in North America has been orthographic design. Linguists who have worked with indigenous groups to develop writing systems have hoped that practical systems could be designed that would serve the purposes of the community and that could also be used in linguistic publications so as to make the latter more accessible to community people. However, it is not uncommon for such writing systems to be rejected by the community people, either immediately or over time. This paper is primarily devoted to working toward an understanding of why people might reject a given writing system.

Smalley et al. (1963) laid out five criteria for an adequate new writing system, in order of importance (with the first being the most important) as they perceived them:

1. maximum motivation for the learner
2. maximum representation of speech
3. maximum ease of learning
4. maximum transfer
5. maximum ease of reproduction

7.2.1 Maximum motivation for the learner

Maximum motivation for the learner refers to the acceptability of the writing system by the speech community it is intended for, which is clearly by far the most important factor. As Fishman wrote (1972:312), "The creation of writing systems is significant only insofar as it leads to the acceptance and implementation of writing systems." In other words, if the people for whom the system is designed are not motivated to use it, the orthography is a failure no matter how perfect its internal design. The reasons for rejecting an orthography are many, relating to both code-internal and code-external considerations. Often, motivation for the learner is lessened because the writing system fails some of the other criteria listed here.

7.2.2 Maximum representation of speech

Maximum representation of speech is what is dearest to the linguist—a writing system that represents all and only the distinctive sounds of the language being written. Yet this is complicated by the fact that different members of the community may have different sound systems, including generational differences due to language change and language decline. In addition, people who are not dominant in the language under consideration may have a different perception of the sound system of the language. Clearly, a writing system representing the speech of native speakers is desirable as part of the language learning process, but maximum motivation to learn it may be lacking due to the failure to meet other criteria such as that of maximum transfer discussed below.

7.2.3 Maximum ease of learning

Maximum ease of learning is of course very important for situations where mass literacy is hoped for. This was a primary reason for orthographic reform in Korea five hundred years ago and in Mainland China in the twentieth century. As we will see, linguists judge LPOs as having maximum ease of learning but non-linguists do not.

7.2.4 Maximum transfer

In multilingual situations, especially where little or no education is available in the minority languages, maximum transfer is closely related to ease of learning—that is, it is important to be able to transfer reading knowledge from one well-learned language to the new system. Transferability of learning from one language to another is the theoretical justification for bilingual education in the United States, and it is also the automatic principle applied when one views a new writing system. (For one example of this issue, see Hyslop, this volume.)

Apropos of maximum ease of transfer, for Latin American languages Fishman (1977:xii) represents the views of Eugene Nida as follows:

> Thus, among the 'practical limitations to a phonemic orthography' Nida (1953) discussed the fact that both the Otomi and the Quechua 'suffer from cultural insecurity' and want their writing systems not only to 'look like Spanish' but to operate with the same graphematic alternances as does Spanish, *whether these are needed or not* in terms of their own phonemic system. (Fishman's italics)

What Nida called "cultural insecurity" may indeed have played a role in the Otomi and Quechua preferences, but probably more important was the notion of ease of transfer.

7.2.5 Maximum ease of reproduction

The last criterion, maximum ease of reproduction, is about whether printing and other technological tools that can publish the new orthography are readily at hand or easily obtainable. Ease of reproduction is one of the main reasons that LPOs replace the exotic IPA characters with letters and letter combinations present in English.

Berry (1977) questioned whether the actual order of criteria was correct and suggested that in the minds of the community members for which an orthography is intended, the priorities would be different. Indeed, in numerous cases, Smalley's number two criterion of maximum representation of the language is overridden by other concerns.

7.3 The bias of familiarity

The motivation for using a writing system depends in large part on a system of dissemination of the knowledge needed to use this orthography. Minority groups have great difficulty finding and maintaining ways to disseminate knowledge about any aspect of their languages, cultures, and histories. Without ongoing access to educational systems pointed directly at such dissemination, LPOs have little or no chance of implementation. Instead, as we shall see, people will always use ease of learning and especially maximum transfer as their highest criteria and will therefore fall back on writing systems that reflect their knowledge of the dominant language orthography.

Both linguists and non-linguists have a "bias of familiarity" that makes each group potentially blind to the ways in which their preferences are viewed by the other group. In general, linguists consider maximum representation of the language (the code-internal factors) to be the most important criterion for a good writing system. The LPO typically compromises primarily for the sake of ease of reproduction by finding Roman-alphabet alternatives to the specialized symbols used in technical research. For linguists, the principle of ease of transfer is clearly adhered to because each Roman symbol or sequence of symbols corresponds to a symbol in the phonetic alphabet. Learnability seems to us linguists to be easy because a student can readily learn the phonetic alphabet in a semester or so.

However, the bias of familiarity may make us fail to recognize that non-linguists and especially second-language learners of minority languages have different issues of transfer than linguists do and, furthermore, may cause us to over-estimate the ease of learning of phonetically based alphabets. Sebba (2007:18) points out that the ease of learning a phonemic system is the subject of debate. Two relevant points can also come out of my own experience over the years of teaching linguistics classes:

1. after an introductory course in linguistics that includes phonetics, many people taking their second course in linguistics have in fact not become at all proficient in the use of the phonetic alphabet;
2. when practice with phonetics involves the writing of English using the IPA, students for whom English is a second language obviously make more errors than native speakers of English, not merely because they are "writing with an accent" but more importantly because they are utilizing a different phonological system than native speakers and are therefore often not able to understand what IPA letter to "hang" a given sound onto.

These facts should show us that there is nothing at all quick and automatic about learning an LPO. Without intensive education of tribal decision makers and educators, phonetically based alphabets may not be chosen for use by native communities and even if chosen, may later be supplanted, especially if there are not ongoing means of education in the LPO.

7.4 Case studies

Sometimes, phonetically based writing systems survive well and sometimes they don't. The phonetically based Navajo [nav] writing system, put into its present form in the 1930s by Robert Young, William Morgan, and John P. Harrington (commonly known as the Young and Morgan system), is still alive and well (Young 1977) and taught in bilingual education programs on the Navajo reservation. Some of the phonetically based systems in Canada are also well accepted and currently well supported by an educational infrastructure, such as Dogrib [dgr], Kaska [kkz], Kwak'wala [kwk], and Slave [den] (Marinakis et al. 2007; Rice and Saxon 2002).[2]

However, in many communities, education in the use of new writing systems for indigenous languages has been spotty or missing altogether so that it cannot be said that the communities have mass literacy in their own

[2] Even for these languages there are only a few people who are fully literate in these writing systems (Keren Rice, pers. comm.).

languages. Without mass literacy, people often decide to use something different than even a well-established LPO.

7.4.1 Navajo

It is interesting, for example, that even in the case of Navajo [nav], the Navajo Code Talkers of World War II did not use the official Navajo writing system but instead one that was closer to English spelling rules. Since the current Navajo orthography was developed just a few years before World War II, and since the code talkers came out of a school system that discouraged any use of the Navajo language, the Young and Morgan system was probably unknown to both the Navajo soldiers and the Armed Forces. The use of the system developed in the 1940s by the military continues today in publications on code talking (e.g., Nez 2011) and in presentations by the code talkers themselves. The system they use lacks the representation of tone and vowel length, uses hyphens between syllables, and includes such English spelling conventions as double consonants and the use of orthographic <ee> for the sound /i/, alternating with <ie> for the same sound. In addition, it uses the letter <l> for both the voiced lateral and the voiceless fricative, represents the glottal stop as a syllable break, and when it represents nasalization of vowels at all, it shows this by a syllable-final <n> as in <lin> for 'horse'. Some examples are provided in table 1.

Table 1. Examples of Navajo Code Talker spelling (with standard spelling)*

Code Talker	Standard	Gloss
wol-la-chee	wóláchííʼ	'ant'
shush	shash	'bear'
moa-si	mósí	'cat'
lha-cha-eh	łééchąąʼí	'dog'
ma-e	mąʼii	'fox'
klizzie	tłʼízí	'goat'
lin	łį́į́ʼ	'horse'

*Standard Navajo spelling from: Glosbe: The Multilingual Online Dictionary, English Navajo Dictionary Online, http://en.glosbe.com/en/nv (accessed Sept. 18, 2012).

I will present as case studies three other languages that are using EPO orthographies: Kumeyaay [dih], Eastern Pomo [peb], and Yurok [yur], located in the southern, central, and northern parts of California respectively.

7.4.2 Kumeyaay

Margaret Langdon provided the main description of Northern Diegueño [dih], also known as Iipay 'Aa or often, nowadays, as Kumeyaay. Around 1970, she devised a practical writing system (presented in Couro and Hutcheson 1973 and in Couro and Langdon 1975), which has the following linguistic practical alphabet:

(1) Langdon's practical alphabet
 ', aa, a, b, ch, d, ee, e, f, g, h, hw, ii, i, k, kw, l, ll, lly, ly, m, n, nn, ny, oo, o, p, q, r, rr, s, sh, t, tt, uu, u, v, w, y, -

The hyphen (which is included in the alphabet in Couro and Langdon 1975) is used to separate two letters which could otherwise be interpreted as some other sound, as in *me-shaalyap* 'butterfly'.

This alphabet corresponds to IPA and the Americanist system, except as follows: double vowels are long; <'> stands for the glottal stop; <hw> and <kw> represent /hw/ and /kw/ respectively; <ll> is the voiceless lateral fricative, <ly> the voiced palatal lateral, and <lly> the voiceless palatal lateral fricative; <n> is dental, <nn> is alveolar; <r> is a flap, <rr> a trill; <sh> is the palatal fricative; <t> is dental, <tt> alveolar.

With Kumeyaay speakers Couro and Hutcheson and her students, Langdon developed a dictionary (Couro and Hutcheson 1973) and a pedagogical grammar (Couro and Langdon 1975) using this orthography. Her orthography is memorialized in the use of the word *Kumeyaay,* such as in the part of Highway 8 in southern California that has been officially named the Kumeyaay Highway.

Nevertheless, this writing system is not being used by many Kumeyaay people who are writing their language today. Two replacement orthographies can be found on the Web, one by Viejas Kumeyaay Sam Brown and another by Roy Cook.[3] I will focus here on Brown's.

[3] See Sam Brown, Kumeyaay Language and Culture, http://www.kumeyaay.org/ and Roy Cook, Kumeyaay Language, http://americanindiansource.com/kumeyaaylanguage.html.

Sam Brown's intriguing introduction to his Web site reads as follows:

> My name is Samuel Brown. I am reservation born and bred. I am a resident enrolled member of the Viejas Band of Kumeyaay Indians..... Both my parents spoke our language but they spoke different dialects. They both came from the Capitan Grande Reservation but my late Mother came from one village and my Father another village. Here lies a great language debate. Which is the TRUE language. I don't really want to get involved in this debate so I will just use the dialect spoken by the Brown family of the Viejas Band.... My first language is English but I have picked up bits of our language since I was a child. I can pronounce words without an American English accent. When true native speakers hear me talk they think I know more than I do because I sound like I do....
>
> Unfortunately the language is passing very quickly. The number of fluent speakers on each reservation can be counted on one or maybe two hands. The phrases presented here are my attempt to preserve some of the language. If you learn the few phrases here you know more language than most people today. All the spelling is just my guess (including English). I am adding stuff to this all the time.

Brown's Web site URL uses Langdon's spelling of "Kumeyaay," but there the similarity stops. For example, the phonemes /ay/ or /aay/ have variant spellings:

(2) Brown's variant spellings of /ay/ or /aay/
<ai> as in *Ha Mutt Hai* /ha mat hay/ 'thirsty' (cf. English *mutt, Thai*)
<ye> as in *Simerrye* /simeray/ 'crazy' (cf. English *rye*)
<i> as in *Ami* /emaay/ 'friend' (cf. English *I*)

English spelling rules and the spelling of particular English lexical items are used frequently on Sam Brown's Web site. Table 2 compares the spelling of a selection of words as rendered by Margaret Langdon and Sam Brown.

Table 2. Comparison of Langdon and Brown orthography*

Langdon	Brown	Gloss
hawka	howka	'hello' (cf. English *how*)
kwahan	QuaHan	'good' (cf. English *qu* as in *quite*)
shewii	shawee	'acorn mush' (cf. English *ee* as in *free*)
mat	Mutt	'earth'
kikshwaypna	KickSchwapNa	'say something' (cf. English *schwa*)
estik	Estick	'small' (cf. English *stick*)
ilmaam	Elmom	'young girl' (cf. English *Mom*)

*Sam Brown, "Let's Speak Kumeyaay," *Kumeyaay Language and Culture*, http://www.kumeyaay.org/firstpage.htm> (accessed January 29, 2010). Capitalization for Brown as on website.

Sam Brown utilizes capital letters in the same way that the Navajo Code Talkers use dashes, namely to represent syllable breaks. Like the Navajo Code Talker orthography, Brown doesn't generally represent vowel length.

Of the five orthographic principles listed above, it appears that the paramount principle followed in this spelling system is (4) maximum transfer.

Sam Brown does not insist that his spelling of words be taken as authoritative. To reiterate his own statement on his Web site, the spelling is "just my guess." I asked him why he doesn't use the Langdon system, and he responded, "She said it was easy, but I couldn't understand it at all" (Sam Brown, pers. comm.).[4]

Why would Sam Brown, a highly intelligent, motivated, and educated person, say that he couldn't understand Langdon's system? From the point of view of someone literate in English, there are various internal difficulties in Langdon's LPO. For example, the convention of using double letters to represent long vowels is unknown to an English reader. When an English reader sees <ee> or <oo>, he will expect those sequences to be pronounced /i/ and /u/. Similarly, the digraphs <ll> and <ly> and the trigraph <lly> all represent Kumeyaay sounds that are not found in

[4] On his Web site, Sam Brown introduces Amy Miller's presentation and description of the Langdon system and writes [quotation unedited–LH], "Some Linguist think that things should always be spelled the same way. Amy Miller spells Kumeyaay using the following. The good this is that it doesn't use all those linguist hieroglyphics that no one can read. Maybe I will try using this some day" (Sam Brown, "Comments from a Linguist," *Kumeyaay Language and Culture*, http://www.kumeyaay.org/amy_miller.htm, accessed September 13, 2012).

English but do exist as letter combinations in English words to represent other sounds; they are likely to be pronounced by the uninitiated as /l/ (as in *all*) or as /liy/ (as in *clearly* or *really*). The way Sam Brown spells words may result in pronunciation errors too, but in the face of no available instruction in the spelling rules, people are more likely to come up with a closer approximation to the Kumeyaay pronunciation of a word using Sam Brown's system than using Margaret Langdon's system.[5]

The lesson to be learned here by linguists is that no matter how logical and efficient the internal design of a writing system, it is unlikely to prevail when (a) there is no ongoing means for educating users in the writing system and its spelling rules; and (b) the system is substantially different in terms of its spelling rules from the language in which the users are literate. Without a system of ongoing community education in literacy in the local language, LPOs will ultimately and repeatedly be abandoned in favor of systems using the spelling rules of the dominant language.[6]

7.4.3 Big Valley Pomo (Eastern Pomo)

The Big Valley Rancheria is one of several communities that used to speak Eastern Pomo [peb]. Presently there are only a few people left who know the language. From 2003 to 2005 the community ran a program to do video documentation of the elders and develop teaching tools for future use, headed by their consultant James BlueWolf. The Eastern Pomo language has also been documented by several linguists, especially Sally McLendon. One of the resources Big Valley used was a wordlist that McLendon prepared some decades ago (McLendon, n.d.). The manuscript uses the Americanist phonetic orthography without compromise (therefore not strictly counting as an LPO).

In conjunction with the documentation program, a weekly class was taught by elders in Big Valley with the help of an assistant who was in charge of the blackboard. I had the opportunity to observe one of the

[5] As a footnote to Kumeyaay writing, a friend from San Diego called me recently to ask for the spelling of the word for horned lizard, saying, "I'd spell it mill-quas, but I know you linguists do it differently." This lack of identification with the Kumeyaay LPO bodes ill for its future.

[6] As of the final version of this paper, the talented Kumeyaay language teacher Stan Rodriguez was teaching a class in Kumeyaay using photocopies of Couro and Langdon (1975), thus for the first time in decades giving learners some exposure to that orthography. However, he also utilizes an informal EPO to elucidate pronunciation.

classes, where the assistant would write words on the board both in English and as they appeared in the McLendon manuscript and would then ask the elder to pronounce them. The elder worked from the English translation to figure out what word it must be because neither she nor anyone else in the class understood the specialized symbols or knew the pronunciation even of the familiar symbols. As the elder and the class worked out the pronunciation, the assistant wrote it on the board using what she and other people in the community have taken to calling "Indian phonics," which utilizes English spelling rules. Following are some examples.

Table 3. Eastern Pomo transcription

McLendon transcription	Pomo class transcription	Gloss
káli	caw lee	'one'
xóč	khoch	'two'
xó.mča	home ca	'three'
do·l	dole	'four'
lé·ma	leh ma	'five'
mí·še	mi shea	'to smell (SG)'
mu·šú	moo sue	'hair'
mu·sáq	moo shuck	'black'
phu·dí·	pooh dee	'to steal'
sa·má·y	saw my	'heart'
cha·wíl	cha will	'left (hand)'
ma·ʔáy	ma eye	'food'
qa·c^{h}íl	caw chill	'cold'
kúruhu·	goo ruh who	'come here'

Like Sam Brown's Kumeyaay, the "Indian phonics" of Big Valley is improvised guesswork which uses English words or common sequences and leaves out vowel length and glottalization. In the class that I observed, the post-velar /q/ was sometimes written as <g>, sometimes as <k>, or other times as <ck>. The voiceless velar fricative was discussed fairly frequently during the class and sometimes written as <kh>, sometimes as

<h>. (Nelson Hopper, who wasn't present that night, prefers an <x>, in keeping with the technical orthography.) Vowel length was not written, but the assistant recognized it and described it to the class in an example: she contrasted *qa·cʰíl* and *kúruhur,* saying that for *qa·cʰíl* "you say it kind of separated" whereas the syllables of the other word are said "faster, all together."

The documentation project resulted in a series of CD-ROMs with words and phrases in audio and video that have been recorded in class and in private sessions with the elders. The staff was trying to decide whether the written form should be in the McLendon form or in "phonics." They were being encouraged from all tribal members who had an opinion to use the phonic notation. The participants in the classes say, with great emphasis, that "Indian phonics is so much easier." They go on to say that the system in the McLendon pamphlet is not understandable and "throws you off." Again, the McLendon orthography is truer to the representation of the sounds of the language but was superseded by an EPO because of the primacy of perceived learnability and transfer. At the end of the three-year project, a Web page on the Big Valley Web site was put up that had a standardized practical orthography lacking the exotic symbols of the McLendon system and allowing two spelling options for many of the sounds, especially vowels. For example, long /i/ can be written as a digraph <ii> or as a trigraph <eee>.[7]

7.4.4 Yurok

Yurok [yur], an Algic language, has an official EPO, which I shall go over in some detail. Yurok was described by Robins in 1958 in a grammar which was recently republished by the Yuroks themselves and distributed to members of the tribe (Robins 1958). However, although not frighteningly technical, the book was designed for linguists rather than for the community and for decades after the book was written, few Yuroks had access to it. Thus, Robins' writing system did not become familiar to the tribe.

In the early 1980s, a faculty member at Humboldt State University in northern California, Tom Parsons, introduced UNIFON to the northern California tribes including the Yuroks (Hinton 1994:216).[8] UNIFON uses letters reminiscent of Roman capitals but strongly altered. It is a phonetic alphabet but one that takes after English spelling rules in that, for

[7] Big Valley Rancheria, "Eastern Pomo Language," Big Valley Band of Pomo Indians, http://www.big-valley.net/lang_home.htm (accessed September 14, 2012).

[8] See http://www.unifon.org/ for a treatise on the history and nature of UNIFON.

example, any sound that would be typically represented as an <a> in English spelling will be represented by a variant of <A> (see figure 1).

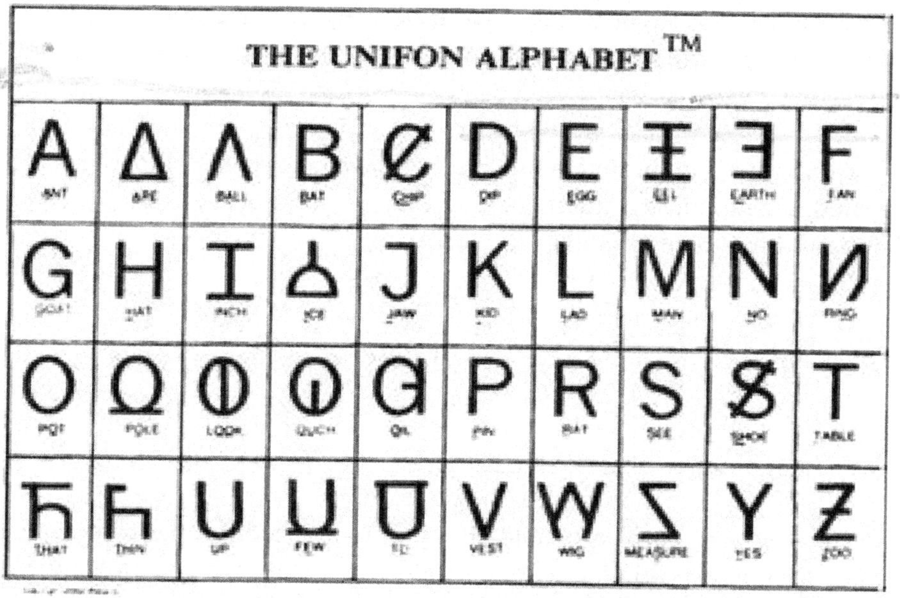

THE UNIFON ALPHABET™

Source: http://www.triune-being.com/Images/Unifon.gif (accessed January 10, 2013.). Some characters in the UNIFON alphabet were modified in 2005. The above chart represents the alphabet at the time that it was presented by Parsons at Humboldt State University (see www.unifon.org).

Figure 1. The UNIFON alphabet as devised by John Malone in 1959.

Through a language program run by Humboldt State University, a sizable number of the native speakers of Yurok and the other languages of the region learned how to read and write using that system, and some of those speakers remained loyal to the system (Hinton 1994; Hinton and Hale 2001). However, it did not fulfill a number of Smalley's criteria: maximum ease of learning, maximum transfer, and maximum ease of reproduction. Furthermore, it was hotly criticized by a number of linguists. In the end, despite a decade or more of the development of materials and publications using that orthography, every language group has now given up using UNIFON.

Asked to assist the Yurok Language Committee in the development of a new writing system in 1997, I presented Robins' writing system along with various changes that had been suggested for Yurok by linguist Jean

Perry with the aim of maximum ease of reproduction. Victor Golla had also worked with the committee previously to suggest a similar writing system. However, a number of people on the language committee were dissatisfied with the systems we presented. Two factors played a big role in the development of the orthography by the committee: the Smalley criterion of ease of transfer and the fact that most of the users would be language learners rather than native speakers of Yurok.

Yurok vowels according to Robins are shown below. His orthography also includes the following diphthongs: uy, ry, o:y, oy, a:y ey, ur, or, ar, er, ir, rw, ew, a:w, ow (Robins 1958:1).

(3) Yurok vowel system

i / i:			u / u:
		ɹ / ɹ:	
	e	o / o:	
		a / a:	

The vowels of Yurok are quite different from Western American English. They have more variation, with a single Yurok phoneme corresponding to what would be two or more different phonemes in English. For example, Yurok /e/ corresponds to [e, ɛ, æ]. Also, Yurok /a/ is quite front, often sounding closer to [æ]. Yurok /o/ varies between [o] and [ɔ], and since Western American English lacks [ɔ], it is often perceived by language learners as /ɑ/. Furthermore, reduced vowels are common in unstressed syllables, deriving from different vowels but sounding like [ʌ].

Originally proposed to the language committee was a writing system like Robins', but one with digraphs replacing non-Roman symbols. In addition, the committee was shown two ways of representing long vowels: either doubled vowels or a vowel followed by a colon. The committee chose doubled vowels. However, based on the bias toward English spelling, some members of the committee did not like <ii> for Robins' <i·> and insisted on using <ee> instead. They ended up preferring <ee> for short <i> as well unless the pronunciation was clearly [ɪ]. We discussed how one could show length and the committee decided that the trigraph <eee> would work. However, this is rarely used.

Second, the representation of syllabic [ɹ] as orthographic <r> did not appeal to the committee, and they decided on <er> instead, with <err>

for the long /ɚ:/. However, there is also a consonant [r] and there are some lexical items with an [er] sequence, and so the solution to this was to spell those words <eyr>.

One of the aspects of the writing system that was contested by linguists was the use of <u> for the reduced vowel. The reduced vowel occurs only in unstressed syllables. The same morpheme can also occur with that syllable stressed in other environments, so the obvious first choice of linguists would be to represent the unreduced form of the vowel in the writing system. But here we begin to see the influence of English on second-language learning of Yurok. The reduced vowel, which can derive from almost any vowel phoneme, sounds like the English vowel phoneme /ʌ/ and is interpreted as distinctive by the non-native Yurok speakers. Therefore, the decision was to use <u> for the reduced vowel (given its frequent usage in English in words such as *mutt, cluck,* or *fun*). This preference was also affected by the Yuroks' knowledge of UNIFON, which uses <U> for that sound. But then how can the sound [u] be represented? The Yuroks' suggestion was to spell it <ue>, as in English *due* or *sue*.

In general the diphthongs are written more or less as Robins wrote them, with the exception of two: <ay> and <aw>, which the committee rejected because of potential confusion with English spelling rules, where they pointed out that the most common pronunciation of <ay> is [ey] (as in *pay*) and the most common pronunciation of <aw> is [a:] (as in *raw*). The solution was to spell [ay] as <aiy> and [aw] as <auw>. The use of a hyphen between syllables is also part of the spelling convention of the new Yurok system.

This system was not satisfying to everyone on the committee, but in the end it was nevertheless the one agreed upon formally.

Table 4. The new Yurok vowel orthography

Robins			New Yurok system		
i / i:		u / u:	i, ee / eeei		ue / uue
	ɹ / ɹ:			er / err	
e	o / o:			u	
	a / a:		e / ey		o / oo
				a / aa	

The variability of Yurok vowels poses a problem to language learners who are learning the language informally from native speakers. The result is that the spelling choices made in the development of teaching materials are sometimes very different from the vowel system of the native speakers. However, a study of two pages of Yurok writing[9] showed that out of 138 vowels, only 26 did not fit the native phonemic system, and of those, 12 involved the use of <u> for the reduced version of /o/, which should not be counted as an error but rather as the transcription of a subphonemic distinction. Most of the remaining vowels that differed from the native system had to do with the lack of indication of vowel length.

Among the consonants, Yurok writers do not indicate syllable-final [h], as in *twey-go* [twegoh]. It was agreed by the committee to spell glottal stops as <’> and glottalized consonants with an apostrophe following the consonant (including glottalized sonorants, which are usually preglottalized). But glottalization, which is rather weakly pronounced by native speakers, appears to be barely noticeable by the Yuroks who are writing the materials and is frequently not indicated. Glottalization is most commonly heard by the writers in preglottalized sonorants, but this is interpreted as a syllable-final glottal stop followed by a syllable-initial sonorant and spelled as illustrated by the words in example (4). This phenomenon is further described in Blevins 2003a and 2003b.

(4) Glottalization

teeˈ-nee-sho	/ti.ˈni.šo/	‘what?’
oˈ-lu-mo	/ˈo.ˈlo.mah/	‘come in’

We must distinguish here between possible infelicities intrinsic to the design of the writing system and spellings based on mishearings or incomplete language learning. The latter would happen regardless of the spelling system used.

Linguists Juliette Blevins and Andrew Garrett who came to work with Yurok later were not fond of the Yurok EPO and presented the language committee with their concerns, most importantly:

1. By writing <u> for the reduced vowel, predictability is lost: the language learner cannot know what the vowel is that is reduced. This has some importance since this vowel will appear in unreduced form in other constructions using the same morpheme.

[9] The “Yurok writing” referred to is an impressive language curriculum by Kay Inong. Thanks are due to Juliette Blevins for providing the LPO alternate spellings.

2. The design is inconsistent. For example, whether something is spelled with an <i> or an <ee> depends on whether the writer hears it as an [ɪ] or an [i]. Not only will the pronunciation differ from token to token of the same word but most of the time the pronunciation is really in between the two sounds, so it is virtually arbitrary which way it would be written. The same problem holds for vowel reduction, which occurs more in some speakers than in others and may disappear in slow speech.[10]

The orthographic issues created some tensions between some of the Yuroks and the linguists. Blevins used a system closer to that of Robins to develop some materials containing phrases for use in the Yurok preschool, but the younger leaders of the Yurok language program would not accept it, insisting that linguists working with the community use the Yurok EPO for any materials that are specifically for the community, although they did not mind the linguists using a scholarly writing system for their scholarly publications. The linguists, on the other hand, hoped that some of their publications, such as dictionaries, grammars, and texts, could be used by both audiences. The difference between linguistic and tribal orthographies meant either that they had to make two versions of these publications or that they would have to include both writing systems in their publications. (Some people were still loyal to UNIFON and wanted any dictionary to also show the UNIFON writing system, totaling three ways of writing each word.) Another problem is that there is not a direct one-to-one correspondence between the linguistic and tribal systems, especially with regard to the reduced sound represented by <u> in the tribal system, which meant that it would be difficult to create an automated transliteration program.

Finally, the linguists wished to use a spelling system that represents the phonemic system of a native speaker, which pitted them against some of the Yuroks who were second-language speakers and who insisted that words should be spelled "like they sound," that is, using some subphonemic distinctions and possibly showing actual shifts that are present in the English-influenced phonemic model of the language learners.[11]

---

[10] These were some of the considerations spelled out in a set of unpublished notes to the language committee by Juliette Blevins and Andrew Garrett in July 2003.

[11] Again, the phonemic shifts that appear to be present in the minds of the Yurok language learners would show up in their spelling no matter what writing conventions were used.

7.4.5 Summary of differences between LPOs and EPOs

English is a very hard writing system to learn (Ellis et al. 2004:441). Nevertheless, it has been pretty thoroughly learned in childhood by anyone educated in an English-speaking country, and despite its complexity, features of it can be used to render other languages to writing, as seen in the examples above. The Yurok system, the early Big Valley system used in Pomo classes, and Sam Brown's Kumeyaay orthography have some differences among them, the main one being that the Yurok system strives for consistency in the representation of sounds whereas "phonic" Eastern Pomo and Sam Brown's Kumeyaay do not. Where Yurok and Navajo Code Talker writing transfer common pronunciations of English sounds to their orthography, Chavez and Sam Brown instead find English monosyllabic words that sound like a given syllable in Pomo or Kumeyaay and use them. The Eastern Pomo and Kumeyaay EPOs might be thought of as syllabic in nature, as opposed to the segmentally based LPOs, since each syllable is designed to match one of the ways that English would spell that syllable without regard to consistency in the spelling of particular sounds. Andrew Garrett (pers. comm.) has suggested that like the other two EPOs, the Yurok EPO should also be thought of as a syllabic system, or more precisely, as a syllable-rhyme system, in that the underlying goal of the system's design is to have a spelling for each perceived different syllable rhyme. Whether the rhyme has one vowel sound or two is irrelevant to how many symbols are used. In all the EPOs discussed here, the use of syllable boundary markers (spaces in Big Valley, hyphens in Navajo Code Talker, and capital letters in Sam Brown's Kumeyaay) can be seen as a clue to the designers' view that the syllable is the basic unit of reading and writing.

Besides the fact that all the EPOs discussed here mark syllable boundaries overtly, there are many features that the three California writing systems and the Navajo Code Talker system have in common. They all utilize English spelling rules, and they all reject linguistic spelling rules that violate the common patterns of English spelling-pronunciation matches. For example, they reject orthographic <ee> to represent /e:/ and reject <ay> to represent the diphthong /ay/. In Sam Brown's Kumeyaay, the use of <ll> to represent the voiceless lateral fricative is also rejected.

The main code-internal differences between LPOs and EPOs are summarized in table 5:

Table 5. Code-internal differences between LPOs and EPOs

Linguistic Practical Orthographies (LPO)	English-based Practical Orthographies (EPO)
• use one symbol (or symbol combination) for one sound	• use various symbols for one sound or one symbol for various sounds
• are modeled on IPA/ Americanist orthographic conventions	• are modeled on English words that have the same sound as a given syllable in the language
• do not indicate syllable breaks	• indicate syllable breaks
• represent phonemic system of native speakers	• tend toward subphonemic representation or English-influenced phonemic system
• preserve suprasegmental features such as vowel length and glottalization	• tend to leave out suprasegmentals

Why is it that Langdon's writing system for Kumeyaay, McLendon's Eastern Pomo orthography, and a modified Robins' system for Yurok are all rejected, as was the Navajo orthography for the Code Talker words? It is primarily that the principle of maximum representation of the sound system is being valued less by the respective communities than the principle of maximum transfer.

Beyond this, linguists and community members have various other system-external needs and preferences that influence their views on writing systems. Linguists focus on descriptive adequacy and documentation of "best speakers" as being among the most important goals of their work, whereas community members increasingly see writing systems as a language teaching tool. Some of the features of EPOs that linguists have a hard time relating to are used commonly in popular language learning materials such as the Berlitz language books. So there are certainly valid points of view about writing for the sake of language learning that may differ from the views of linguists. In the end, EPOs will appear over and over again in language programs despite their infelicities because they appear to be "user-friendly," appealing to the bias of familiarity to people who are literate in English.

7.5 Some compromises to consider

7.5.1 Orthographic considerations

English spelling rules can't be applied to sounds that aren't in English, but one problem with some LPOs is that they use letters and letter combinations that are confusing because they evoke an English pronunciation. Kumeyaay <ll> for example should just sound like <l> according to the expectations of literate English speakers, so it shouldn't be used to sound like the voiceless lateral [ɬ]. Sam Brown uses <lh> instead, and at the other end of the state, the Yuroks use <hl>. Both representations are chosen partly because the <h> shows the voicelessness and partly because it doesn't look like a common English sequence and so is not likely to be confused with an English sound. The Yurok Language Committee was especially sad to give up one adaptation of a UNIFON letter, a capital *H* with a circle around the bar, which stood for their voiceless lateral fricative. Since this is a sound that is not in English, everyone felt that this was one case where it was highly appropriate to use something other than an English letter.

Similarly, when I worked with the Havasupais in the development of their writing system, they refused to use the letter <t> for their dental stop, even though there was no alveolar stop in the language, because this was a salient difference between English and Havasupai and they feared that using the letter <t> for their dental stop would encourage people to mispronounce it. They made up a letter instead: a *t* with a double cross (Crook, Hinton, and Stenson 1977). In retrospect, it is apparent that in Langdon's Kumeyaay LPO, the use of <t> and <n> for the Kumeyaay dentals and <tt> and <nn> for the alveolars is unconsciously based on the Americanist principle used by linguists for California languages, where in the case of pairs of apicals, the front one (whether dental or alveolar) tended to be represented by the simpler symbol such as <t> or <n>, while the back one (whether alveolar or retroflex) was represented by the more complex symbol <ṭ>. Readers of English who do not have a linguistic background would instead expect the symbols <t> and <n> to be used for the apical, whose pronunciation is closer to English.

Thus, one lesson from this is that the use of letter combinations that can easily evoke an English pronunciation might be better avoided if possible, and letters standing for common sounds in English will be better understood if they are used for similar sounds in the Native language.

7.5.2 Multi-orthographic materials

A second point is that when linguistic and community writing systems cannot be reconciled for one reason or another, using both is a potentially wise compromise. For one thing, using both systems will allow each group to become more accustomed to the other's writing system, and the "bias of familiarity" will no longer be a divisive factor. Indeed, each group stands to benefit from knowing both systems. The local community may become proficient enough in reading the linguistic orthography to be able to make better use of the linguistic materials available in scholarly publications; and the linguists may gain interesting linguistic insights from the community system. For example, Juliette Blevins gained important corroboration of native-speaker intuitions about syllabification for her paper on Yurok stress (see Blevins 2003b), through the examination of the hyphens used at syllable boundaries in the Yurok writing system. Furthermore, frequently, some of the discrepancies between LPOs and EPOs can disappear with time. For example, the Yurok second-language speakers are using the <u> for reduced vowels less and less frequently as they become more fluent in Yurok themselves, becoming more likely to write the underlying full form of the vowel instead. Linguists may also change toward the use of some of the conventions of the community system. This kind of evolution is enhanced by keeping both systems side by side in materials. (In this connection, see Karan this volume for the importance of not rushing language standardization.)

The use of a dual orthography was the final compromise made by the Yurok linguists, as can be found in the wonderful Web-based dictionary set up and maintained by Andrew Garrett (Garrett n.d.). A small sample from the search index shows the layout:

(5) Sample from Yurok dictionary[12]

cha'amew	[cha-'a-mew]	'be boiled'
cha'anar	[cha-'a-neyr]	'be new'
chechekw	[che-chekw]	'fin of fish, bone of fish, small fish bones'
chechomeyo'r	[che-cho-mey-yor']	'run at a trot'
chechu's	[che-chue's]	'boils, simmers'

Another example of materials using a dual system of writing is a Miami phrasebook designed by Daryl Baldwin, a linguist and a member of the Miami Nation. He uses a linguistic writing system in the development of language learning materials but also uses an EPO as a pronunciation guide.

(6) Sample from Miami phrasebook[13]

'blanket'	waapimotayi *(wah-pim-o-TAH-yih)*
'board'	peepakisiki *(pey-pah-kih-SHICK-ih)*
'bottle'	sakinteewi *(sah-kin-DAY-wih)*
'bow'	mihtehkoopa *(mih-teh-KOOP-ah)*

7.5.3 Using the web

A strategy that might be useful to linguists can be learned from Sam Brown. Despite the fact that Margaret Langdon has published many books and articles using the Kumeyaay LPO that she developed, her system is now less familiar to the general Kumeyaay population than Sam Brown's. Sam Brown's writings are on the Web. Links to his Web site can be found on the Web sites of Kumeyaay-owned casinos and other businesses, and his is the first Web site that comes up with a Google search. Even though Sam Brown does not tout his system as authoritative, his orthography now has great familiarity to Kumeyaay language enthusiasts while the Langdon system, presented in a book that is now out of print (Couro and Langdon 1975), languishes in libraries.

---

[12] Garrett n.d., accessed January 29, 2010.

[13] Miami Tribe of Oklahoma, n.d.

7.5.4 Beating the bias of familiarity

Another point to consider is that there is a relatively short window of opportunity for linguists developing new writing systems to share their views with speech communities before a writing system becomes finalized and entrenched. Once a writing system is in use, changing it becomes less and less desirable, as written materials proliferate in the system, the commitment to it is strengthened, and the bias of familiarity sets in. In the past, linguists have been barred from a community for making the mistake of trying to improve on an established writing system. (For two case studies describing situations where bad orthography decisions had to be reversed, see Karan, this volume.)

7.6 Conclusion

If we look back on the history of Native American orthography, there is an interesting pattern of how the design of writing systems acceptable to the community shifts along with language shift. For the primarily monolingual Cree [cre] and Cherokee [chr] nations of the eighteenth and early nineteenth century, syllabic writing systems prospered. These had no relationship to English. Since its monolingual and then literate inventor, Sequoyah, had inspected English-language manuscripts, Cherokee certainly has the look of English writing. The similarity is, however, purely visual: there is no sound correlation between the Cherokee syllabics and anything that looks like an English letter. Cree, on the other hand, has no visible similarity to the Roman alphabet. It is fairly certain that James Evans, the developer of the Cree syllabary, based it partly on a shorthand system that was prevalent in the early 1800s. Both these syllabic systems were rapidly accepted by their communities, whose attitudes were unencumbered by exposure to English literacy.

In the years intervening between those times and today, we see many manuscripts written primarily by outsiders—linguists, missionaries, army officers, doctors, and so forth—using either linguistic or English-based writing systems; but a large number of the official orthographies accepted into communities tended to be based on the linguistic principles. Certainly this was the case with most of the twentieth century orthographies, such as Navajo and other writing systems developed from the '30s through the '70s.

And of course linguistically based writing systems still abound. However, I suspect that the California trend toward English-based writing is connected closely to language shift. Most of the languages under discussion here have very few speakers left at all, and the main people bearing the responsibility for language preservation and revitalization are not native speakers but rather people whose first language is English and who are educated completely in English. That fact, combined with the present-day primary function of these new writing systems as a language teaching tool to other English speakers trying to learn their ancestral tongue biases people almost inexorably toward an EPO.

Even though we know that LPOs can work well once they are learned, linguists must accept that our own criteria for a good orthography may well be overridden. It may be hard to accede to this because there is always the feeling that if people were just able to take a semester of linguistics they might well agree with the linguists about the best design of a writing system. But most people do not take linguistics courses. System-external principles are likely to prevail, and many of them are even important and reasonable. Linguists acting in the capacity of consultants to the community must be willing to recognize that they are not the final decision makers about the writing system, and for the sake of the maintenance of mutual trust they must learn when to give in gracefully.

I close with one more quote from Fishman (1977:xiii) about linguists working with communities to design writing systems: "Once having stepped outside of the charmingly closed circle of code-internal considerations, Pandora's box had been opened never again to be shut."

References

Berry, Jack. 1977. 'The making of alphabets' revisited. In Fishman, 1–16.

Blevins, Juliette. 2003a. The phonology of Yurok glottalized sonorants: Segmental fission under syllabification. *International Journal of American Linguistics* 69(4)(October):371–396.

Blevins, Juliette. 2003b. Yurok syllable weight. *International Journal of American Linguistics* 69(1)(January):4–24.

Couro, Ted, and Christina Hutcheson. 1973. *Dictionary of Mesa Grande Diegueño*. Banning, Calif.: Malki Museum Press.

Couro, Ted, and Margaret Langdon. 1975. *Let's talk Iipai 'Aa.* Banning, Calif.: Malki Museum Press.

Crook, Rena, Leanne Hinton, and Nancy Stenson. 1977. Literacy and linguistics: The Havasupai writing system. In James E. Redden (ed.), *Proceedings of the 1976 Hokan-Yuman Languages Workshop,* University of California, San Diego, 21–23 June, 1976, 1–16. University Museum Studies 11. Carbondale, IL: Southern Illinois University.

Ellis, Nick C., Miwa Natsume, Katerina Stavropoulou, Lorenc Hoxhallari, Victor H. P. Van Daal, Nicoletta Polyzoe, Maria-Louisa Tsipa, and Michalis Petalas. 2004. The effects of orthographic depth on learning to read alphabetic, syllabic, and logographic scripts. *Reading Research Quarterly* 39:438–468.

Fishman, Joshua A. 1972. The uses of sociolinguistics. In Joshua A. Fishman, *Language in socio-cultural change: Essays by Joshua A. Fishman,* 305–330. Stanford: Stanford University Press.

Fishman, Joshua A. 1977. *Advances in the creation and revision of writing systems.* The Hague: Mouton Press.

Garrett, Andrew. 2011. *An online dictionary with texts and pedagogical tools: The Yurok language project.* Oxford University Press. http://linguistics.berkeley.edu/~garrett/garrett-ijl.pdf (accessed November 14, 2012).

Hernandez, Pedro. 2004. Revitalization, development, and diffusion of indigenous languages, starting with their writing: The experience of CEDELIO. In Meyer, L, and Maldonado, B. (eds.), *Between national standards and communal ways of life: Innovative educational experiences from indigenous Oaxaca today,* 81–111. Oaxaca, Mexico: Publication branch of the State Institute for Public Education of Oaxaca. Collection Voces del Fondo, Molinos de Viento series.

Hinton, Leanne. 1994. *Flutes of fire: Essays on California Indian languages.* Berkeley: Heyday Books.

Hinton, Leanne, and Ken Hale, eds. 2001. *The green book of language revitalization in practice.* San Diego: Academic Press.

Hollyman, Jim, and Andrew Pawley. 1981. Bruce Biggs: A foreword. In Jim Hollyman and Andrew Pawley (eds.), *Studies in Pacific languages and cultures in honour of Bruce Biggs,* 7–23. Auckland: Linguistic Society of New Zealand.

Jones, Henry. 1995. Optimal orthographies. In Insup Taylor and David R. Olson (eds.), *Scripts and literacy: Reading and learning to read alphabets, syllabaries and characters.* Dordrecht, The Netherlands: Kluwer.

Kim-Cho, Sek Yen. 2002. *The Korean alphabet of 1446.* Amherst, N.Y.: Humanity Books.

Kim-Renaud, Young-Key, ed. 1997. *The Korean alphabet: Its history and structure.* Honolulu: University of Hawai'i Press.

Luyx, Aurolyn. 2003. Whose language is it anyway? Historical fetishism and the construction of expertise in Bolivian language planning. *Current Issues in Comparative Education* 5(2):92–102.

Marinakis, Aliki, Mary K. Richardson, Leslie Saxon, and Mary Siemens, eds. 2007. Reading and writing in Tłı̨cho˛ Yatıì. Tłı̨cho˛ Community Services Agency, Behchokò˛ , Northwest Territories, Canada Ms.

McLendon, Sally. n.d. A brief word list of Eastern Pomo.

Miami Tribe of Oklahoma. n.d. Iilaataweeyankwi: Our language. Ms.

Nez, Chester. 2011. *Code talker.* New York: Berkley Caliber.

Nida, Eugene. 1953. Practical limitations to a phonemic orthography. *Bible Translator* 5:58–62.

Rice, Keren, and Leslie Saxon. 2002. Issues of standardization and community in aboriginal language lexicography. In William Frawley, Kenneth C. Hill, and Pamela Munro (eds.), *Making dictionaries: Preserving indigenous languages of the Americas,* 125–154. Berkeley: University of California Press.

Robins, R. H. 1958. *The Yurok language: Grammar, texts, lexicon.* Berkeley: The University of California Press.

Sebba, Mark. 2007. *Spelling and society: The culture and politics of orthography around the world.* New York: Cambridge University Press.

Siefert, Frank. 2006. Orthography development. In Jost Gippert, Nikolaus P. Himmelmann, and Ulrike Mosel (eds.), *Essentials of language documentation,* 275–299. New York: Walter de Gruyter.

Smalley, William A., et al. 1963. *Orthography studies: Articles on new writing systems.* Helps for Translators 6. London: United Bible Societies.

Young, Robert W. 1977. Written Navajo: A brief history. In Fishman, 459–470.

8

Breaking Rules for Orthography Development

Pamela Munro

Orthographies should follow the "one-symbol-per-sound, one-sound-per-symbol" rule, generally speaking—but there must be exceptions. In this paper, I consider how two orthographies were adapted in ways that break this rule, for the Zapotecan (Otomanguean) language Tlacolula Valley Zapotec of Oaxaca, Mexico, and for Gabrielino/Tongva/Fernandeño, a Uto-Aztecan language formerly spoken in southern California. In Zapotec, we under-write contrasts; in Tongva, we write contrasts that aren't real. These rule-breaking approaches help learners and are more acceptable to speech communities, so any theoretical cost is probably justified.

8.1 Introduction*

As the studies in this volume demonstrate, orthographies may vary substantially and yet function effectively for user communities. In this

* I thank, first, the Tlacolula Valley Zapotec [tvz] speakers who have taught me so much about their language (especially my collaborator Felipe H. Lopez) and my fellow Tongva language

paper, I will review some basic orthography rules and then present two case studies—from the Tlacolula Valley Zapotec [zab] language of central Oaxaca, Mexico, and the "sleeping" Gabrielino/Tongva/Fernandeño [xgf] language of southern California—showing how these rules have been violated in the development of effective orthographies for these languages.

8.2 Orthographies and orthographic rules

Readers of this volume most likely already have an idea what an orthography should and should not be and what "rules" it should follow. Here, by way of introduction, I review these concepts briefly.

8.2.1 What orthography is (and isn't)

An orthography is a systematic, standardized writing system for a particular language, designed to be appropriate for representing the sounds and phonology of that language. A standard orthography allows users to write words so that others familiar with the orthography can read them, and to read words others have written using the same system, with no need to memorize spellings for every word.

Speakers who are literate in another language may develop ad hoc systems for writing their language, often coming up with inconsistent spellings on a word-by-word basis—especially if their language of literacy is one like English, with a massively irregular orthography of its own (see Hinton, this volume). Although these efforts may not be orthographies as such, they often represent the beginning of orthography development.

Orthography is not phonetic transcription or some other universal system. Since any two separate languages seldom have the same sound inventory and never the same phonology, an orthography designed for one language will rarely work perfectly for a second language (though in some cases only minor adaptation may be needed).

learners (listed in footnote 10), as well as Eric Bacović, the late William Bright, Mike Cahill, Mario Chávez Peón, Leanne Hinton, Brook Danielle Lillehaugen, Martha Macri, Marcus Smith, and all the others who have helped me figure things out about this fascinating topic. Work on TVZ has been supported by the Chicano Studies Research Center, the Department of Linguistics, and the Academic Senate of UCLA; the UCMexus Foundation; the National Science Foundation; and a Department of Education Title VI grant, "San Diego Consortium: NRC and FLAS," subcontract to UCSD (Charles L. Briggs, PI), subcontract to UCLA (Pamela Munro).

Even though an orthography is a standard writing system, this does not mean that every word needs to have one standard spelling (or pronunciation), or that some speakers' pronunciations can be labeled as non-standard. A standard orthography can be used to represent many different pronunciations, or even regular dialect variants (see, for example, the Lisu and Lahu case study in Adams, this volume).

Generally, it is best if an orthography can be typed on a standard keyboard—not just a computer keyboard (where Unicode allows nearly limitless character and diacritic options), but also the keyboards of cell phones and other such devices. This desideratum is especially important for younger users.

Sometimes, however, users may favor an orthography with unique (or at least unusual) characters, perhaps with important cultural connections. A prime example is the Cherokee [chr] alphabet (actually, a syllabary) developed in the 1820s by Sequoyah, a native speaker who was illiterate in English, as represented in figure 1.[1] Despite the typographic problems this system presents (and its failure to represent various contrasts), it enjoys wide acceptance among Cherokees (both speakers and non-speakers) and has almost certainly increased Cherokee literacy (see Walker 1969, Walker and Sarbaugh 1993).

[1] Wikimedia Commons: File:Ceroka silabaro.png, http://commons.wikimedia.org/wiki/File: Ceroka_silabaro.png (accessed November 13, 2012). In the standard transcription used in figure 1 (similar to that of Feeling 1975), the letter <v> represents the nasalized schwa phoneme, the sequence <qu> represents [kw], <dl> is a voiceless unaspirated affricate with lateral release, and <tl> is the corresponding aspirated affricate. Stops and affricates shown here as voiced are all voiceless unaspirated, while those represented as voiceless are aspirated (or, in some cases, sequences of voiceless unaspirated plus [h]).

a	e	i	o	u	v [ə̃]
Ꭰ a	Ꭱ e	Ꭲ i	Ꭳ o	Ꭴ u	Ꭵ v
Ꭶ ga Ꭷ ka	Ꭸ ge	Ꭹ gi	Ꭺ go	Ꭻ gu	Ꭼ gv
Ꭽ ha	Ꭾ he	Ꭿ hi	Ꮀ ho	Ꮁ hu	Ꮂ hv
Ꮃ la	Ꮄ le	Ꮅ li	Ꮆ lo	Ꮇ lu	Ꮈ lv
Ꮉ ma	Ꮊ me	Ꮋ mi	Ꮌ mo	Ꮍ mu	
Ꮎ na Ꮏ hna Ꮐ nah	Ꮑ ne	Ꮒ ni	Ꮓ no	Ꮔ nu	Ꮕ nv
Ꮖ qua	Ꮗ que	Ꮘ qui	Ꮙ quo	Ꮚ quu	Ꮛ quv
Ꮜ s Ꮝ sa	Ꮞ se	Ꮟ si	Ꮠ so	Ꮡ su	Ꮢ sv
Ꮣ da Ꮤ ta	Ꮥ de Ꮦ te	Ꮧ di Ꮨ ti	Ꮩ do	Ꮪ du	Ꮫ dv
Ꮬ dla Ꮭ tla	Ꮮ tle	Ꮯ tli	Ꮰ tlo	Ꮱ tlu	Ꮲ tlv
Ꮳ tsa	Ꮴ tse	Ꮵ tsi	Ꮶ tso	Ꮷ tsu	Ꮸ tsv
Ꮹ wa	Ꮺ we	Ꮻ wi	Ꮼ wo	Ꮽ wu	Ꮾ wv
Ꮿ ya	Ᏸ ye	Ᏹ yi	Ᏺ yo	Ᏻ yu	Ᏼ yv

Figure 1. The Cherokee syllabary with standard phonemic values.

The Cherokee case, in turn, raises another important point about orthographies: they must be acceptable not only to users but to other stakeholders as well (see Cahill's contribution on non-linguistic factors in orthographies, this volume).

8.2.2 Orthographic rules

Orthographic rules specify how a given character or letter (or the combination of a given character with a diacritic) in the system should be pronounced, and which character should be used to encode a given sound. Specific orthographic rules and practices vary from language to language: each language's orthography is different.

8.2.2.1 A simple example of variation among orthographies

Orthographies often represent the same sound differently, or use the same symbol to represent different sounds. Consider the case of the letter <j> in four familiar European languages:

(1) The letter <j> in four languages
In English, <j> represents the sound [dʒ], as in *juvenile* or *junior.*
In French, <j> represents the sound [ʒ], as in *jeune* 'young'.
In Spanish, <j> represents the sound [x], as in *joven* 'young'.
In German, <j> represents the sound [j], as in *jung* 'young'.

Even when people are making an effort to write consistently, how they represent a sound they hear (or how they interpret the pronunciation of something written) can be affected dramatically by the language or languages they know (see Hinton, this volume).

8.2.2.2 Two rules for good orthographies

There are two basic technical rules for good orthographies.[2] First, every symbol or combination of symbols (for example, a sequence such as <ch>) must always represent the same sound (or more precisely phoneme) of the language. (The more precise phrasing is important, because, of course, phonemes may have different realizations in different contexts and should still ideally be represented the same way.) Second, every sound (or more precisely, every phoneme) of the language must always be represented the same way.

8.2.2.3 Orthographies vary

Established orthographies vary considerably in terms of how well they follow the two rules in §8.2.2.2. English violates both rules. A single English letter sequence may be pronounced in more than one way. Consider, for example, the <ough> in *cough, through, rough, though, thought,* and *plough.* Similarly, English phonemes (especially, but not limited to, vowels) are often written in more than one way: consider the [ey] sound in *way, weigh, aid, ate, hey,* and

---

[2] See Snider, this volume, for further discussion on this topic.

vein. Sounding out unfamiliar written words or spelling unfamiliar spoken words can be very difficult for untrained English speakers.

Spanish, in contrast, does a much better job with the first rule—a Spanish speaker almost always knows how to pronounce a word from its spelling (though some letters, such as <x>, may present difficulties). However, spelling unfamiliar spoken words is more difficult for Spanish speakers. Many speakers pronounce <y> and <ll> alike, so they may be uncertain of how to spell a word with the [j] sound. Similarly, there is confusion among the use of <s, z> and (in some cases) <c>, and between <j> and <g>, and less-literate speakers are often puzzled about where to use the letter <h>.

8.2.2.4 Orthographic rules need to be flexible

Some orthographies are sensitive to morphology as well as phonology, which can lead to violations of the rules in §8.2.2.2. A morpheme may be written the same way even though it is pronounced differently in different contexts. For example, the English plural suffix is always written <s> after a non-alveopalatal, even though it is regularly pronounced as [z] when it follows a voiced sound (compare the sound of <s> in *pots* [s] versus *pods* <z>).

My two orthographic case studies illustrate two very different ways in which orthographic rules must be broken to be effective.

8.3 Case study 1: Tlacolula Valley Zapotec

8.3.1 Background

Tlacolula Valley Zapotec (TVZ) [zab], a language of the Valley-Isthmus branch of the Zapotec family, is spoken in a number of pueblos in the Tlacolula District of central Oaxaca, Mexico (including San Lucas Quiaviní, San Juan Guelavía, Tlacolula de Matamoros, Santa Ana del Valle, Teotitlán del Valle, and others), just southeast of Oaxaca City, as well as by several thousand immigrants to the Los Angeles area.[3] The language has a full New Testament translation (*La Liga Bíblica,* published in 1995) and has been the subject of intensive study by a number of researchers based on fieldwork both in Oaxaca and in Los Angeles.[4]

[3] The *Ethnologue* (Lewis 2009) identifies TVZ as "San Juan Guelavía Zapotec." This name privileges one community (of perhaps 20) where the language is spoken and thus does not seem appropriate.

[4] Dissertations have been written on the language by Mario Chávez Peón (2010); Michael R. Galant (1998); Kristine Jensen de López (2002); Felicia A. Lee (1999); Brook Danielle Lillehaugen

My collaborators on UCLA's TVZ research project include Dr. Felipe H. Lopez, a native speaker originally from San Lucas Quiaviní; Dr. Brook Danielle Lillehaugen of the University of Nevada in Reno; and many others.

8.3.2 TVZ sounds and the academic orthography

Table 1 presents the consonants of TVZ (a fairly typical inventory for Valley Zapotec) in what we now refer to as the "academic" orthography for the language. Felipe Lopez and I developed this orthography for use in our dictionary (Munro and Lopez et al. 1999), using generally Hispanic orthographic conventions. For example, <qu, gu>, replace <c, g>, respectively before front vowels. The alveopalatal/retroflex fricative and lenis/fortis sonorant contrasts carry a very low functional load.

Table 1. TVZ consonants in the academic orthography*

	Labial	Dental-alveolar	Alveo-palatal	Retroflex	Velar
Stop (fortis)	p	t			c/qu [k]
Stop (lenis)	b	d			g/gu [g]
Affricate (fortis)		ts	ch [č]		
Fricative (fortis)	f	s	x [š]	x: [ʂ]	j [x]
Fricative (lenis)		z	zh [ž]	zh: [ʐ]	
Nasal (fortis)	mm	nn			nng (fortis [ŋ])
Nasal (lenis)	m	n			ng [ŋ]
Lateral (fortis)		ll			
Lateral (lenis)		l			
Flap		r			
Trill		rr			
Glide (lenis)	w		y [j]		

*Munro and Lopez et al. 1999:1–2.

Although the consonant inventory shown in table 1 is complicated, it is TVZ's vowel inventory that is really difficult. TVZ has six vowel

(2006); and Gabriela Pérez Báez (2009). Masters' theses have been written as well, with additional work in progress.

qualities: [i, e, ɯ, a, o, u]. We represent the high back unrounded vowel [ɯ] as <ë> and the others with the usual vowel symbols. TVZ has at least four phonation types, including modal (plain, represented, e.g., as <a>); checked (post-glottalized, represented, e.g., as <a'>); breathy (represented, e.g., as <ah>); and creaky (represented, e.g., as <à>, with the creaky high back unrounded vowel represented as <ê>). Up to three (or perhaps four) vowel units with either the same or different phonation may occur in a syllable nucleus. Each of these different syllable nuclei (more than twenty of which are illustrated in table 2) is uniquely associated with a specific tone—either high, low, rising, or falling. Table 2 presents examples in the academic orthography of the dictionary with their associated tones.[5]

Because there are so many different vowel complexes and each has its own tone, tone need not be separately marked in the dictionary—and indeed native speakers do not seem particularly sensitive to tonal distinctions, though they do sometimes refer to phonation differences as differences in tone.

However, even linguists find the details of the academic orthography just presented hard to use and to remember. The complexity of our proposed system initially led to considerable native speaker skepticism.

Ad hoc attempts at writing TVZ are generally inconsistent. For example, figure 2 is a headline (*Dìi'zh x:tèe'n binguul* 'word of the elder') from the Tlacolula de Matamoros newspaper *El Tlacolulense*. The writer has used <sh> (not a standard Hispanic letter combination but one that is sometimes borrowed from English) for the alveopalatal lenis fricative, which we represent as <zh> (which is voiced in most positions, though devoiced word finally), and has used <s> to represent the voiceless retroflex fricative (even though TVZ also has a normal /s/). Most interestingly, however, the writer represents every vowel with a single plain vowel, despite its actual phonation and tone.

[5] There are several competing analyses and orthographic proposals in addition to what I report here and in §8.3.3. Jones and Knudson (1977) present a somewhat different analysis of TVZ phonology, which underlies the orthography (developed by Ted Jones and his colleagues) used in *La Liga Bíblica* (1995) and in other materials developed by Jones and his collaborators. Chávez Peón (2010) and Rojas Torres (2006) have made other orthographic proposals. Munro 2003a is an earlier description of the issues discussed here.

Table 2. TVZ vowel complexes, in the academic orthography*

Pattern	TVZ	Gloss	Tone
<a'>	cha't	'kiss'	high
<aa>	syudaa	'city'	high
<ah>	zah	'grease'	low
<ahah>	lohoh	'face'	low
<àa>	dàany	'mountain'	low
<a'a>	da'ad	'father'	rising
<a'aa>	gami'iizh	'blouse'	rising
<àaa>	nnàaan	'mother'	rising
<a'ah>	cu'uhb	'tejate'	falling
<a'ahah>	gahllgui'ihihzh	'sickness'	falling
<a'àa'>	zhi'ìi'zh	'pineapple'	falling
<a'àa>	zhi'ìilly	'sheep'	falling
<àa'>	rcàa'z	'wants'	falling
<àa'ah>	dàa'ah	'petate'	falling
<àa'a>	zhìi'iny	'son'	falling
<ààa'>	mnnààa'	'woman'	falling
<ààa'ah>	rcwààa'ah	'throws'	falling
<aah>	baahlly	'flame'	falling
<aa'>	bax:aa't	'toad'	falling
<aa'ah>	baa'ah	'earlier today'	falling
<aàa'>	yaàa'	'up'	falling
<àaa'>	àaa'	'yes, that's right'	falling

*Examples are taken from Munro and Lopez et al. 1999.

EL TLACOLULENSE

Dish sten bin gul

Palabra del anciano

Figure 2. Headline from the Tlacolula newspaper *El Tlacolulense.*

The treatment of the vowels in figure 2 is most likely motivated by speakers' frequently expressed belief that words with essentially the same segmental inventory are "spelled the same" even if they contain vastly different vowel patterns. Table 3 presents examples of words with contrasting tone and phonation types illustrating this phenomenon. Above each column is the probable "same spelling" for that group of words.

Table 3. Some TVZ words that speakers would say are "spelled the same"

Tone	<bel> ?	<gyia> ?	<na> ?	<nda> ?
High	Be'll 'Abel'	gyiia 'will go home'		
Low	behll 'fish'	gyihah 'rock' gyìa 'agave root'	nah 'now' nnah 'says' nàa 'is'	ndàa 'sensitive'
Falling	bèèe'll 'snake' bèe'l 'naked' bèe'll '(woman's) sister' beèe'l 'meat'	gyii'ah 'will drink' gyìia' 'flower' gyìi'ah 'market'	nnàa'ah 'heavy' nnaàa' 'hand'	ndàa' 'loose' ndàa'ah 'had broken' ndaàa' 'hot' nda'ah 'had been poured'

8.3.3 The *Cali Chiu?* project and the minimalist orthography

In 2004, Brook Lillehaugen, Felipe Lopez, and I began collaborating on *Cali Chiu?: A course in Valley Zapotec,* a first-year college course in TVZ that has now been used in six years of classes taught by Lopez at UC San Diego and UCLA.[6] The book now has four volumes, including a considerable amount of supplementary material (cf. Munro 2005).

[6] *Cali chiu?* 'Where are you going?' is a common TVZ greeting.

Following the intuition represented in table 3, we decided to replace the academic orthography of the dictionary with a "minimalist" spelling system that writes, for example, all twenty-plus syllable nuclei containing /a/ (all those in the first column of table 2) as <a> and merges consonant contrasts with a low functional load (as was done for /l, ll/ and /n, nn/ in table 3). Thus both /x/ and /x:/ are written <x>; /zh, zh:/ are both <zh>; /m, mm/ are both <m>; /ng, nng/ are both <ng>; and so on. (Still, most consonants are written the same in the academic and the minimalist orthographies.)

Normally, our book uses only the minimalist spelling just described.[7] The first time vocabulary words are introduced, however, they are followed by a "pronunciation guide" in the academic orthography (which is used to discuss the sounds in the first unit), as in example (2).[8]

(2) Pronunciation guide
bel {bèèe'll} 'snake'
bel {bèe'l} 'naked'
bel {bèe'll} '(woman's) sister'
bel {beèe'l} 'meat'

Different people have different learning styles and the bracketed pronunciation guides may be more useful to some than to others, so students are never tested on pronunciation-guide representations. Lopez reports that his students are happy with this orthography and use it well—and it is now his choice to use himself.

8.3.4 Consequences of the TVZ orthography change

The new minimalist orthography for TVZ violates the first basic rule of orthography design—namely that every letter or letter combination must

[7] There are a few extra wrinkles. Inflectional clitics are always written with a separate letter, even when they appear to merge with a preceding syllable. Thus, for example, the speakers whose intuitions are represented in table 3 might well include the first person singular independent pronoun *nàa'* in the <na> column, but we would in fact write it <naa> because it contains a base *na* followed by the first person singular clitic =*a*.

[8] In the textbook, pronunciation guides are enclosed in square brackets, but I have used curly brackets in example (2) to differentiate the pronunciation guides from phonetic transcriptions such as those used in table 1.

always represent the same sound of the language—just as the English words in the sentence pairs in example (3) violate the same rule.

(3) English
  a. He made a *bow* with the ribbon.
     He made a *bow* to the queen.
  b. I *read* this book yesterday.
     Now I *read* this book every day.

This violation makes the orthography less intimidating to learners and does not seem to impede communication among those familiar with the language.

We are continuing to revise the *Cali Chiu?* textbook and are working on a Spanish translation. Brook Lillehaugen and Rosa María Rojas Torres have already taught from draft materials of the Spanish version in undergraduate classes at the Escuela Nacional de Antropología e Historia (ENAH) in Mexico City. Lillehaugen et. al (2007) have written a well-received book on Tlacolula area plants in the minimalist orthography (using the Tlacolula de Matamoros dialect of TVZ). Lopez and I plan to revise our dictionary using minimalist spellings, with the academic spellings retained as pronunciation guides. A long-term project is an edited collection of TVZ speakers' narratives about their experiences immigrating to the US, to be published in the new orthography.

8.3.5 Postminimalist writing in TVZ

Several years ago, Román López Reyes (a teacher in San Lucas Quiaviní) established the Colectivo Literario Quiaviní, a group of students who write poetry and stories in TVZ (e.g., in Chávez Peón and López Reyes 2009). However, these authors write using a form of the academic orthography (which is seen as more authoritative since it is formally published), not the much easier minimalist orthography. Sadly, the drafts of their work show many inconsistencies of the sort the minimalist orthography was designed to avoid (the academic orthography is, after all, a very difficult system!). Orthography design and adaptation is a long and difficult process!

8.4 Case study 2: Gabrielino/Tongva/Fernandeño

8.4.1 Background

Gabrielino/Tongva/Fernandeño was the language spoken in the Los Angeles area at the time of first contact with Europeans, a member of the Takic branch of Uto-Aztecan (see figure 3).[9]

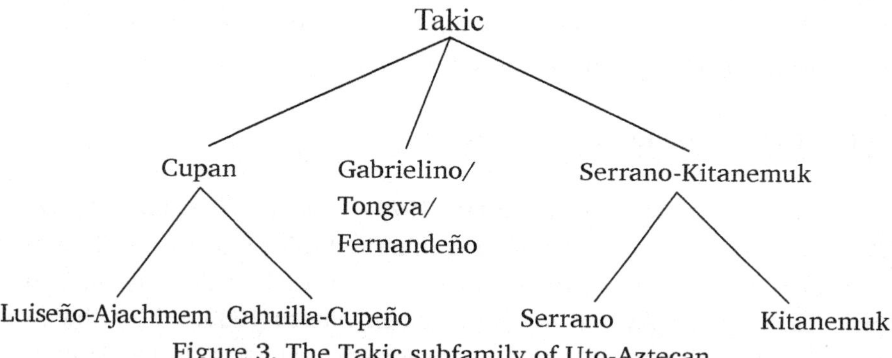

Figure 3. The Takic subfamily of Uto-Aztecan.

Traditionally, this language has been known to linguists as Gabrielino (in the Los Angeles Basin) and Fernandeño (in the San Fernando Valley). More recently the language has been called Tongva by descendants of speakers in Gabrielino areas, and I'll refer to it this way below. Since 2004 I have been meeting monthly with members of the Gabrielino/Tongva language committee, developing heritage language-learning materials.[10]

Tongva has been "sleeping" (the term *extinct* is considered offensive by many heritage learners) for more than fifty years. The language was last documented in the 1930s by the linguist/ethnologist J. P. Harrington (1884–1961). Harrington recorded vast amounts of data on American Indian languages (particularly those of California) for the Bureau of American Ethnology; his notes are now in the Smithsonian Institution.

[9] Figure 3 presents the best-known members of the Takic branch, but not, for example, Tataviam (Munro 2001) or Nicoleño (Munro 2003b). There is no consensus about Takic's internal classification. I represent it here with three coordinate sub-branches (following Kroeber 1907), but others have proposed linking Gabrielino/Tongva/Fernandeño with either Cupan (Bright 1974) or Serrano [ser]–Kitanemuk (Miller 1984).

[10] Current participants in the group include Virginia Carmelo, Jacob Gutierrez, Brent Scarcliff, Julia Bogany, Carolyn Berry, and myself. Others who have been involved have included the late Carol Ramirez, Jesus Gutierrez, the late Mary Gutierrez, Citlali Arvizu, Tonantzin Carmelo, Mary Garcia, Linda Gonzales, and L. Frank Manriquez.

There are four microfilm reels of Tongva data, which are being transcribed by volunteers working with the J. P. Harrington Project at UC Davis. Unfortunately, this is not as much data as one might guess (or hope), because there were many things Harrington did not get around to asking, and there are many other things that for reasons of his own he asked on multiple occasions. But it's still sufficient to give a clear picture of the language.

In addition to Harrington's data, earlier recordings from other observers have been collected in McCawley 1996.

8.4.2 Tongva sounds and writing

I began work on Tongva in the late 1970s, systematizing and analyzing data from Harrington's notes, having inherited this project from Geraldine Anderson and William Bright. During this initial work, I developed a practical orthography for Tongva (used in Munro 1983, 2000) that was similar to those in use for Takic languages such as Luiseño [lui] and Cahuilla [chl]. For consonants, this orthography included *'* [ʔ], *ch* [č], *h, k, kw* [kw], *l, m, n, ng* [ŋ], *p, r, s, sh* [š], *t, v, w, x,* and *y* (and, in Spanish loans, *b, f, g,* and *z*).[11] The language has five phonemic long vowels, which are written double as <aa, ee, ii, oo, uu>, and three phonemic short vowels, written as <a, e, o>.

For my fellow Tongva students, the difficult sounds are the glottal stop (written with an apostrophe,[12] as in *kwitii'* 'boy'); [ŋ], especially when syllable initial (written as <ng>, as in *yongaavewot* 'condor' or *ngooxavavet* 'metate'); and [x] (as in *xaay* 'not').[13]

For the linguist, however, the greatest difficulty with this system is finding the best orthographic representation of the Tongva vowels. In Harrington's recordings, each word has one stressed, long vowel (in other

---

[11] Most likely this list should also include *d*, but we have so far not found any words recorded with that sound.

[12] Following the style for this paper, I use a right single quote (') to write the glottal stop here. Normally, however, I turn off smart quotes and write a straight apostrophe ('), which avoids the tendency of word processors to make any initial apostrophe a left quote.

[13] Like <j> (§8.2.2.1), <x> has multiple orthographic uses: in English, it represents [ks]; in TVZ and many other Latin American languages , it represents [š] (see §8.3.2); in Tongva, it represents [x]; in Spanish, <x> can represent [x] as in *México,* [ks] as in *éxito,* [s] as in the most frequent pronunciation of *mixteco,* or [š] as in *mexica.*

words, all stressed vowels are long).[14] Harrington wrote unstressed vowels less consistently but contrasted only three short vowels: <a>; <e> (recorded usually as [e] but occasionally as [i]); and <o> (recorded usually as [o] but occasionally as [u]).[15] (The same word might be recorded once with [e] and another time with [i], or once with [o] and another time with [u], but the mid vowels are much more common and clearly were Harrington's preference.)

8.4.3 Tongva plural formation

I've developed a set of grammar lessons that I continue to revise on the basis of input from my fellow Tongva learners. Several of these lessons deal with the formation and use of noun plurals. Initially, I was quite uncertain about how to present this material.

The language forms plurals mainly by reduplication (sometimes along with a plural suffix, either *-am* or *-om*), as in example (4).[16]

(4) Reduplicated plurals

Gloss	Singular	Plural
'tuna cactus'	naavot	nanaavot
'mountain'	xaayy	xaxaayy
'road'	peet	pepeet
'(type of) oak'	toomshar	totoomshar
'cane'	naaxovar	nanaaxovar

The first consonant and vowel of the singular are copied at the beginning of the plural noun. All plurals are stressed on their second syllable (thus, they all have a short, unstressed initial-syllable vowel and a long

[14] This is a slight idealization: there are a few words where Harrington marked stress but not length, and a few where he marked neither. It is not the case, incidentally, that all long vowels are stressed: most possessed nouns with plural possessor prefixes contain two long vowels.

[15] This Tongva pattern is similar to that of the closely related language Luiseño, which contrasts only unstressed /a, i, u/. In stressed syllables, however, Luiseño has a clear contrast between short and long vowels.

[16] Alternatively, some nouns only use the suffix, and there are also a few irregular plurals. Many nouns have more than one plural. On the basis of comparative data, we might expect there to be potential differences between collective and distributive plurals, but there seems to be no evidence of any semantic distinctions in the data.

second-syllable vowel). In the words in example (4), the first two vowels of the plural noun are identical, except for their length/stress.

The plurals of other nouns look less regular, however, as shown in example (5).

(5) Irregular plurals

Gloss	Singular	Plural
'house'	kiiy	kekiiy
'bear'	huunar	hohuunar
'owl'	muuhot	momuuhot
'hummingbird'	piinor	pepiinoram

In the words in example (5), the short (first) copy in the plural and the long stressed vowel in the singular don't look the same.

Nouns that have stress on the second vowel of the singular also have a first vowel short, second vowel long in the plural. Sometimes the first two vowels of the plural are the same, as in example (6).

(6) Plurals with identical first two vowels

Gloss	Singular	Plural
'willow'	shaxaat	shashaaxat
'sycamore'	sheveer	shesheever
'tray basket'	novoor	nonoovor

Alternatively, however, in other words with second-syllable stress in the singular, the first and second vowels of the plural are different, as in example (7).

(7) Plurals with different first and second vowels

Gloss	Singular	Plural
'song'	mokaat	momuukat
'blackberry'	pekwaar	pepiikwar
'deer'	shokaat	shoshuukat

Additionally, still other vowels in the word may look different in the plural, as with the last vowel in 'squirrel' in example (8).

(8) Plurals with different vowels

Gloss	Singular	Plural
'squirrel'	xongiit	xoxoonget

Presenting data like that in examples (5), (7), and (8) in a language lesson would require learners to memorize the plurals of every noun, even though the reduplication process seems quite regular.

8.4.4 A new way to write the Tongva vowels

One clue to what is going on is that there are no unexpectedly irregular plurals whose first vowel is *a*. The problem with the apparently irregular plurals in examples (5), (7), and (8), then, is not the data, but the spelling system. In the orthography presented in §8.4.3, there are only three contrasting unstressed vowels, /a, e, o/, written as <a, e, o>.

Thus, even though as linguists we believe that the first vowel of *kekiiy* 'houses' in example (5) is a short copy of the /ii/ in the singular *kiiy* (alternating in pronunciation between [i] and [e]), the system requires us to write it as <e> (because the orthography in §8.4.3 has no short unstressed <i>). Similarly, even though we believe that the first vowel of singular *shokaat* 'deer' in example (7) is a short copy of the stressed /uu/ in the plural *shoshuukat* (pronounced as either <o> or <u>), the system makes us write it as <o>.

Relaxing the rules about writing unstressed/short vowels, and allowing the use of unstressed/short <i, u> makes all the singular/plural pairs look more regular (not just those whose first vowel is /a/). Example (9) shows the singulars and "irregular" plurals of examples (5), (7), and (8) rewritten in this new system.

(9) "Irregular" plurals rewritten

Gloss	Singular	Plural
'house'	kiiy	kikiiy (*kekiiy)
'bear'	huunar	huhuunar (*hohuunar)
'owl'	muuhot	mumuuhot (*momuuhot)
'hummingbird'	piinor	pipiinoram (*pepiinoram
'song'	mukaat	mumuukat (*mokaat, *momuukat)
'blackberry'	pikwaar	pipiikwar (*pekwaar, *pepiikwar)
'deer'	shukaat	shushuukat (*shokaat, *shoshuukat
'squirrel'	xongiit	xoxoongit (*xoxoonget)

The orthographic changes illustrated in example (9) affect other areas of the grammar as well, since possessed nouns with singular possessors illustrate the same types of problems seen in §8.4.3. Clearly, this change in the orthography makes presentation of these key grammatical areas more regular and thus less problematic.[17]

8.4.5 Consequences of the Tongva orthography change

The revised Tongva orthography is no longer strictly phonological (since it suggests a grammatical difference between unstressed/short <i/e> and <u/o> that the data does not support). Thus, this orthography violates the rule that the same phoneme should always be written the same way (§8.2.2.2).

This change will undoubtedly tempt learners to make a pronunciation difference where original native speakers would not have done so. But this is probably not too crucial.

Another problem concerns the status of unstressed/short vowels that don't alternate with stressed/long vowels. Thus, in the revised system described in §8.4.4, an orthographic unstressed/short high vowel <i> or <u> is unambiguous (we know that it alternates with a stressed/long /ii/

[17] Some things will still need to be memorized about plural formation (unfortunately): (1) Does the reduplicated plural use an ending (as with the *-am* of *pipiinoram* 'hummingbirds')?; (2) Is reduplication even used? (Some nouns use only the ending, and a few appear not to have plurals.) On the other hand, many words in the data were recorded with two or even more plural forms, so it's likely that speakers would have accepted a variety of plural forms.

or /uu/), an orthographic unstressed/short mid vowel <e> or <o> could be either an alternant of a stressed /long /ee/ or /oo/ or, alternatively, a nonlow vowel unspecified for height. For example, the second vowel of *piinor* 'hummingbird' never alternates, and we thus have no idea whether it should be written <o> (the default in this system) or <u>. This also is probably not too important, especially for learners!

The great advantage to the new orthography is that it is much easier to teach and learn, since it makes it much easier for learners to see the relationship between singular and plural nouns (and other such alternations). Thus, despite its violation of an orthographic principle, the change is positive.

8.5 Conclusions

In this paper, I have described two fundamental rules for orthography design, and then presented two case studies that illustrate how each rule can be violated to produce an orthography that is less intimidating and easier to learn. Ideally, an orthography should follow the "one-symbol-per-sound, one-sound-per-symbol" rule, but sometimes this rule must be modified to serve language and community needs.

References

Bright, William. 1974. Three extinct American Indian languages of Southern California. In the *American Philosophical Society, Year Book,* 573–574.

Chávez Peón, Mario. 2010. The interaction of metrical structure, tone and phonation types: Prosodic patterns in Quiaviní Zapotec. Ph.D. disssertation. University of British Columbia.

Chávez Peón, Mario E., and Román López Reyes, en representación del Colectivo Literario Quiaviní. 2009. Zidgyni zyala rnalaza liu: 'Vengo de la luz del amanecer, recordándote'. Cuatro poemas y un cuento del zapoteco del Valle. *Tlalocan* XVI:17–49.

Feeling, Durbin. 1975. *Cherokee-English dictionary.* Edited by William Pulte, in collaboration with Agnes Cowen and the Dictionary Committee. Tahlequah, Okla.: Cherokee Nation of Oklahoma.

Galant, Michael R. 1998. Comparative constructions in Spanish and San Lucas Quiaviní Zapotec. Ph.D. dissertation, UCLA.

Jensen de López, Kristine M. 2002. Baskets and body-parts. Ph.D. dissertation. Aarhus University (Denmark).

Jones, Ted E., and Lyle M. Knudson. 1977. Guelavía Zapotec phonemes. In William R. Merrifield (ed.), *Studies in Otomanguean phonology,* 163–180. Summer Institute of Linguistics and the University of Texas at Arlington Publications in Linguistics 54. Dallas.

Kroeber, Alfred Louis. 1907. Shoshonean dialects of California. *University of California Publications: American Archaeology and Ethnology* 4:65–165.

Lee, Felicia A. 1999. Antisymmetry and the syntax of San Lucas Quiaviní Zapotec. Ph.D. dissertation. UCLA.

Lewis, M. Paul, ed. 2009. *Ethnologue: Languages of the world.* Sixteenth edition. Dallas: SIL International. Online version: http://www.ethnologue.com/.

Liga Bíblica, La. 1995. *Xtiidx Dios Cun Ditsa (El Nuevo Testamento en el zapoteco de San Juan Guelavía y en español).* n.p.

Lillehaugen, Brook Danielle. 2006. Expressing location in Tlacolula Valley Zapotec. Ph.D. dissertation. UCLA.

Lillehaugen, Brook Danielle, Pamela Munro, and Roberto Antonio Ruiz, with Josefina Antonio Ruiz and Juana Ramos Jiménez. 2007. *Da Cwan cun Didshza xten Guëzh Bac* [Plants in Tlacolula de Matamoros Zapotec/ Plantas en el zapoteco de Tlacolula de Matamoros]. www.lulu.com.

McCawley, William. 1996. *The first Angelinos: The Gabrielino Indians of Los Angeles.* Banning, Calif.: Malki Museum Press–Ballena Press.

Miller, Wick R. 1984. The classification of the Uto-Aztecan languages. *International Journal of American Linguistics* 50:1–24.

Munro, Pamela. 1983. Selected studies in Uto-Aztecan phonology. *International Journal of American Linguistics* 49:277–298.

Munro, Pamela. 2000. The Gabrielino enclitic system. In Eugene H. Casad and Thomas L. Willett (eds.), *Uto-Aztecan: Structual, temporal, and geographic perspectives,* 183–201. Hermosillo, Sonora, Mexico: Universidad de Sonoral (Editorial Unison).

Munro, Pamela. 2003a. Preserving the language of the Valley Zapotecs: The orthography question. Presented at the conference on Language and Immigration in France and the United States: Sociolinguistic Perspectives, University of Texas. http://www.utexas.edu/cola/insts/france-ut/_files/pdf/resources/munro.pdf (accessed February 5, 2013).

Munro, Pamela. 2003b. Takic foundations of Nicoleño vocabulary. In David R. Browne, Kathryn L. Mitchell, and Henry W. Chaney (eds.), *Proceedings of the Fifth California Islands Symposium,* 659–668. Santa Barbara, Calif.: Santa Barbara Museum of Natural History.

Munro, Pamela. 2005. Zapotec grammar without tears (except perhaps for the grammarian). Rosemary Beam de Azcona and Mary Paster (eds.), *Papers from the Conference on Otomanguean and other Oaxacan Languages.* Survey of California and Other Indian Languages Report 13:87–106. Berkeley, California: Survey of California and Other Indian Languages.

Munro, Pamela, with John Johnson. 2001. What do we know about Tataviam?: Comparisons with Gabrielino, Kawaiisu, and Tübatulabal. Presented at Friends of UtoAztecan Meeting, Santa Barbara.

Munro, Pamela, Brook Danielle Lillehaugen, and Felipe H. Lopez. In preparation. *Cali Chiu? A course in Valley Zapotec.*

Munro, Pamela, and Felipe H. Lopez, with Olivia V. Méndez [Martínez], Rodrigo Garcia, and Michael R. Galant. 1999. *Di'csyonaary X:tèe'n Dìi'zh Sah Sann Lu'uc (San Lucas Quiaviní Zapotec dictionary/Diccionario Zapoteco de San Lucas Quiaviní).* Chicano Studies Research Center Publications. Los Angeles: UCLA.

Pérez Báez, Gabriela. 2009. Endangerment of a transnational language: The case of San Lucas Quiaviní Zapotec. Ph.D. dissertation. State University of New York (Buffalo).

Rojas Torres, Rosa María (coordinadora). 2006. *Alfabeto práctico para la lecto-escritura del dìxzâ de Santa Ana del Valle, Oaxaca.* México: Instituto Nacional de Lenguas Indígenas.

Walker, Willard. 1969. Notes on native writing systems and the design of native literacy programs. *Anthropological Linguistics* 11:148–166.

Walker, Willard, and James Sarbaugh. 1993. The early history of the Cherokee syllabary. *Ethnohistory* 40:70–94.

9

A Yanesha' Alphabet for the Electronic Age

Mary Ruth Wise

This case study of alphabet development, use, and change through nearly six decades summarizes the phonological properties of Yanesha' (an Arawakan language spoken in Peru) that challenge alphabet makers. It also sketches the history of Yanesha' alphabet decisions, as well as the history of formal and informal literacy programs and literature production in Yanesha'. Finally, it recounts the recent decision-making process for the revised Yanesha' alphabet, in which Yanesha' bilingual teachers and community leaders were the chief players. The resulting official alphabet enables the Yanesha' to produce their own school texts and other literature using any computer with a Spanish keyboard.

9.1 Introduction[*]

The first literacy books in Yanesha' [ame], an Arawakan language spoken in Peru, were printed in 1952 using an experimental alphabet (Fast and Fast 1952a, 1952b), and the first Yanesha' bilingual school was established by the Peruvian Ministry of Education in 1953. During the next few years, additional bilingual schools were established and adult literacy classes were offered in a number of Yanesha' communities. Forty-six books were printed using an alphabet formulated by SIL personnel according to SIL's agreement with the Ministry of Education (e.g., Duff 1957 and Duff-Tripp 1981).[1] As a result of having a standard writing system and bilingual education opportunities, several thousand Yanesha' learned to read and write fluently in their own language as well as in Spanish; in fact, illiteracy became almost non-existent except among the elderly.

Today, however, almost all of the Yanesha' language books are out of print, and the methodology required for language arts textbooks in the bilingual schools has changed. New materials are urgently needed. To meet this need, a committee of Yanesha' bilingual teachers began writing new textbooks in 2008. But they quickly ran into difficulties: they had to download special fonts in order to key some of the frequent graphemes—a tilde over five consonants, in addition to Spanish <ñ>, to indicate palatalization and a dieresis in the digraph <c̈h> for the retroflex affricate. Furthermore, the printers that were available to them did not have the capacity to print these special characters. In January 2010 this committee of teachers invited me to consult with them on changing their alphabet to one that would serve them well in the electronic age. On June 16, 2011, the Ministry of Education issued a resolution making the changed alphabet official.

This paper recounts the process leading to the change in the Yanesha' alphabet. In §9.2, I summarize the Yanesha' phonology with special attention to the properties that present a challenge for alphabet development. In §9.3, I sketch the history of earlier Yanesha' alphabet decisions, as well as formal and informal literacy programs and literature production. In §9.4, I describe the recent decision-making process and the resulting alphabet that

---

*I am indebted to Mike Cahill, Elke Karan, Patricia Kelley, and Keren Rice for many helpful suggestions in the preparation of this paper. My debt to the many Yanesha' friends who not only taught me their language but also permitted me to live among them and share their everyday lives is incalculable.

[1] In Peru, SIL International is known as Instituto Lingüístico de Verano (ILV).

enables Yanesha' speakers to write their language on any computer with a Spanish keyboard.

First, a note on the Yanesha' and their language: Yanesha' (also known as Amuesha) is spoken by about 5,000 people among an ethnic population of about 10,000. In many areas children are no longer learning the language and are monolingual in Spanish. There are some forty communities in the departments of Junín and Pasco and a few in Huánuco. Their territory is constantly being reduced by the influx of new settlers, primarily from the Peruvian Andes.

Yanesha' is highly agglutinative; example (1) is a typical verb.[2]

(1) 0-oma:ʐ-amʲ-eˀt-ampʲ-es-j-e:s-n-e:n-a
3-go.downriver-intermittently-TH-APPL-TH-DISTR-TH-PM-PROG-REFL
'several people are going downriver by canoe (or raft) in the late afternoon, stopping often along the way'

9.2 Summary of Yanesha' phonology

Yanesha' has twenty-six phonemic consonants (three of which are rare) and four vowels. Consonant clusters occur word medially and word finally. Syllable types are: VC, VCC, CV, CVC, and CVCC. The first two occur only word initially. There are no unambiguous vowel clusters.

9.2.1 Summary of phonemes

The Yanesha' consonant phonemes are listed in table 1. Palatalized and labialized allophones need to be considered for formulating an alphabet and are listed within square brackets. Voiceless allophones of the voiced consonants and voiceless palatal off-glides are not listed in the table since they occur syllable or word finally and are irrelevant for alphabet decisions.

[2] The following abbreviations are used in this paper: 0 Zero morpheme; 1 First person; 3 Third person; APPL Applicative; C Consonant; DISTR Distributive; FIN Finish; GEN Genitive; OBJ Object; PF Perfective; PM Late in the afternoon or nocturnal; PROG Progressive; REFL Reflexive; SG Singular; TH Theme; V Vowel.

Table 1. Consonant phonemes*

	Labial	Alveolar	Alveopalatal	Retroflex	Velar
Stop	p [p, pʷ]	t			k [k, kʷ]
palatalized	pʲ [pʲ, p]	tʲ (or tʃʲ)			kʲ [kʲ, k]
Affricate		ts	tʃ	tʂ	
Nasal	m [m, mʷ]	n			
palatalized	mʲ [mʲ, m]	nʲ			
Fricative		s	ʃ		x [x, xʷ]
	βʲ [βʲ, β]			ʐ	ɣ [ɣ, ɣʷ]
Flap		ɾ			
Approximant	w	lʲ	j		

*Forms in square brackets represent allophones. The first of these occurs before /a/ and /o/ and word finally; the second occurs only before /e/. Daigneault (2009) lists the palatalized alveopalatal /tʲ/ as /tʃʲ/. Fast (1953) considered it to be alveolar. Fast (1953) did not list a palatalized velar nor did he include the palatalization of the labial fricative. He wrote aspiration of vowels [Vʰ] as <Vj> since he considered vowel aspiration to be an allophone of /x/.

In addition to the consonants listed in table 1, /ɸʲ/ and /ŋ/ occur in a few words with onomatopoeic roots, and /l/ occurs in songs and in words imitating the speech of the Inca.

The primary vowel phonemes are /e, a, o/.[3] The vowels tend to be raised to [i, æ, u], respectively, in the environment of palatalized consonants, but there is generally free variation of vowel quality, as follows: /e/ [i~ɪ~e~ɛ], /a/ [æ~a~ə], /o/ [u~ʊ~o~ɔ]. Distribution of vowel phones with labial and velar consonant phones is described in §9.2.2. All three vowels occur before and after alveolar, alveopalatal, and retroflex consonants—plain and palatalized alike—and before and after the labial-velar approximant /w/.[4]

Each of the vowels may be short, lengthened, or followed by aspiration or a glottal stop, so that the syllable nucleus may be either simple or complex: /apaː/ 'dad, father'; /aːp/ 'caigua (a vegetable)'; /aʰp/ 'pacae (a fruit)'; /aˀpa/ 'he/she stayed'. The glottalized vowels are often re-articulated preceding voiced consonants, as in /neˀmaːɾ/ [neˀᵊmaːɾ] 'my baby'. A short vowel between voiceless consonants in the first two syllables of a word is often voiceless.

[3] These could also be listed as /i, a, u/.

[4] /w/ is listed in the labial column of table 1 since some native speakers perceive it as the fricative allophone of Spanish /b/. In distribution, however, it is more like alveolar, alveopalatal, and retroflex consonants than labials or velars.

There is a fourth phonetic vowel, [ɨ], which occurs only following velar consonants. A sequence of /k/, /x/, or /ɣ/ plus /ɨ/ is the distributional analog of the labialized allophones of labial consonants plus /e/. In fact, in some dialects the preceding velar consonant is labialized as shown in table 1. However, in a few words, following /x/, which has no palatalized counterpart, [ɨ] contrasts with [e]. Therefore, a fourth vowel with limited distribution (only following velars, and never word initially) is added to the inventory. (For more detailed descriptions of Yanesha' phonology, see Fast 1953, Wise 1958, and Duff-Tripp 1997.)

9.2.2 Palatalization and labialization of consonants

All phonetic plain stops and nasals have palatalized counterparts that are clearly contrastive. The labial palatalized fricative does not have a contrastive plain counterpart. The sets in example (2) show the palatalization contrasts.

(2) a.	/pa:moˀts/	[pa:moˀts]	'his/her relative'
	/pʲa:moˀts/	[pʲæ:moˀts]	'your (sg) relative'
b.	/mo:ʐe:nʲets/	[mo:ʐi̠:nʲɪts]	'song'
	/mʲo:ʐa:ɾe:n/	[mʲo:ʐa:ɾɛ:n]	'it is windy'
c.	/te/	[tɪ]	'species of bird'
	/tʲeˀ/	[tʲɪˀ]	'now'
d.	/na:/	[na:]	'I'
	/nʲa:/	[nʲa:]	'he/she/it'
e.	/nekaˀjo:ɾ/	[nekaˀjo:ɾ]	'my macaw'
	/nekʲaˀm/	[nekʲaˀᵊm]	'my sleeve'

Phonetic plain labial and velar stops and the labial nasal have labialized counterparts. The sets in example (3) show the contrasts between phonetic plain and phonetic labialized consonants.

(3) a.	/pʲeˀlʲ/	[peˀlʲ]	'species of green worm'
	/pelʲ/	[pʷelʲ]	'wart'
b.	/mʲetʃeˀ/	[mɪtʃɪˀ]	'jicama'
	/metʃetʲ/	[mʷetʃitʲ]	'quiet, serene'
c.	/neʰkʲeˀ/	[neʰkɪˀ]	'my arm'
	/keˀ/	[kɨˀ, kʷɨˀ]	'macaw'

The labial consonant phones have the following distribution in CV(C) syllables:

Table 2. Distribution of labial consonant phones

Phoneme	Stops	Nasals	Fricatives
Palatalized	[p^{j}a, pe, p^{j}o]	[m^{j}a, me, m^{j}o]	[β^{j}a, βe, β^{j}o]
Plain	[pa, p^{w}e, po]	[ma, m^{w}e, mo]	

Note that there are three labial stop phones ([p, p^j, p^w]) and three labial nasal phones ([m, m^j, m^w])—plain, palatalized, and labialized—but only two phones contrast before each of the vowels: [p] contrasts with [p^j], and [m] contrasts with [m^j] before /a/ and /o/, while [p] contrasts with [p^w], and [m] contrasts with [m^w] before /e/. Only [p, p^j, m, m^j] occur syllable and word finally. The voiced labial fricative allophones [β^{j}a, βe, β^{j}o] have the same distribution as the palatalized labial stop allophones [p^{j}a, pe, p^{j}o] and the palatalized nasals [m^{j}a, me, m^{j}o].

Velar consonant phones have the following distribution in CV syllables:

Table 3. Distribution of velar consonant phones

Phonemes	Stops	Vl fricative	Vd fricative
Palatalized	[k^{j}a, ke, k^{j}e]		
Plain	[ka, k^{w}ɨ/kɨ, ko]	[xa, xe, x^{w}ɨ/xɨ, xo]	[ɣa, ɣ^{w}ɨ/ɣɨ, ɣo]

Of the velar consonant phones, only [k, ɣ] occur as the first member of a word-medial consonant cluster in my data. Only [k, x, ɣ] occur word finally.

The labialized labial phones [p^w, m^w] and their velar analogs [k^w, x^w, ɣ^w] are considered allophones of /p, m, k, x, ɣ,/ respectively, since they occur when a root or affix ending with one of those consonants is followed by a morpheme-initial /e/. Compare, for example, the labialized stop phones in example (4b, c, d) preceding /eːn/ 'PROG' with the plain stop in (4a).

(4) a. 0-ot-eːn > [oteːn] /oteːn/
3-to.say-PROG
'he/she says'

b. 0-ana^{h}p-e:n > [ana^{h}p^{w}e:n] /ana^{h}pe:n/
3-to.answer-PROG
'he/she answers'

c. 0-na:m-e:n > [ema:m^{w}e:n] /ena:me:n/
3-to.beg-PROG
'he/she begs'

d. 0-kel^{j}k-e:n > [kil^{j}kɨ:n] ~ [kil^{j}k^{w}ɨ:n] /k^{j}el^{j}ke:n/
3-to.write-PROG
'he/she writes'

The labialized phones [p^w, m^w] contrast respectively with sequences of /p, m/ plus /w/, as illustrated in example (5).

(5) a. 0-ana^{h}p + -e:n > [ana^{h}p^{w}e:n] /ana^{h}pe:n/
3-to.answer-PROG
'he/she answers'

b. 0-ana^{h}p + -w-e:n > [ana^{h}p^{o}wen] /ana^{h}pwe:n/
3-to.answer-FIN-PROG
'he/she finishes answering/is answering completely'

(There are morpheme-medial sequences of /k/ plus /w/, but no examples of morpheme-final /k/ followed by morpheme-initial /w/ occur in my data.)

Similarly, the sequences [pe, me, βe, ke] are considered to be realizations respectively of /p^j, m^j, β^j, k^j/ followed by /e/, since they occur when a root or affix ending with a palatalized consonant is followed by a morpheme beginning with /e/; that is, the palatalization is not heard preceding a front vowel except that the vowel quality tends to be high. This is shown in example (6). Note that the palatalization is heard in (a) preceding a low vowel but not in (b); however, in (b) the vowel is raised to a high vowel.

(6) a. ne^h-p^j-0-a > [ne^{h}p^{j}æ] /ne^{h}p^{j}a/
1-to.do-PF-REFL
'I did'

b. ne^h-p^j-e:n-^{j} > [ne^{h}pi:n^j] /ne^{h}p^{j}en^j/
1-to.do-PROG-3OBJ
'I do it'

Again, sequences of /p/ or /m/ plus /j/ contrast with palatalized /p^j/ and /m^j/ and, thus, pose a challenge for alphabet development.

9.2.3 Phonological challenges for alphabet development

The palatalized consonants and the retroflex affricate in Yanesha' present the main challenge for alphabet development. In neighboring Arawakan languages of the Kampan subgroup, palatalized consonants pose no problem since in those languages consonants occur word finally only rarely and then only in onomatopoeic words. Furthermore, the only word-medial consonant clusters in those languages consist of a nasal followed by either a stop or an affricate. Thus, unlike for Yanesha', palatalization can be written as <Cy>, a consonant followed by <y> (the Spanish grapheme for /j/ is <y>). For example, /tʲapa/ 'chicken' (in all of the Kampan languages) can be written as <tyapa>. In some of the languages, other palatalized consonants, such as /kʲ/, can be written as <Cy> or <Ci> with no problem since they never occur syllable or word finally.

In Yanesha', however, all consonants except /kʲ/ occur word finally; all except /kʲ/ occur as the first member of a consonant cluster; and all occur both word and syllable initially. Thus, palatalized consonants contrast with orthographic sequences of Consonant+y so that palatalization cannot be written as <y>. Compare example (7a) with (7b).

(7) a. /noːtʲeːɾ/ [noː.tʲɪːɾ]
'my bird'
b. /notjeːɾ/ [notᶦ.jɪːɾ]
'I told him/her various (things) again'

As exemplified in (7b), in most word-medial, cross-syllable consonant clusters, there is an open transition between the consonants. But native speakers insist that there is no vowel between the consonants in words such as /tʃopnom/ [tʃopᵊ.nom] 'it continued to grow', /amnaːɾ/ [amᵊ.naːɾ] 'five', or /notjeːɾ/ [notᶦ.jɪːɾ] 'I told him/her various (things) again'.

Neither can palatalization be written as <i> or <e>, since palatalized consonants occur both word and syllable finally so that writing palatalization as a vowel would add a syllable. For example, /nanoːʐamʲ/ [na.noː.ʐamʲ] 'my chair' cannot be written <*nanorrami> or <*nanorrame> since either of those spellings would be pronounced as four rather than three syllables.

On the other hand, syllable-initial palatalized consonants could be written as <Cy> or <Ci/e> since there are no unambiguous vowel clusters in the language. For example, /pʲa/ [pʲæ] 'you (SG)' could be written as <pya>, <pia>, or <pea>. The problem with this is that palatalization would have to be written one way syllable initially and another syllable finally.

The retroflex affricate also presents a problem since the "obvious" solutions of <tr> and <chr> are precluded by the sequences /t/+/ɾ/ and /tʃ/+/ɾ/.

Writing the short vowels presents no real problems since (a, e, o) and (ë)—the last one for the high central vowel—are available on all Spanish keyboards. Symbolizing vowel length, aspiration, and glottalization is problematic primarily because few speakers of the language are consistently aware of those contrasts in syllable nuclei and many insist they should be written simply as short vowels. Furthermore, unless they are written with diacritics, writing all of the complex syllable nuclei would increase the length of already long words.

9.3 History of Yanesha' alphabets and literacy

The first books in Yanesha' (see Fast and Fast 1952a, 1952b) used the consonant symbols listed in table 4.

Table 4. Consonant graphemes in first alphabet

Labial	Alveolar	(Alveo)palatal	Retroflex	Velar
p	t			k
py	ty			
	ts	ch	chr	
m	n			
my	ñ			
	s	sh	rr	j
b				g
	r			
w	ll	y		

Labialized /p/ and /m/ were written as <pw> and <mw> respectively. The /C+w/ sequence had not yet been recognized; nor had the /C+y/ sequence or the /t/ or /tʃ/+/ɾ/ sequences (probably because the open transition, described above after example (7) was originally transcribed as a full vowel). Long vowels were written as double vowels, glottalized vowels were written as <V'>, and vowels followed by aspiration as <Vj>. (The aspiration was considered to be an allophone of /x/).

Soon after the first books were printed using this initial alphabet and the first bilingual school was established, Martha Duff and I began gathering more data and using those first books with young adults who were literate in Spanish. The sequences of /C+y/, /C+w/ , and /t/ or /tʃ/+/ɾ/ came to light, and we began to discuss the implications with Peter Fast and other experienced colleagues in SIL, as well as with Yanesha' who were literate in Spanish.

An important consideration in the discussions was to make the alphabet look like Spanish as much as possible, in part because of the attitudes of neighboring Spanish speakers toward speakers of indigenous languages. Thus, as in Spanish, we decided to use <c/qu> for /k/ and <hu/u> for /w/. Word-final /k/ was written as <c> and word-final /w/ as <u>. Labialized allophones of /p/ and /m/ were written as <pu> and <mu> (paralleling similar Spanish usage in words such as *pueblo* 'town' and *mueble* 'piece of furniture').

Spanish <rr> (alveolar trill) for the retroflex sibilant matched well with Andean Spanish pronunciation of words like *carro* 'car'. Spanish <ll> for the palatalized lateral approximant also fit well with a similar sound in some widely known varieties of Quechua, although <ll> is pronounced as [j] in Peruvian Spanish.

Since Spanish distinguishes the alveolar nasal from the palato-alveolar by a tilde (~), there was consensus to use a tilde over <p, m, b, t, c> to indicate palatalization. In order to do so, a tilde had to be installed as a dead key on typewriters which were used to write the language.[5] (Later, special fonts were required for keyboarding Yanesha' on computers.)

The retroflex affricate was written as <c̈h>. The dieresis was already present on Spanish typewriter keyboards as a dead key. Later on it presented a problem since on Spanish computer keyboards it can be used only over vowels.

The vowels were written as <a, e, ë, o>. There was general agreement to continue writing the glottal stop with an apostrophe but to discontinue

[5] A dead key is a modifier key on a typewriter that is used to attach a specific diacritic to a base letter.

indicating vowel length and aspiration. (Fast had written double vowels and <V+j> in the 1952 books.)

The consonants, as they were written preceding each of the vowels, are shown in table 5.

Table 5. Consonants in CV syllables in 1955 alphabet

Labial	Alveolar	(Alveo)palatal	Retroflex	Velar
pa, pue, po	ta, te, to			ca, quë, co
p̃a, pe, p̃o	t̃a, t̃e, t̃o			c̃a, que, c̃o
	tsa, tse, tso	cha, che, cho	čha, čhe, čho	
ma, mue, mo	na, ne, no			
m̃a, me, m̃o	ña, ñe, ño			
	sa, se, so	sha, she, sho	rra, rre, rro	ja, je, jë, jo
b̃a, be, b̃o				ga, guë, go
	ra, re, ro			
hua, hue, huo*	lla, lle, llo	ya, ye, yo		

*Syllable finally, /w/ was written as <u>.

Writing /w/ syllable initially as <hu> following labial consonants, in contrast with <pu> and <mu> for the labialized allophones of /p/ and /m/, worked well in words like the pair in example (8).

(8) a. [ana^{h}p^{ə}.wɪːɾ] /ana^{h}pweːɾ/ <anaphuer>
'he/she finished answering him/her in return'

b. [ana^{h}.p^{w}ɪːɾ] /ana^{h}peːɾ/ <anapuer>
'he/she answered him/her in return'

However, it caused confusion after <c> for /k/. Thus, /pekweˀ/ 'look!' had to be written <pecue'> and not <pechue'> to avoid reading it as the non-existent but phonologically potential word /petʃweˀ/ pechue'. Few people knew the rules for writing /w/.

As for the complex syllable nuclei /Vˀ, V^{h}, Vː/, readers learned to recognize the glottal stop, but few have ever written it consistently. The ambiguity resulting from writing /V, V^{h}, Vː/ all simply as <V> (<a, e, ë, o>) caused many readers to go back and read the first syllables of long words over again—a problem that probably would have been averted if complex syllable nuclei had been written consistently in prefixes and stems (usually the first two or three syllables of a word).

Several new bilingual schools were established and a series of new reading textbooks were produced by Duff in 1957 and 1958 (for example, Duff 1957). When the students had read everything available, Duff suggested that the teachers have the students write stories in their notebooks and read each other's work.[6] The next year, those stories, with names of the authors listed prominently (see, for example, Duff 1958), were used as the basis of more advanced textbooks—the beginning of native-authored texts. From 1957 to 1981 some 2,200 pages of textbooks and library books were produced for the bilingual schools; in addition, 1,332 pages of Bible translation, Bible stories, and songs were published for the churches. The grammar and dictionary (Duff-Tripp 1997, 1998) provided 911 more pages of bilingual material. The last reprints of any of these materials were published in the year 2000.

9.4 The change process and the official alphabet

By the time most of the books were out of print, the Ministry of Education had instituted new methodology for language arts textbooks. In January 2008, when three Yanesha' teachers began writing a new book for first grade, they had to acquire the special fonts needed for keying Yanesha', but then they were unable to print them on the printers available to them. It was time for an alphabet change. To accomplish this, five preliminary meetings and an "alphabet congress" were called by Yanesha' leadership and/or the Ministry of Education over a period of sixteen months. These

[6] When the bilingual schools began, the Yanesha' teachers had limited education themselves because of a lack of schools in their area; none of them had completed primary school. Each year during the school vacation, they studied another half grade—barely keeping ahead of their students. But by the 1970s most of them had completed their secondary education. In 1984 the Instituto Superior Pedagógico Bilingüe-Yarinacocha (ISPBY), a normal school specializing in bilingual intercultural education, was established and trained teachers until 2011. At present several Peruvian universities and other teacher training schools also offer the opportunity for bilingual teachers to obtain the appropriate degrees and credentials for obtaining a teaching post. Almost all Yanesha' communities have a school; some, however, are only nominally bilingual since their teachers are monolingual Spanish speakers or bilingual in Spanish and an indigenous language other than Yanesha'. Such situations continue, but at present the Peruvian Ministry of Education is proactive in promoting true bilingual intercultural education.

gatherings resulted in the Yanesha' alphabet that was approved by the Ministry of Education in June 2011.

9.4.1 Initial discussions and proposed changes

In January 2010, a Yanesha'-speaking professor at the Universidad Nacional Intercultural de la Amazonía (UNIA) and the committee of three bilingual teachers who were preparing new language arts textbooks in Yanesha' invited me to work with them in making changes to their alphabet so that they could prepare their materials easily on computers with Spanish keyboards. The five of us, along with a literate Yanesha' grandmother (grandmothers are highly respected and loved by the Yanesha'), and the secretary of culture of one of their socio-political organizations, met several hours each afternoon for a week.[7]

We all agreed that I, as invited linguistic consultant, would make suggestions, but they would make the decisions. I presented two alternatives for the palatalized consonants: <g+ C>, as in Italian, or <C + h>, as in Portuguese. I had a personal preference for <h> for two reasons: (1) they already used it in the alveopalatal consonants <ch> and <sh>; and (2) I had learned some lessons from an earlier experience in a related language.[8] Nevertheless, I tried not to unduly influence the decision makers.

Soon all of the Yanesha' present were leaning toward <C+h>. However, they said, "We feel that /tʲ/ is somehow different from the others." And they were correct: it acts like the other palatal and palatalized consonants in nouns but not in verbs.

With a few exceptions, the initial vowel of several nominal suffixes depends on the final consonant of the preceding morpheme: following a palatal or palatalized consonant or /ɾ/, the vowel is /e/, as in (9a) and (9b); following a non-palatal or non-palatalized stop or nasal, the vowel is /a/,

[7] During the first meeting, I learned that they were not the first to propose changes. In his 2003 thesis for the ISPBY, one teacher proposed replacing the tilde to represent palatalization with <y> and to use <k> and <w>.

[8] A young Nomatsigenga [not] man was transcribing texts in his language for me. When he came to syllables like/ʃa/ and /tʃa/ he asked me how to write them. I suggested *sha* or *sia* and *cha* or *tsia*. He chose *sha* and *cha*; to my surprise he then wrote *tha*, *rha*, etc. for all [ia] sequences. I began to think how much simpler typesetting in Yanesha' would be if we had thought of C plus *h* instead of using tildes.

as in (9c); following an approximate (except /lʲ/) or a non-palatal or non-palatalized fricative of affricate, the vowel is /o/, as in (9d).[9]

(9) a. n-oːtʲ-Vːɾ > /noːtʲeːr/
1-bird-GEN
'my bird'
b. ne-tʃeːtʃ-Vːɾ > /netʃeːtʃeːɾ/
1-peanut(s)-GEN
'my peanut(s)'
c. ne-kaːk-Vːɾ > /nekaːkaːɾ/
1-fish-GEN
'my fish'
d. ne-tʃoˀs-Vːɾ > /netʃoˀsoːɾ/
1-rat-GEN
'my rat'

In verbs, however, palatalization of the preceding consonant is the most frequent realization of a third-person singular object. In that context /t/ plus palatalization is not /tʲ/ but /tʃ/. Compare, for example, the final consonants in (10a) and (10b):

(10) a. 0-anaʰp-0-ʲ > /anaʰpʲ/
3-answer-PF-3OBJ
'he/she answered him/her'
b. 0-ot-0-ʲ > /otʃ/
3-say-PF-3OBJ
'he/she/said to him/her'

After comparing examples and thinking it over for a day or two, they decided to write <th> to parallel <ph, mh, bh, kh>, that is, to substitute <h> for all of the tildes except in <ñ>.

For /ʈʂ/, I suggested <x>, but the next day they had decided among themselves to write <c'h>. (They would continue to use the apostrophe for glottal stop also.)

A day or two later, one of them suggested—and everyone agreed—to write <k> and <w> rather than <c/qu> and <hu/u>. No changes were ever suggested for the other consonants or for the vowels /a, e, ë, o/.

[9] See Wise 1963:133n5 and Duff-Tripp 1997:145–146 for more details.

The Yanesha' speakers studying at UNIA applauded the changes when they were consulted. So, with some fifty people agreeing, the proposed changes were presented to the Dirección General de Educación Intercultural Bilingüe y Rural (DIGEIBIR)—the Department of Intercultural, Bilingual, and Rural Education—of the Ministry of Education as a first step toward official recognition.

9.4.2 Steps toward consensus

A four-page pamphlet was prepared and widely distributed in order to promote the alphabet changes among all of the Yanesha'. It was soon evident that not everyone agreed with the proposed changes. Some objected to making any changes at all; others objected to the particular changes proposed. People expressed that:

- the tildes give them a sense of special identity;
- they knew the old alphabet well and liked to write in it;
- it would be too hard to remember the changes;
- they should not depend on computers; and
- <h> is silent in Spanish.

To the last objection, I pointed out that <h> is silent only word initially and between vowels, but not in <ch> and <sh>.[10]

In August, an informal meeting to discuss changing the alphabet was held in the centrally located community of Loma Linda; all residents who were interested were invited. At that time a two-day alphabet workshop in Loma Linda was planned for October and invitations were sent to representatives of all of the communities.

Only about a third of those invited came in October; just two representatives came from downriver. The teachers who initially proposed the changes led the discussions, and I explained the linguistic pros and cons of various alternatives. There was lively discussion—some of it heated. A university student suggested that they write <poe> and <moe> rather than <pue> and <mue> since they had no /u/ in their language. Everyone agreed to that and, in the end, all participants signed a request to the Ministry of Education to make the changes official, although one or two teachers did so reluctantly.

[10] The grapheme <sh> is not a standard Spanish grapheme, but in Peruvian Spanish it occurs in many words of indigenous language origin.

In January 2011, the teachers who were continuing to work on their textbook for first grade language arts decided that the apostrophe in <c'h> for the retroflexed affricate separated the parts of a word too much. They chose <x>, modified to <xh> after discussion.

In the meantime, Yanesha' from several isolated villages requested a meeting to orient them on the proposed changes. In February 2011, a two-day workshop was organized and the Ministry of Education sent two representatives.[11] As they discussed the proposed changes, some commented that there were too many instances of <h>; so they decided to write <tz> rather than <th> for /tʲ/—reflecting the earlier reaction that it is somehow different from the palatalized labial and velar consonants. They also raised the question of [ɸʲ] and [ŋ] in onomatopoeic words and [l] in songs. They chose <f>, <ng>, and <l> for those sounds. Again, the meeting ended with general consensus.

Then, the Ministry of Education proposed another workshop in mid-March in a community easily accessible by road. That was the first meeting with representatives from far downriver; two of the older (and now retired) bilingual teachers attended for the first time. Again, there was heated discussion and many opposed changing the alphabet which they had learned long ago. But other retired teachers reminded them that the proposed changes were for the future of the language—for the children. In the end, they all agreed to the changes proposed except that they reverted back to <th> rather than <tz>.

9.4.3 The alphabet congress

From April 27 to 29, 2011, the final alphabet-focused event was held. The DIGEIBIR organized and sponsored the Congreso de Aprobación del Alfabeto de la Lengua del Pueblo Yanesha (Congress for the Approval of the Alphabet of the Language of the Yanesha'). Approximately 150 Yanesha' attended, many of whom were not in any of the previous meetings and were opposed to using <h> for palatalization; again it was necessary to explain why neither <y>, <i>, nor <e> would work.

In the end, one of the main opposition leaders did an about-face and said, "Let's do it!" Within a few minutes, the vote was unanimous for the major

[11] The October 2010 and February 2011 workshops were made possible by grants from the Ralph Hull Foundation and by contributions from a private donor.

changes; discussion about <k> and <w> (instead of <c/qu> and <hu>) went quickly. The letters and digraphs that the congress participants voted to approve are shown in CV syllables in table 6. All of these graphemes can be keyed on any Spanish keyboard, including the small One Laptop Per Child computers that the Ministry of Education has distributed in some of the Yanesha' bilingual schools.

Table 6. Consonants in CV syllables using the official alphabet

Labial	Alveolar	(Alveo)palatal	Retroflex	Velar
pa, poe, po	ta, te, to			ka, kë, ko
pha, pe, pho	tha, the, tho			kha, ke, kho
	tsa, tse, tso	cha, che, cho	xha, xhe, xho	
ma, moe, mo	na, ne, no			
mha, me, mho	ña, ñe, ño			
	sa, se, so	sha, she, sho	rra, rre, rro	ja, je, jë, jo
bha, be, bho				ga, gë, go
	ra, re, ro			
wa, we, wo	lla, lle, llo	ya, ye, yo		

It is understood that the graphemes that occur in onomatopoeic roots and other "special" language—such as <f> for [ϕ^j], <ng> for [ŋ], and <l> for [l]—will be used but not form part of the official alphabet.

Similarly, symbolization of the complex syllable nuclei will be recognized but is not part of the official alphabet. In three workshops organized by the Ministry of Education (in October 2011, May 2012, and August 2012) for the preparation of educational materials and a spelling guide for the teachers, participants discussed how to distinguish vowel length and aspiration. Their latest idea (using <a> as a representative vowel) is to write <a> (long) and <á> (aspirated). They continue to write <a'> (glottalized). The advantage of the diacritic for aspiration is that it does not add to the length of words and its omission is not as noticeable as the omission of a letter such as <h>. The disadvantages of not indicating length are that there will be words written as homonyms that in fact are not, and children who have not learned Yanesha' in the home will need to be taught correct pronunciation of long versus short vowels. In any case, those children will need some special instruction since vowel aspiration is to be written only on prefixes and stems (not on inflectional suffixes). Whatever the Yanesha' decide, it will probably be many years before they write the acute accent and apostrophe consistently, even on roots. However, one man who is very conscious of the complex syllable nuclei has begun to write the diacritics consistently on prefixes and roots but not on suffixes.

The order of the alphabet is important to the Yanesha'—they evidently feel that <xh> for the retroflexed affricate should be next to its plain counterpart, <ch>, just as the palatalized consonants are next to their plain counterparts. The following is the alphabet they voted for and that was approved by the Ministry of Education's *Resolución Directoral* 1493-2011-ED, signed June 16, 2011:

(11) a, b, bh, ch, xh, e, ë, g, j, k, kh, ll, m, mh, n, ñ, o, p, ph, r, rr, s, sh, t, th, ts, w, y

The movement toward alphabet change originated with the speakers of the language and the outcome is what they chose. As they implement their new alphabet in the electronic age, other questions come to mind: What new domains of use of the language will emerge? Will the new alphabet help in maintaining and even revitalizing the Yanesha' language?

References

Daigneault, Anna Louisa. 2009. An ethnolinguistic study of the Yanesha' (Amuesha) language and speech community in Peru's Andean Amazon, and the traditional role of *ponapnora*, a female rite of passage. M.A. thesis. Université de Montréal.

Duff, Martha. 1957. *Ema': Amuesha 1.* Pucallpa, Peru: Ministerio de Educación Pública.

Duff, Martha. 1958. *Nochcar: Amuesha 5.* Pucallpa, Peru: Ministerio de Educación Pública.

Duff-Tripp, Martha. 1981. *Apa ñaña ach.* Libro No. 3 para la Lectura y Escritura. Pucallpa, Peru: Ministerio de Educación.

Duff-Tripp, Martha. 1997. *Gramática del idioma yanesha' (amuesha).* Serie Lingüística Peruana 43. Lima: Instituto Lingüístico de Verano.

Duff-Tripp, Martha. 1998. *Diccionario yanesha' (amuesha)—castellano.* Serie Lingüística Peruana 47. Lima: Instituto Lingüístico de Verano.

Fast, Peter W. 1953. Amuesha (Arawak) phonemes. *International Journal of American Linguistics* 19:191–194.

Fast, Peter W., and Mary Fast. 1952a. *Amuesha 1.* Lima, Peru: Ministerio de Educación Pública.

Fast, Peter W., and Mary Fast. 1952b. *Amuesha 2.* Lima: Ministerio de Educación Pública.

Wise, Mary Ruth. 1958. Diverse points of articulation of allophones in Amuesha (Arawak). *Miscellanea Phonetica* 3:15–21.

Wise, Mary Ruth. 1963. Six levels of structure in Amuesha (Arawak) verbs. *International Journal of American Linguistics* 29:132–152.

10

Kurtöp Orthography Development in Bhutan

Gwendolyn Hyslop

In our collaborative work documenting and describing the Tibeto-Burman language Kurtöp, we considered many linguistic and non-linguistic factors. While the adaptation of a Roman-based orthography was relatively straightforward, the application of the 'Ucen (Tibetan-like) script to Kurtöp posed many challenges. This chapter discusses the factors which we considered and the difficulties we encountered in applying 'Ucen, a script originally devised for an older variety of Tibetan.

10.1 Introduction*

Kurtöp [xkz] (a.k.a. Kurtotpikha), a Tibeto-Burman language of Bhutan, had been almost completely undescribed until recently (Hyslop 2011).

* Documentation of Kurtöp has been generously supported by the Hans Rausing Endangered Languages Documentation Project and the National Science Foundation. While I take full responsibility for the ideas put forth in this paper, I gratefully acknowledge the assistance of Karma Tshering, Kuenga Lhendup, Namgay Thinley, Chris Fynn, and participants at the

As part of an ongoing, collaborative effort at documenting endangered languages, we have been involved with the Bhutanese government in orthography development for Kurtöp. The Bhutanese government formally recognizes two scripts: Roman for English (the language of education) and 'Ucen for Dzongkha [dzo] (the national language). Therefore, in developing an orthography for Kurtöp, both Roman and 'Ucen orthographies were requested by the government and the Kurtöp speech community. The adaptation of 'Ucen, the writing system devised originally for Old Tibetan, turned out to be particularly challenging, due primarily to the fact that Kurtöp is not a direct descendant from Classical Tibetan and has both a phonology and a phonological history which deviate from the languages for which 'Ucen is most regularly used.[1]

Of Bhutan's approximately twenty indigenous languages, only Dzongkha has a written history and is regularly represented in writing. With approximately 15,000 speakers, Kurtöp falls somewhere in the middle in terms of number of speakers. Larger languages like Dzongkha and Tshangla [tsj] have over 100,000 speakers each, while Bhutan's smaller languages, such as Gongduk [goe] and Chali [tgf], have 1,000 or fewer speakers.

Although Kurtöp was undescribed until recently, there is some history of literacy in Kurtöp. Specifically, a particular Kurtöp-language text locally referred to as the *Priu Zhung* was written and passed down by monks to be chanted during the annual *priu* (local festival) in the Kurtöp-speaking village of Jasabi. We consulted this text in devising the orthography but concluded that (1) it was heavily laden with Classical Tibetan loans and therefore not representative of the colloquial language; and (2) the conventions used led to transference issues with Dzongkha, and confusability. Local scholars who had access to the text agreed they could read the text and associate it with Kurtöp (as opposed to Dzongkha or Tibetan) but confessed it took some time to do so.

In an article on orthography development for the Bhutanese language Tshangla by Andvik (2012), following UNESCO 2004, outlines the

2009 Dzongkha Development Commission orthography convention. Consultation with these individuals and governmental bodies has been integral in development of the Kurtöp orthography. I am also grateful for comments from Mike Cahill and Keren Rice on a previous version of this paper.

[1] Old Tibetan is ascribed to the language spoken in the Yarlung Valley, considered to be the cradle of the Tibetan Empire. The language was first put into writing in 650 A.D. Classical Tibetan, on the other hand, refers to a written standard which emerged over time following the collapse of the Tibetan Empire (Hill 2010).

importance of an orthography being relatively easy to learn (learnability) while also allowing for transference to the dominant language (transferability). Both criteria will also be shown to be important in the development of the Kurtöp orthography.

The remainder of this paper has the following structure. First, §10.2 presents the linguistic factors we addressed and includes an overview of Kurtöp phonology, while §10.3 examines the non-linguistic factors we addressed. Following this, §10.4 describes the process of applying the 'Ucen orthography to Kurtöp, including those aspects of the orthography which could be transferred in a straightforward manner and those which were more difficult. Finally, §10.5 presents a summary and conclusion.

10.2 Linguistic factors

10.2.1 Kurtöp phonology

Before delving into the linguistic factors we considered in adapting the 'Ucen orthography to Kurtöp, we provide an outline of Kurtöp phonology. Consonants, vowels, and suprasegmental contrasts are presented below, based on Hyslop (2011).

10.2.1.1 Consonants

Table 1 presents the Kurtöp consonant phonemes. All of the consonants presented here may constitute a simple syllable onset while only those indicated in parentheses may also be syllable codas. Possible complex onsets are: /pr, pj, p^hj, p^hr, br, bj, bl, kw, k^hw, gw, mr, mj/. The complex onsets involving palatal glides exhibit a great deal of synchronic variation, such as [pj~pc~c], [p^hj~pch~ch], and [mj~ɲ]. This variation will have ramifications for choices on how to represent complex onsets, discussed in §10.4.2.3.

Table 1. Kurtöp consonant phonemes

	Labial	Dental	Retroflex	Palatal	Velar
Stops	(p), pʰ, b	(t), tʰ, d	ʈ, ʈʰ, ɖ	c, cʰ, ɟ	(k), kʰ, g
Affricates		ts, tsʰ			
Fricatives		(s), z		ç	
Nasals	(m)	(n)		ɲ	(ŋ)
Laterals		(l), l̥			
Rhotics		(r)			
Glides	w			j	
Aspirates					h

10.2.1.2 Vowels

All varieties of Kurtöp have the five cardinal vowels /ɑ, e, i, o, u/ and diphthongs /ui, au, oi, iu/. Educated speakers, under influence from Dzongkha and Lhasa Tibetan [bod], often pronounce /ui/ and /oi/ as [yː] and [øː] respectively, in addition to realizing /u/ and /o/ as [y] and [ø] respectively in contexts in which the vowel is followed by a coronal coda.

10.2.1.3 Suprasegmentals

Kurtöp contrasts high and low tone word-initially following sonorant onsets. Following obstruents, tone is predictably high if the obstruent is voiceless (including voiceless aspirated) and low if the obstruent is voiced.[2] Vowel length is also minimally contrastive in open syllables.

10.2.1.4 Syllable shapes

The maximal syllable shapes in Kurtöp are CCVC and CCVV, with CV, CVC, CCV, and CVV being other possibilities. As indicated in table 1, possible syllable codas are: /p, t, k, s, m, n, ŋ, r/. The liquid /l/ is also a possible coda but found only in loans.

[2] Technically, the voicing distinction following the palatal fricative has collapsed in favor of the tonal contrast, such that a voiceless palatal fricative now contrasts high versus low tone on the following vowel. For more details, refer to Hyslop 2009.

10.2.2 What to represent

An important first question we addressed was which aspects of the phonology to represent. For the more robust contrasts, where minimal pairs abound, such as voicing contrasts, the obvious answer was to represent the contrasts. It was not clear, however, what to do with contrasts such as tone and vowel length which have a much smaller functional load. The eventual decision was to represent both vowel length and tone, as speakers felt it important to be able to represent those differences.

10.2.3 Deep versus shallow representation

In deciding how to represent Kurtöp in the 'Ucen orthography, the first question was to decide whether to employ a "deep" or a "shallow" representation. Kurtöp exhibits several allomorphs for a number of verbal suffixes and nominal clitics. A detailed description of all Kurtöp allomorphy is beyond the scope of this article (see Hyslop 2011 for a full account), but table 2 will suffice to illustrate one example of morphophonological alternation, where the perfective suffix *-pala* has allomorphs *-wala* and *-sala*.[3] The decision to represent the allomorphy in these cases appears to be in line with observations made by Snider, this volume, about postlexical forms being preferable orthographic representations.

[3] If not otherwise indicated by phonetic symbols, data in this chapter are represented in Roman letters designed for Dzongkha by George van Driem and Karma Tshering and adapted to Kurtöp. The symbols correspond to the IPA as follows: <k> [k]; <kh> [k^h]; <g> [g]; <ng> [ŋ]; <c> [c]; <ch> [c^h]; <j> [ɟ]; <ny> [ɲ]; <tr> [ʈ]; <thr> [ʈ]; <dr> [ɖ]; <t> [t̪]; <th> [t̪h]; <d> [d̪]; <p> [p]; <ph> [p^h]; <b> [b]; <m> [m]; <ts> [ts]; <tsh> [ts^h]; <sh> [ç]; <zh> [ʝ̞]; <s> [s]; <z> [z]; <l> [l]; <lh> [l̥]; <r> [r]; <a> [ɑ]; <e> [e]; <i> [i]; <o> [o]; <u> [u]; <ö> [ø]; <ü> [y]; <'CV> high tone on following vowel; <^> long vowel.

Table 2. Alternation in Kurtöp perfective *-pala*

Stem type	Bare stem	Gloss	Stem with *-pala*
-k	kuk	'gather'	kû-wala
-ng	thong	'drink'	thong-wala
-r	chir	'chop'	chir-wala
historical -l	phre	'separate'	phre-wala
-t	dot	'sleep'	dot-pala
-n	gin	'wear'	gin-pala
-p	phap	'bring down'	phap-pala
-m	ngom	'be excessive'	ngom-pala
open syllable	se	'die'	se-sala

In all such morphophonological alternations, we opted to be faithful to the surface representation. Thus, allomorphy shown in the ergative/instrumental/genitive case markers, locative case markers, negative prefix,[4] imperative suffixes, and unmarked perfective suffixes[5] is represented.

Some phonological processes, however, were preferred to be ignored in the orthography. First, the language tends to drop word-final vowels in multi-syllable words, so that words like *gemale* 'go-FUT' and *getaki* 'go-IPFV' are often realized as *gemal* and *getak* respectively. Second, as it is a requirement in Kurtöp that tone occur on the first syllable of the word, the addition of the negative prefix *ma-/me-/mi-* to a verb stem conditions the movement of the stem tone to the initial syllable, or the negative prefix. For example, *ma-ŋáp* 'NEG-dry.out' is realized as *máŋap*. In this case, tone will be represented only on the verb stem and not on the negative prefix.

10.3 Non-linguistic factors

Non-linguistic factors in the development of the Kurtöp 'Ucen orthography were an important facet of our process and involved a considerable amount

[4] The different forms of the negative prefix may also encode a change in tense. Thus, *ma-* indicates past tense while *me-/mi-* indicates non-past. In the latter case, the use of the mid or high vowel is dependent on the vowel of the verb stem: high vowels condition *mi-* while non-high vowels condition *me-*.

[5] Kurtöp has five perfective suffixes which encode a range of evidential/mirative/epistemic contrasts. The only perfective affix to exhibit any allomorphy is the "unmarked" perfective *-pala*. See Hyslop (2011) for a full description.

of discussion and careful thought. Below, we outline the non-linguistic policies and factors that played part in our decision making, including Bhutanese government and religious practices and policies, and provide an introduction to the 'Ucen writing system. Many of these factors are mentioned in Cahill, this volume, as common non-linguistic factors involved in orthography development, though in Kurtöp the role of religion, script choice, and transferability has been especially nuanced.

10.3.1 Governmental and religious practices and policies

Until recently, Dzongkha, the national language of Bhutan, was the only language native to Bhutan that was written and that maintained any written history.[6] Dzongkha orthography is a matter of constant debate in Bhutan but discussion of Dzongkha orthography is beyond the scope of this paper. Let it suffice for our purposes to maintain that Dzongkha is traditionally written in various versions of the 'Ucen writing system and thus it was expected that Kurtöp writing would use the 'Ucen writing system as well. Because of this, we needed to keep Dzongkha conventions in mind with regard to possible issues with transference.

In addition to representing the national language, Dzongkha, the 'Ucen orthography is also used to write Chöke, the liturgical language, which is also known as Classical Tibetan. Buddhism is the state religion in Bhutan and plays a very important role in society. Buddhist scripture is written exclusively in Chöke and these writings are considered sacred. Although Dzongkha is not Chöke, because it is traditionally written in the same orthography as Chöke, by extension its written form is often considered sacred as well. In one recent incident, Bhutanese storekeepers were using old Dzongkha newspapers to wrap betel nut packages for sale in their shops in the capital. Some monks and Buddhist scholars found the use of the printed Dzongkha to be an offense to Buddhism and pleaded over national news to stop this re-use of newspapers and promoted burning of the used

[6] Both Nepali, spoken in Bhutan as a first language, and English, spoken in Bhutan as a fluent second language (and as the medium of education) have a history of writing and established writing conventions. Neither language, however, is considered to be indigenous to Bhutan in the sense that Dzongkha is. English is taught in schools, together with Indian English writing conventions, but Nepali is not taught, and most fluent speakers of Nepali have little or no knowledge of the standard Nepali writing system and its conventions. Further, Nepali is generally not considered a language indigenous to Bhutan as it was brought by Nepalese immigrants only in the past century.

newspapers instead.[7] Using 'Ucen with Kurtöp therefore also necessarily involved tending to these sensitive issues.

In Bhutan, 'Ucen is actually represented by two scripts: the standard Tshui and the cursive Joyi.[8] The former was developed to write Tibetan in the seventh century A.D. The general belief is that one of the emperor's ministers, Thonmi Sambhotra, was sent from Tibet to India to learn the art of writing and brought back with him a modified North Brahmi script designed exclusively for the Tibetan language as it was spoken in the seventh century.[9] However, some scholars question the validity of this belief (e.g., van Driem 2001:835 cites Snellgrove 1987).

General knowledge in Bhutan is that writing was first brought into Bhutan through Padma Sambhava when he visited Bhutan in the eighth century A.D. According to local beliefs, Padma Sambhava was accompanied by his disciple Denma Tsenmang, who was also a renowned Tibetan translator. Denma Tsenmang is attributed with the creation of Joyi, which is a sort of cursive used today for writing Dzongkha in Bhutan.

Bhutanese children begin to learn to read and write Dzongkha from the beginning of their education. In addition to being able to read and write in the Joyi script, Bhutanese children will also learn to read the Tshui script, but *writing* of Tshui is generally reserved for monks. For this reason, children's books and Dzongkha education materials are all produced in the Joyi script.

In deciding how to represent Kurtöp using 'Ucen we debated between using Tshui and Joyi. Because Joyi was considered to be indigenous to Bhutan in a way that Tshui was not, and because Joyi has less association with Buddhism than Tshui (and thus avoids offending Buddhist sensibilities when their sacred script is used for secular texts), we decided, in

---

[7] While I am not a Buddhist scholar, I presume that burning the old newspapers was on par with cremation and thus an acceptable means to dispose of something considered sacred.

[8] In Written Tibetan, Tshui is known as ཚུགས་ཡིག་ <tshugs.yig> and Joyi as མགྱོགས་ཡིག་ <mgyogs.yig>. Joyi is also known in Written Tibetan as ལྷོ་ཡིག་ <lho.yig> lhoyi or མོན་ཡིག་ <mon.yig> mönyi (Tshering 2010:5).

[9] The origin of the Brahmi script itself is somewhat of a mystery. The first specimens appear on the Ashokan edicts, in the third century B.C., with scholars debating four possible origins. The indigenous theory speculates that Brahmi was home grown in India, independent of the Indus Valley writing, Semitic, Chinese, or any other writing system, but this is mainly speculative. Another theory, that Brahmi is the descendant of the older Indus Valley writing, is intriguing but lacking in evidence, since a gap of around 1,400 years exists between the two. The theory that Brahmi was borrowed from Semitic orthographies, specifically Aramaic, is plausible, though irrefutable evidence remains to be seen. Finally, scholars speculate that Brahmi may be based on Kharoṣṭhi, a script that is generally believed to have derived from Aramaic and was present at the time when Brahmi was actively used (Rogers 2005:205–211).

consultation with the Bhutanese government, to focus exclusively on Joyi for now. Tshui and Joyi scripts are illustrated in figure 1 (representing the words *Tshui* and *Joyi,* respectively).

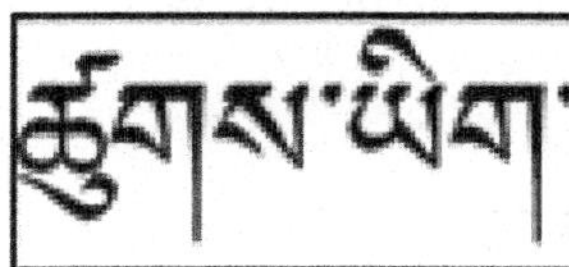

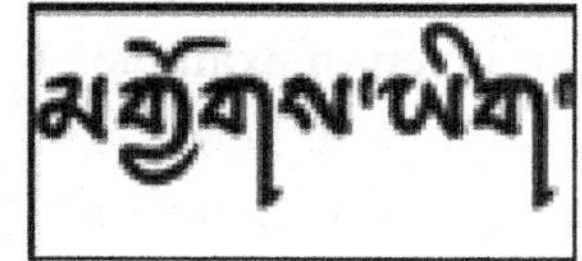

Figure 1. Tshui (left) and Joyi (right) scripts.

10.3.2 The 'Ucen syllable and Classical Tibetan

Being an abugida (also called an alphasyllabary), in which vowels are encoded via modifications to consonantal symbols, 'Ucen required additional understanding before it could be applied to Kurtöp. This section outlines the basic features of the 'Ucen syllable and how it was applied to an older variety of Tibetan. This knowledge was a prerequisite to the application of 'Ucen to Kurtöp.

Figure 2 represents the various positions within the 'Ucen syllable. For each position, it gives the (Romanized) Dzongkha name (not the Tibetan transliteration) and the English abbreviation. In English terminology, the *R* represents the root (usually a consonant, but it can be a vowel if the word lacks an onset), *C* represents a consonant, and *V* represents a vowel. Each box represents a particular position in the syllable, where a given subset of available characters may be assigned.

	'yang V		
	gocen C2		
'nyönju C1	*mingzhi* R	*jêju* C3	*yangju* C5
	dokcen C4		
	'yang V		

Figure 2. The 'Ucen syllable.

The ’Ucen syllable consists minimally of a *mingzhi* (R) and maximally of a *’nyönju* (C1), *mingzhi* (R), *gocen* (C2), *dokcen* (C4), *’yang* (V), *jêju* (C3), and *yangju* (C5). Lack of a V character in a syllable signals a low back vowel. By way of example, we will illustrate the structure of the word *bsgrubs* ‘achievement’ given in example (1).

(1) the Tibetan word *bsgrubs* ‘achievement’
    བསྒྲུབས་

Figure 3 shows how the syllable structure of this word is represented.

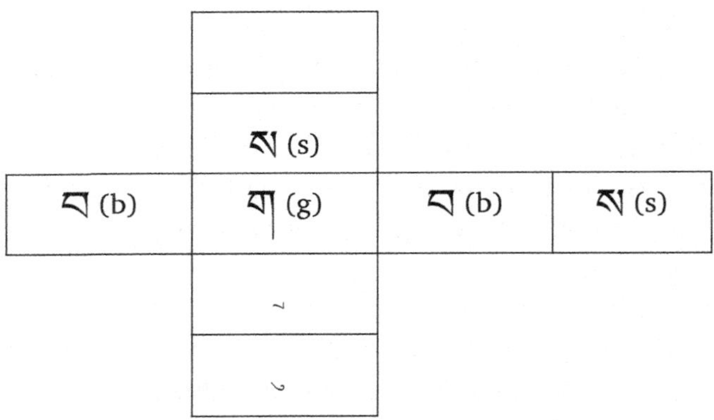

Figure 3. The Tibetan word *bsgrubs* ‘achievement’.

Old Tibetan, which was toneless, allowed for complex onset and coda consonant clusters. The *mingzhi,* or root, was the minimum position required in an Old Tibetan word. A *mingzhi* by itself represented a simple consonant onset. The *’nyönju* (C1), *gocen* (C2), and *dokcen* (C4) positions could also be filled to represent a complex onset. The vowels /i, e, o/ were indicated by symbols in the upper *’yang* (V) position while /u/ was indicated with a symbol in the lower *’yang* (V) position. If the syllable onset consisted of more than one consonant, a *’nyönju* (C1) would be used. If the syllable was closed with a coda, a *jêju* (C4) would be used. In the unusual case that a complex coda was present, a *yangju* (C5) could also be present.

The remainder of this section addresses the phonology of Classical Tibetan, based on DeLancey (2003). For a thorough discussion of Old Tibetan phonology, the reader is referred to Hill (2010). A discussion of the precise linguistic differences between the two languages (Classical Tibetan and Old Tibetan) is beyond the scope of this chapter. The consonant phonemes of Classical Tibetan (along with the corresponding Tshui symbols) are represented in table 3 (DeLancey 2003:256).[10]

Table 3. Classical Tibetan consonant phonemes and corresponding Joyi symbols

	Labial	Dental	Palatal	Velar	Glottal
Stops	p, p^h, b པ ཕ བ	t, t^h, d ཏ ཐ ད	c, c^h, ɟ ཅ ཆ ཇ	k, k^h, g ཀ ཁ ག	
Affricates		ts, ts^h, dz ཙ ཚ ཛ			
Fricatives		s, z ས ཟ	ç, ʝ ཤ ཞ		
Nasals	m མ	n ན	ɲ ཉ	ŋ ང	
Laterals		l, ɬ ལ ལྷ			
Rhotics		r ར			
Glides	w ཝ		j ཡ		
Aspirates					h ཧ

Table 4 presents the vowel phonemes of Classical Tibetan with the corresponding Tshui symbols (DeLancey 2003:256). The Tshui names for the diacritic marks are given in parentheses. The unmarked Tshui symbol represents the low vowel /a/.

[10] At the time of preparing this chapter, the Joyi font for Kurtöp was still being developed by the Dzongkha Development Commission.

Table 4. Classical Tibetan vowel phonemes and corresponding Joyi symbols*

	Front	Back
High	i ཀི་ *(kiku)*	u ཀུ་ *(zh'abju)*
Mid	e ཀེ་ *(drembo)*	o ཀོ་ (naro)
Low		ɑ ཀ་

*The vowels are represented following the consonant /k/. The Classical Tibetan terms for the diacritics appear in parentheses. The low form is the unmarked form.

Since the time when Old Tibetan was codified as a written language, several phonological changes have taken place. Complex onsets and codas have simplified, expanding the number of places of articulation, and many codas have disappeared, leaving tonal splits, lengthened vowels, nasalized vowels, or other vowel changes in their places. Tone has also developed as conditioned by contrasts on syllable onsets. For example, the Tibetan word <bsgrubs> is today pronounced as [ɖùp].

Modern Tibetan is still fairly easy to read, to the extent that one is aware of the sound changes that have taken place since the language was put to writing. However, the current use of Tibetan conventions to represent a language that exhibits nearly 1,400 years of phonological change poses some serious challenges to the application of 'Ucen to Kurtöp in Bhutan (where the literate population is well schooled in the Chöke conventions). The focus of the next section is how we overcame these challenges.

10.4 Application to Kurtöp

10.4.1 Straightforward transfer

A number of features of Kurtöp were easy to represent in the 'Ucen orthography. For example, the three-way contrast in the voicing of stops in syllable-initial position transferred straight to the Chöke corresponding symbols. Example (2) illustrates this with [k, k^h, g].

(2) 3-way voicing contrast of stops

ཀ་	<ka>	[kɑ]	'snow'
ཁ་	<kha>	[kʰɑ]	'mouth, language'
ག་	<ga>	[gɑ]	'saddle'

Recall that in Kurtöp only sonorants or some voiceless obstruents may serve as syllable codas. As in Chöke, syllable-final stops are represented with the voiced correspondent of the symbol while the remaining codas are faithfully represented. Example (3) shows how 'Ucen is used to represent Kurtöp codas.

(3) representation of codas

ཀད་	<kad>	[kɑt]	'voice'
ཕབ་	<phab>	[pʰɑp]	'bring down'
ཀས་	<kas>	[kɑs]	'ladder'[11]
གར་	<gar>	[gɑr]	'encampment'
ཕེལ་	<phel>	[pʰel]	'flourishing'[12]
ཐང་	<thang>	[tʰɑŋ]	'plane'
གན་	<gan>	[gɑn]	'fall.backwards'
ཀིམ་	<kim>	[kim]	'step'

In Kurtöp, coda /k/ tends to be deleted with compensatory lengthening of the previous vowel in its place. Because this is a regular rule, and because coda /k/ can often be recoverable in various morphological contexts (such as the addition of the imperfective suffix in the case of a verb stem), we chose to always represent coda /k/, as shown in example (4).

(4) representation of coda /k/

ཀུག་	<kug>	[ku:]	'bend'
ཀུག་ཏ་	<kugta>	[kuktɑ]	'bend.IPFV.MIR'

Kurtöp's five vowels were also easy to represent using the symbols which corresponded to Chöke's five vowels. However, this was not an easy decision

---

[11] Note that coda *-s* is only present word finally in southern varieties of Kurtöp, such as the variety spoken in Gangzur. In Kurtöp spoken in Dungkar *geok* (a geographical unit perhaps akin to 'county'), coda *-s* has been lost, leading to contrastive vowel length word finally. In these varieties, coda *-s* may still be present word-internally.

[12] Coda *-l* is present only in borrowings; native words have lost coda *-l* through diachronic processes. This particular word is a borrowing from Chöke.

to make, as the symbols have evolved in Dzongkha so that they are often associated with fronted pronunciations. For example, in Tibetan, coronal codas triggered fronting of the vowel and lengthening, and eventually were lost. More educated speakers, familiar with the Tibetan and Dzongkha conventions, tended to pronounce non-front vowels followed by a coronal coda with a fronted pronunciation. However, we did not feel this needed to be represented in the orthography. Words exemplifying each of Kurtöp's five vowels are shown in example (5).

(5) representation of vowels

ཀི་	<ki>	[ki]	'potato'
ཀེ་	<ke>	[ke]	'behind.RELN'
ཀུ་	<ku>	[ku]	'dig'
ཀོ་	<ko>	[ko]	'door'
ཀ་	<ka>	[kɑ]	'snow'

10.4.2 Problems and solutions

Recall that, unlike Classical Tibetan, Kurtöp has tone, vowel length, and retroflex consonants. In this way, Kurtöp is similar to Dzongkha. Unlike Dzongkha, and similar to Classical Tibetan, however, Kurtöp has retained complex onsets. The three features tone, vowel length, and complex onsets posed the greatest problems in applying the 'Ucen orthography to Kurtöp, with retroflex consonants posing additional problems. This is described below.

10.4.2.1 Tone

To mark high tone following sonorant consonants, Chris Fynn, font developer for the Dzongkha Development Commission, designed a tone diacritic that appears above the *mingzhi* in the same space as a *'yang* (if present). The high tone mark can be seen above the symbols in figure 4.

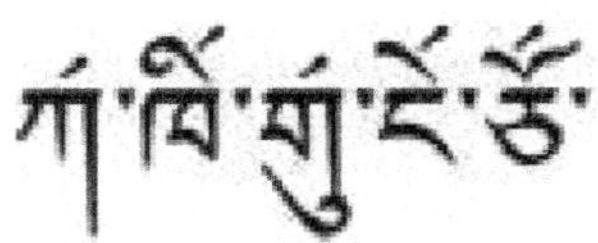

Figure 4. High tone in 'Ucen for Kurtöp.

While it will be possible to apply the high tone diacritic to any character in 'Ucen, it will be used in practice only in those environments where tone is contrastive and not easily represented with another feature (such as voicing); that is, the high tone mark will be employed as needed for sonorant-initial words.

10.4.2.2 Vowel length

To represent the distinction made by vowel length, the letter <འ> is written on the long forms. It is added below the *mingzhi* as a *dokcen,* above a vowel diacritic if one is present. Table 5 shows examples of vowel length as indicated in 'Ucen. The top row shows words with a long vowel while the bottom row shows the corresponding short vowel forms.

Table 5. Kurtöp vowel length represented in 'Ucen

	<â/a>	<î/i>	<ê/e>	<ô/o>	<û/u>
Long	ནཱ་ <nâ> 'COP.EXIS.MIR'	ཚཱི་ <tshî> 'calculation'	ཤཱེ་ <shê> 'glass'	ཚཱོ་ <tshô> 'here'	མཱུ་ <mû> 'NEG.COP.EXIS'
Short	ན་ <na> 'ear'	ཚི་ <tshi> 'sticky'	ཤེ་ <she> 'over.pour'	ཚོ་ <tsho> 'lake'	མུ་ <mu> 'mushroom'

10.4.2.3 Complex onsets

The largest obstacle to overcome when devising the Kurtöp 'Ucen orthography was the complex onset clusters that are present in Kurtöp but no longer in Dzongkha. Classical Tibetan had complex onsets, which, among other possible options, were represented by a combination of symbols representing the first member of the cluster and diacritics representing the second member of the cluster. Some examples are: ཀྲ <kr>, ཀྱ <ky>, and ཀླ <kl>.

Because of sound changes that took place since Tibetan was put into writing, most Tibetan dialects today do not have the same phonemic sequences that these symbols initially represented. For example, children studying Dzongkha learn to pronounce ཀྲ as [ʈ], ཀྱ as [c], and ཀླ as [l] with a high tone on the following vowel. Adopting the same conventions that were used in Chöke to represent complex onsets for Kurtöp leads to difficulties in transference from Kurtöp to Dzongkha. For example, if Kurtöp children learn to read པྲ་ <pra> as [prá], the fact that the same combination of characters would be pronounced as [ʈá] in Dzongkha leads to added difficulty in transference. (For further discussion on transference issues, see Hinton, this volume.)

We explored several alternatives to the Chöke conventions, and a decision was finalized during the DDC orthography convention in 2009. A known, but rarely used, convention in 'Ucen orthography is the ability to combine "half" consonants in vertical arrangements. This convention was historically devised in order to represent other combinations in Sanskrit or other languages. Scholars and administrators decided this would also be the most viable option to represent the complex onsets present in Kurtöp and other Bhutanese languages. Learnability is enhanced by the fact that no new characters are introduced, though a new convention must be learned. Transferability to Dzongkha will not pose too great a problem, since the combination of two full characters in one vertical alignment is not a Dzongkha convention. At the time of the DDC orthography convention in 2009, the Bhutanese 'Ucen fonts were not equipped to handle this vertical stacking. At the request of the researchers, Chris Fynn, font developer for the DDC, agreed to revise the Joyi font in order to accommodate these combinations. Anticipating the application of this font to other Bhutanese languages, Chris Fynn has arranged for a wide selection of complex onsets to be represented.

An example of complex onsets in Kurtöp is shown in Tshui in figure 5. Here, the initial /k/ is shown with the typical *dokcen* <y, r, l> and then followed by the initial /k/ with the "half" consonants <y, r, l>. Note that in the case of /kl-/, a half consonant does not work in Tshui, as the *dokcen* form is no different from what a half form would be. Thus, in the case of Tshui, we have proposed to add a *wazur* beneath the *dokcen* /l/ when it is intended to be fully pronounced. In Joyi we do not have this problem as the *dokcen* /l/ is different from the half /l/.

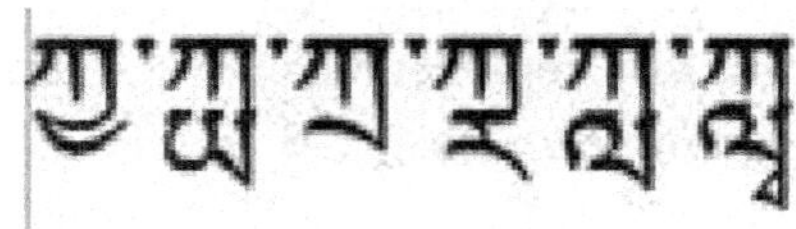

Figure 5. Representing complex onsets in 'Ucen for Kurtöp.

Kurtöp labial-initial onset clusters /pj, p^hj, bj, mj/ involving a palatal glide as the second member have rapidly undergone change, such that it is only the oldest generation of speakers who have retained the pronunciations with palatal glide offsets. In the case of the obstruents, later generations of speakers have fortified the palatal glide into a fricative or stop, while the youngest and most educated speakers have lost the labial altogether and retain only a palatal stop in lieu of the older cluster. Regarding the sonorant, most speakers today have a palatal nasal /ɲ/ in place of /mj/. Because these sound changes mirror the sound changes of Classical Tibetan <pj, p^hy, by, my> to Lhasa Tibetan /c, ch, ɟ, ɲ/, we decided to adopt the Chöke/Dzongkha conventions in these cases. Transference to Dzongkha in these cases is straightforward. The representation of Kurtöp labialglide onsets is shown in example (6).

(6) representation of labialglide onsets

པྱ	[pj ~ pç ~ pc ~c]
ཕྱ	[p^hj ~ p^hç ~ p^hc ~ c^h]
བྱ	[bj ~ bʝ ~ bɟ ~ ɟ]
མྱ	[mj ~ ɲ]

10.4.2.4 Retroflex consonants

Retroflex consonants were also challenging to represent. When Old Tibetan was first written down, the language did not have any retroflex consonants. They are now present in Lhasa Tibetan and other Tibetan dialects, having been innovated from a series of stop-plus-rhotic clusters. Thus, words with retroflex consonants in Dzongkha are generally written as stop-plus-rhotic clusters, such as in ཕྱེད་ཀྲ་ <phyed.kra> [pchéʈə] 'adultery fine'. With many recent borrowings from Nepali, Hindi, and English, and without a prescribed standard, many Bhutanese are using the same strategy to represent retroflex sounds.[13] Thus, ཀྲ <kr>, ཁྲ <k^hr>, and གྲ <gr> are often used to represent [ʈ, $ʈ^h$, ɖ], respectively in borrowed words.

In theory, there is an alternative to representing retroflex consonants in non-Tibetan words in Bhutan. Throughout the history of Written Tibetan,

[13] Though English does not have retroflex stops, Bhutanese speakers—like Hindi and other South Asian language speakers—map the English alveolar stops to their retroflex series. Interestingly, then, the English dental fricatives are mapped to the dental series of stops.

a special series of *lokpa,* or reversed characters, has been used to represent sounds in Sanskrit borrowings that were not present when Tibetan was first codified into a written system. Three were used, in particular, to represent retroflex consonants which were present in Sanskrit. These were: ཊ [ʈ], ཋ [ʈ^h], and ཌ [ɖ]. For the Kurtöp 'Ucen orthography, then, we had two choices: (1) use a combination of stop-plus-rhotic cluster or (2) use the *lokpa* series of symbols. When presented with these options, the members of the DDC orthography convention preferred the former option. The reasons for this were that most Bhutanese were unfamiliar with the *lokpa* symbols, and those who were familiar with these symbols associated them with a Sanskritic religious context.

Thus, we opted for the former choice. Rather than use the velar series (ཀྲ ཁྲ གྲ) or labial series (པྲ ཕྲ བྲ) with the rhotic diacritic, we decided to use the dental series with the rhotic diacritic, which, we felt, would be easier to learn than the velar or labial series. There would be no problem with transference, since this combination is also used as one of the strategies to represent retroflex sounds in Dzongkha. Kurtöp retroflex stops are represented in 'Ucen in example (7).

(7) representation of retroflex stops

ཏྲ	[ʈ]
ཐྲ	[ʈ^h]
དྲ	[ɖ]

10.5 Summary and conclusions

In our linguistic research documenting and describing Kurtöp, we also worked with the local community and Bhutanese government to devise Roman and 'Ucen-based orthographies. There were many linguistic and non-linguistic factors we had to consider. With regard to the former, we debated whether a deep or shallow representation would be used, and with regard to the latter, we considered governmental policies, local history, and religious practices. Speakers overwhelmingly favored a shallow and faithful representation. Considering the non-linguistic factors, we opted for a Joyi (cursive) version of the 'Ucen writing system, though the font is still being finalized.

While the Roman orthography was relatively straightforward, devising an 'Ucen-based orthography was difficult, primarily because of the fact that literate Bhutanese read and write Dzongkha based on Chöke, the liturgical language. That is, the writing system is based on a language that was spoken approximately 1,400 years ago, but since then Dzongkha pronunciation has changed drastically. Reading modern Dzongkha and Tibetan requires that the student infer 1,400 years of sound change, rendering the pronunciation of the word to be something drastically different from what it would appear on the surface. This fact caused tremendous transference difficulties in devising a Kurtöp orthography. Our solutions, which differ from the strategies proposed by Andvik (2012), Bodt (2012), Chamberlain (2004), and van Driem (1995) for similar issues, were to use existing (though often rare) conventions that created minimal transference confusion while also maximizing learnability.

References

Andvik, Erik, 2012. Tshangla orthography. In Gwendolyn Hyslop, Stephen Morey, and Mark W. Post (eds.), *North East Indian Linguistics* 4, 121–144. New Delhi, India: Cambridge University Press/Foundation.

Bodt, Timotheus A. 2012. *The new lamp clarifying the history, peoples, languages and traditions of Eastern Bhutan and Eastern Mon.* Wageningen, the Netherlands: Monpasang Publications.

Chamberlain, Bradford Lynn. 2004. The Khengkha orthography: Developing a language in the Tibetan scriptal environment. M.A. thesis. Arlington, Tex.: Graduate Institute of Applied Linguistics.

DeLancey, Scott. 2003. Classical Tibetan. In Randy LaPolla and Graham Thurgood (eds.), *The Sino-Tibetan languages,* 255–269. New York: Routledge.

Driem, George van. 1995. *Een eerste grammaticale verkenning van het Bumthang, een taal van Midden-Bhutan: Met een overzicht van de talen en volkeren van Bhutan* [A first grammatical exploration of Bumthang, a language of central Bhutan: With an overview of the languages and peoples of Bhutan]. Leiden, the Netherlands: Research School CNWS.

Driem, George van. 2001. *Languages of the Himalayas: An ethnolinguistic handbook of the greater Himalayan Region.* Leiden, The Netherlands: Brill.

Hill, Nathan W. 2010. An overview of Old Tibetan synchronic phonology. *Transactions of the Philological Society* 108(2):110–125.

Hyslop, Gwendolyn. 2009. Kurtöp tone: A tonogenetic case study. *Lingua* 119:827–845.

Hyslop, Gwendolyn. 2011. *A grammar of Kurtöp.* Ph.D. dissertation. Eugene: University of Oregon.

Rogers, Henry. 2005. *Writing systems: A linguistic approach.* Malden, Mass.: Blackwell Publishing.

Snellgrove, David Llewellyn. 1987. *Indo-Tibetan Buddhism: Indian Buddhists & their Tibetan successors.* 2 vols. Boston, Mass.: Shambala Press.

Tshering, Karma. 2010. The mismatch between Dzongkha phonology and the Chöke writing system. University of Oregon. Ms.

UNESCO. 2004. *Manual for developing literacy and adult education programmes in minority language communities.* Asia-Pacific Programme of Education for All, United Nations Educational, Scientific and Cultural Organization. Bangkok: UNESCO.

11

Case Studies of Orthography Decision Making in Mainland Southeast Asia

Larin Adams

This chapter takes a look at case studies of successful and unsuccessful language development projects in Mainland Southeast Asia (MSEA). The MSEA situation is complicated by political boundaries, religious identity, and varying scripts. Apparently successful projects are characterized by building on pre-existing unity within language groups. Less successful projects are characterized by misplaced involvement or by underinformed involvement on the part of outsiders and insiders. In all cases careful linguistic analysis is less important than the social factors involved.

11.1 Linguists as activists

The reality of endangered and dying languages has caused many linguists to alter their perspectives on the goal of linguistic research. A growing number of linguists seek not only to describe aspects of dying languages but also to undertake actions that will increase the likelihood that endangered languages will continue and thrive into the future. Probably the most sought-after outcome which leads to long-term language health is widespread literacy in the endangered language. It is a critical step in Fishman's Graded Intergenerational Disruption Scale (Fishman 1991) and has been noted as one of nine crucial factors in preserving languages in UNESCO (2003). The process of a group moving from preliterate (lacking an alphabet) to fully literate in their own language is sometimes called language development. However, becoming involved in the language development process as an outside linguist often presents unusual challenges. In this paper I look briefly at three case histories of language development in Mainland Southeast Asia (MSEA). This area includes the countries of Cambodia, Laos, Myanmar, Thailand, and Vietnam.

11.1.1 Basis of information

Unlike some authors in this volume who have invested decades into language work and orthographies, I have had only a few years of exposure. As a result I speak more as an outside observer than as a full participant in the process of helping orthographies and literacy grow and thrive. I teach at a university in Chiang Mai, Thailand. Each year the university attracts a few members of minority groups to receive training in linguistics. Following this training for which they receive an M.A., many of them return to their home countries to do linguistic research and encourage language development. My comments are based on their experiences as well as the experiences of other linguists in the area.

Minority languages can be compared to ice floating in the water of the majority language and culture. Ice, in this metaphor, exists either as diffuse slush or as a hardened solid block. Slush is like fragmented minority groups on the cusp of merging with the water or majority culture. Solid blocks of ice, on the other hand, are robust language groups which are preserving their identity and have a high resistance to melting into the majority language. A larger and more cohesive language group (metaphorically a large solid block of ice) will maintain a strong group identity much longer than a group of partially linked dialect groups with little interaction.

In truth, it is not always clear which outcome—assimilation or separatism—is best for the people involved, but we all feel a significant loss when a cultural perspective and language disappears from our world. And while it is naïve to think that the future of any minority group will not involve dramatic changes, most people assume that a language group is better prepared for its future if the majority of group members acquire literacy in their own language and the national language.

Language development, however, is not inherently the kind of unifying force one would expect. In what follows we provide some examples of situations where orthography decisions that are part of language development could potentially be regarded as more divisive than unifying.

11.1.2 Observations on language development

In the course of this paper, several "observations" of language development in process are presented. Some of them are motivated by the case studies given here and others are simply provided without extensive justification. The first two observations are provided as largely self-evident, with little other justification.

Observation 1: Group size matters.

Decisions which result in serving a larger community are to be preferred over those which benefit a smaller community. The underlying assumption is that over time a group's identity will best be preserved if it is a large group, as opposed to a set of small groups. While this need not be the case, it seems more often true than not. The limiting factor here is comprehensibility and unity (see Observation 2). In general, if comprehensibility is not extensively impaired, then orthography decisions which favor serving a larger group are to be preferred over those that create divisions into smaller groups. This aspect of language development is called *extensibility*. It refers to the range of dialects for which a given orthography can be used. See Hasselbring (2006) for a review of the many issues of extensibility.

Observation 2: Unity matters.

A language group's long-term survival depends upon them behaving as a unified group. It does not matter how they label themselves; to succeed they must use their language and culture in as many domains as possible. Both language and culture replicate through use and if the proposed orthography cannot or is not used by large subgroups then the group's identity is not helped by language development. An orthography that is correctly extended will be used in many domains by the dialects for which it is intended. An orthography that is extended too far will not be used and can interfere with the development of a smaller, more unifying orthography and in this way become a force for disunity rather than unity.

11.1.3 Orthography defined

Before proceeding further, there are a few terms that need to be defined. The term *orthography* is used to mean a system for representing a language in written form. This includes decisions on individual characters, word breaks, punctuation, diacritics, and capitalization. This use of *orthography* is synonymous with *writing system*. Separate from *orthography* is the notion of *script*. Scripts are the graphical form of letters and symbols. Often scripts are classed by which other script they resemble. These might be called *base scripts*. Common base scripts in MSEA are Thai, Khmer, Lao, Burmese, and Roman. Usually, a language community will select a base script as part of doing language development. However, it is not uncommon for a community to have more than one script associated with their language. As mentioned above, *language development* is used as a label for the process of creating a writing system (orthography) and having that writing system adopted into widespread use by the community.

11.1.4 General problems in MSEA: scripts are not neutral

One surprise to me has been the volatility that surrounds script decisions. Many of the national scripts in MSEA are historically derived from Sanskrit [san], but they each have a unique form and express tones, voice, registers, etc. in slightly different ways. When a minority group in MSEA develops an orthography, it generally has three choices:

1. use a variation of the national script,
2. use a romanized script, and
3. develop its own script.

Options (1) and (2) are the most common, although option (3) is not unheard of. Sometimes, the national government has a policy enforcing option (1). Usually, a national policy exists because of the perception that using a script based on the national script will facilitate literacy transference from the minority language to the national language (see Hyslop, this volume). There are however, two serious consequences to using a national-based script. One consequence is that because many minority groups are spread across national borders, it is impossible to provide one writing system for the whole group that meets the competing requirements of the respective governments. Case study III looks at how one border group is dealing with a version of this issue by simultaneously using multiple scripts.

A second problem comes from competing religious identities. From a religious perspective, villages within most minority groups can divide into Buddhist, Christian, Muslim, or animist. Often in the past there has been some kind of attempt to develop an orthography by someone in the group. Sometimes this effort was influenced by western missionaries, sometimes it was a Buddhist-led effort, and perhaps most often it was a dream of a single person. Whatever the source, the particular base script chosen often acquires the religious affiliation of the first users. If, for example, a Thai-based script is first used by Christians, then it becomes the "Christian" orthography. Then, if Buddhist villages do not want to be identified with the "Christian" orthography, they may choose an alternate base script (e.g., a Roman-based script). Each "religious" branding of a base script is unique to that language group and may actually be reversed in a neighboring group.

This religious branding is a significant impediment to successful language development as it can fragment a group instead of uniting it. Religious branding is often accentuated if the orthography is developed with only a small group of local people. The resulting orthography is colored by those individuals' religious affiliation and any other personal animosity others may hold toward them. However, if orthography development can include representative members from all religious groups from the start, then this religious branding can be significantly ameliorated (though other problems may emerge).

In MSEA, both Buddhist and Christian (Catholic or Protestant) villages are often part of associations that have significant organizational structure. Since both religions often have a level of coordination across multiple village boundaries and their own leadership hierarchy, they provide useful connections to engage the influential members of the language group. However, many animist villages have not developed regional organization and lack any easy means to identify true indigenous leaders.

11.1.5 Case studies

For a number of reasons, in this chapter, the actual names of the language groups involved are sometimes not used. One reason is that some of these groups find themselves interacting with a government which views activities not done in the national language as potentially subversive. For this reason, drawing undue attention to particular groups could have an unnecessarily negative effect on their relationships with their government. A second reason for not giving specific names is that it is difficult to speak of some of these matters and not sound paternalistic or judgmental toward either the group or individuals in the group. An external view of a group's decision-making process is not the same as the perspective of those involved in the process. Thus, some decisions are presented here as flawed but they actually might be quite sound when viewed from within the group. It seems inappropriate for an outsider to report negatively on a particular individual or language group. Thus, to limit the effects of negative reporting, the language names are changed.

11.2 Case Study I: E and H

The following case history has been simplified somewhat, but the general outline of events illustrates some of the complications of engaging in language development as a linguist.

11.2.1 The plot

The plot for this story follows the following sequence: Contact of SIL by H; Money; Contact of SIL by E; Conflict; Survey; The rise of S; More conflict; End of external (SIL) involvement.

11.2.1.1 Contact of SIL by H

In language development it is vital that the members of the community making decisions about orthographies and literacy training are respected and influential community members. If such influential people are not engaged in the project then all orthography and literacy achievements will be owned by a small clique and not adopted by the community at large. So, one crucial function for outsiders is to make sure that the people they engage with are truly able to make group decisions. While good progress can be made on a language *description* with a single individual or a small group of speakers, the same cannot be said for language *development*.

SIL is an international organization which has a reputation for supporting some successful language development projects. This reputation has the effect that numerous groups contact SIL in hopes of gaining assistance in doing literacy development. While this reputation has the positive side effect of attracting interested *individuals*, it does not necessarily mean that interested *groups* have been identified. Often individuals have a private agenda that does not reflect the wishes of the language group.

Language group H was one of the groups that initiated contact with SIL about getting involved with literacy and Bible translation. However, *H* here really means a single individual (J) claiming to be a spokesman of a representative cultural committee. In actuality, there was no independent way initially to evaluate this claim. Later a visit to the region confirmed the status of J as a genuine representative of H. He had been sent to the capital city in order to find help in developing an orthography, starting a literacy program (train teachers, provide production workshops, pay for publishing), and translating the Bible into H.

When J contacted SIL, he said that the language project would include both groups H and E, since E was a very closely related dialect and one that was traditionally considered tightly related to H. Since H seemed to have high vitality based on self-reporting from the initial contact with J, and since H had even formed a literacy committee that spanned several Christian groups across a few villages, three members of H were invited to a literacy workshop.

11.2.1.2 Money

One aspect of the literacy training workshop attended by people from H was that following the workshop the participating members were given funds to pursue literacy promotion activities in their own villages. Ideally, these activities not only include providing instruction in reading to non-readers, but they might also include publication of literacy by-products such as calendars or brochures for special events. These funds might also be used to put on a special literacy celebration which helps establish a cultural committee. In the case of H, the total amount of funds provided was equivalent to one year's salary. In reality, it is very difficult to monitor how these funds are actually used.

One effect of people returning from the workshop in the capital (after an all expenses–paid trip) with lots of money was to create interest from other people. However, in this case the secondary interest now appears to have been more about money and less about literacy.

11.2.1.3 Contact by E

The next literacy workshop a few months later included a new delegation of E speakers. They claimed to be representative of the E group previously mentioned by J. In actual fact, E had no organizational equivalent of H that could have deputized this delegation of E speakers. However, this was not known by SIL and the E speakers were treated as co-owners to the language project.

11.2.1.4 Conflict

However, during the workshop some differences (only slightly linguistic) developed between H and E and, as a result, the E deputation demanded their own independent project (and funding). Attempts to mediate the differences failed. In retrospect, the E deputation probably had only pecuniary interests and did not care about the success of literacy. However, an outside organization like SIL could not ascertain that fact and instead opted to fund both groups—thereby somewhat legitimizing the E deputation.

Although small dialectal differences were seized by the E group to demand a separate project, there was plenty of obvious evidence that mutual intelligibility was not an issue. While SIL accepted E as an independent project, the conflicting information led SIL to decide to seek more objective evidence by surveying the villages said to be E and H villages. The survey was to be done with the help of J, but he was only part of the team; the remaining team members were nationals from different ethnic groups.

11.2.1.5 Survey

The reality of language survey is that nothing can proceed without the willing involvement of the groups to be surveyed. This means that prior to a survey, contacts with village leaders need to be made and permissions established. In this case, both groups had substantial Christian minorities through which contacts with leaders could be made. However, on arrival the contact for the E group refused to allow survey in E group villages. Eventually, they agreed to the survey but stipulated that the E group villages be done last. The survey (consisting of a wordlist, some sociolinguistic data, and a little comprehension testing) proceeded in the H area.

The H area is significantly separated geographically from the E area. Early in this survey a surprising finding developed. Some H villages had a substantial S minority which was shown to have only 30 percent lexical similarity with H and E. While many H speakers understood S, it turned out that they understood S only if they had been raised around S speakers. H and E speakers who had not been raised around S speakers showed no comprehension of S; thus it was clearly another language.

However, during the survey some S speakers started saying that they were really the H people and the H people were just a splinter of the E people. Soon it became apparent to the surveyors that some E people were attempting to influence the outcome of the survey by running ahead of the surveyors and planting the same information in H villages with S people.

11.2.1.6 The rise of S

It bears mentioning at this point that the national government involved has a finite number of categories for minority groups. These categories have come about in a non-systematic fashion. Sometimes names were proposed using good historical-comparative linguistics, sometimes using geographic names, sometimes using colloquial names in the national language, and sometimes using ethnonyms of the people groups. The result is that some groups are multiply identified to the government and some groups have no official identification. In the H and E case, they both had an official government identity but S did not, so that if S took over H's identity then it would now be identifiable to the government and to NGOs like SIL. This explains why the S people were willing to go along with the attempt of some E people to skew the survey results.

After the survey, a few more facts about the E and H people became known. The H group is clearly larger than the E group. In fact, the E group has no villages that are completely E; they are always part of a village whose majority is another ethnic group—usually a group called M. The M group has had literacy and a Bible translation for more than thirty years. Further, the E children are not exhibiting high language vitality. They have been observed primarily speaking M in their villages.

The H group, on the other hand, has a number of H-only villages. Also, the H have a long-standing cultural committee which includes representatives of the major religious groups. The E group has nothing like this. Further, the S are actually a group whose language is like the language of wider communication (M). In fact, some decades ago the M began to move into H villages to evangelize them. These evangelization efforts have led to the M renaming themselves four times in an attempt to spread their literacy and Bible into the groups they evangelize. However, the M dialect is not comprehensible by the H (or E), although it is comprehensible by the S.

11.2.1.7 Decline into conflict

At this point the narrative loses linearity. For some time both H and E presented themselves at literacy workshops—eventually accompanied by an S group demanding their own language development project separate from the M language which they have been using in church and with which they have 90 percent lexical similarity. It had become obvious that what once looked like a viable single language development project had now devolved into four different groups, at least two of which were probably not represented by legitimate community members. And it also had led to a high level of conflict between the groups. This conflict was either started or accelerated by beginning a language development project—and the resulting fragmentation actually was creating disunity and delaying literacy for all the groups. Ultimately, this made E, H, and S much more like slush floating in the sea of the majority language than into stronger communities ready to interact with their national language and culture.

11.2.1.8 End of external involvement

Given this situation and a growing chorus of legal and physical threats against SIL personnel if they did not do various things demanded by one or more of the groups, SIL was forced to cease working with any of the groups. Thus, language development that was stimulated by external involvement resulted in accentuating or even creating division in a group that needs to work together if it is to survive in the face of a growing national culture.

11.2.2 Observations

Several observations can be made from these events, four of which are discussed briefly. Many of these observations have been made with more subtlety in discussions by Robbins (1992) and Nida (1987).

Observation 3: Know who you are working with.

An outside linguist brings attention, energy, focus, and probably money into the language group. If not the first to do so, the linguist is probably currently the most important person doing so. In one way or an other, the linguist will ultimately decide who leads the language development process. Two undesirable choices for this are (a) the linguist or (b) a person not approved of by the true leaders of the group. An acceptable and good choice is a talented set of people approved of by the community. An acceptable but less desirable choice is a talented person who is not offensive to the community and is genuinely working toward community consensus with regard for economic gain.

In this case the H group appears to have provided the best choice—an approved and talented set of people. However, for quite some time this was only assumed and not verified information. And conversely, the people representing the E group were definitely not representative. However, SIL treated these groups equally. In effect they did *not* know who they were working with.

Observation 4: An orthography cannot extend group identity beyond any pre-existing political or social organization.

Many times a linguistic survey will identify groups that should work together and share a language development project. And in many of those cases when initial meetings are held with apparent stakeholders, there is agreement to work together. However, experience shows that if the people do not already have a history of working together in a structural organization that defines authority (e.g., government or religious) and that has a tradition of compromise, then they will not work together in a language development project—especially when making orthography decisions. Orthography decisions almost always define a "winning" dialect and a "losing" dialect and without a previous background of negotiating conflict successfully, groups will not acquire this ability during orthography development.

When H attempted to bring along E into its literacy plans it attempted to create a unity beyond any existing social organization. One consequence of this is that there was no place to turn when misunderstanding occurred.

Observation 5: Literacy and orthography decisions are often a proxy forum for other social, religious, or political issues.

Although orthography decisions could be viewed as purely linguistic decisions, usually they are not treated that way by group participants. Instead, the need to make a decision is often an occasion to air previously held differences. In the E and H example, a slight linguistic variation became a reason for E and H to split and to express their conflict. Orthography making seems to tighten unity only if unity already exists. If unity does not exist, the orthography decision-making process leads to conflict and disunity.

Observation 6: Most of the time money creates more problems than it solves.

A literacy program that has to be heavily funded to function is probably doomed to fail. Literacy is really a low-budget enterprise. If you have to generate a big, flashy program to gain interest, then that interest will attract the wrong people and dissipate as soon as the funds for the program go away.

In the E and H case study, the observation that money is often a negative influence held true since most of the unseemly events observed seemed to be primarily geared to gaining control of the money that goes along with language development.

This sad situation developed from many people having good intentions and just a few having bad intentions. However, it is clear from an outsider's perspective—in this case the SIL linguists involved—that many of the problems arose from acting before having adequate information. Outside linguists are often like oversize dogs in a chicken coop, causing lots of damage (stress) even if our goal is to "guard" the language from dying. The effects of non-linguistic NGOs who venture into literacy are often even more damaging to the long-term survival of the group's identity.

The information and cultural awareness that is needed for an outsider to be a positive force for the future of a minority group can only be gained by the humble process of learning the language and culture in a posture of humility. Attempts to "administer" are not only inherently colonial but doomed to fail.

11.3 Case Study II: Lisu and Lahu

There have been some very successful literacy movements in MSEA among some minority groups. Two of the better known ones are the Lisu [lis] in China and Myanmar and the Lahu [lhu] across a similar area that extends into Thailand. There are two interesting features that both groups show. They are: (1) a high degree of linguistic compromise and (2) religiously based regional organization.

Based on this commonality, these two groups are treated as exemplars of the same kind of successful language development process. Both of these groups have had substantial (Christian) minorities who have thousands of readers and a stable orthography which has existed for decades.

While both of these groups have had alternate orthographies proposed over the years (and continuing into the present), the Lisu have settled into a single dominant one (the Frazier script) and the Lahu have settled essentially for another single orthography—though at least one secondary orthography is supported by a few. While the history of their script development is somewhat murky, in both cases it was clearly motivated by missionary linguists. But it is the long-term success of language development in these groups—without continued missionary input and without government support—that makes observations about their current status interesting.

The bulk of these observations have to do with the substantial degree of linguistic compromise in their orthographies. While these scripts are used largely by Christians, these Christians come from a wide range of dialects. In many contexts, these dialect differences could have led (and still may lead) to different orthographies. As the orthographies have matured and become a literate standard, the differences between the written dialect and the dialects of other users have persisted, and yet an overall unity has been maintained.

When looking at the standard written form of Lisu, not only are there the expected phonological differences between dialects, but there are grammatical function words and even variant word orders in some dialects that do not match the dialect used for literacy among the Lisu. This dialect was based more on central Lisu and is colloquially called "Bible Lisu."

Table 1 lists some examples that distinguish Northern Lisu from Bible Lisu.

Table 1. Cross-dialect variation in Lisu

	Northern Lisu	Bible Lisu
Word order: Verb, Ability, and Negation	Verb–Negation–Ability	Negation–Ability–Verb
Word order: Noun and Demonstrative	Noun–Demonstrative	Demonstrative–Noun
Sentence-final particle	/a/	/a-lo/

Speakers of Northern Lisu are very aware of these differences as shown by the ease at which they provided the above examples. However, they generally seem to accept without hesitation that this degree of variation is a necessary part of maintaining a consistent Lisu identity. Hasselbring (2006) suggests that syntactic variation among dialects is a much stronger impediment to extensibility than variant phonology. This seems intuitively correct and yet the Lisu have achieved significant cross-dialect extensibility of their orthography in spite of noticeable variation in the word orders of different dialects.

Lahu is similar to Lisu in that the dialect has served the needs of several different Lahu varieties. The dominant Lahu dialect is Lahuna; it differs from the other dialects in many ways.

Table 2 shows the heavily used sentence-final marker for several Lahu dialects. This marker is also widely used as a general subordination marker for possessives, relative clauses, and nominalizations. What is interesting is that each major Lahu dialect has distinctive sentence-final markers. However, in the orthography, only the Lahuna sentence-final marker is used. As with the Lisu, there is no way to call these allophonic variations. Instead, the non-Lahuna readers learn a literate Lahu that uses different grammatical markers than their own dialect.

Table 2. Lahu dialects and sentence final markers

Dialect	Sentence-final marker
Lahuna	[ve]
Lahusi (Thailand)	[t͡ʃhē]
Lahusi (USA)*	[sē]
Lahuaga	[ka]
Lahunyi	[a]

*The Lahusi who have migrated to the USA live primarily in two communities: in California and in Minnesota. Interestingly, these communities have changed their final particle from/ t͡ʃhē/ to /sē/.

While most Lahu Christians are Lahuna or Lahusi, it appears that the choice to use only the Lahuna particles is not a significant impediment to comprehension. In comprehension tests in which Lahusi speakers listened to written Lahuna they often achieved more than 90 percent comprehension.

The broadest observation from both the Lisu and Lahu examples is that using the orthography (and by extension the established written standard) involves significant compromise—especially from the perspective of speakers whose dialect differs from the dialects used in the Bible translations. And yet, that compromise is a crucial part of what makes the orthographies successful. Also, as the orthographies are extended to align with existing regional structures that have a tradition of authority and consensus (the respective Protestant denominations), their literacy efforts have been a unifying force.

These observations can be captured in the following statements.

Observation 7: Language development demands regular compromises.

This observation was already made in the E and H case where there was no will to compromise, and as a result language development failed. In the case of the Lisu and Lahu language groups, they have had a century of compromise that resulted in relatively successful language development.

And in each case speakers are aware of the compromise. They feel that their identity as a group supersedes having an orthography that exactly matches their dialect.

Observation 8: Always work with a religious body if it exists.

This observation was hinted at above where the need to have a pre-existing unity (and history of authority and compromise) was proposed. Since most minority groups do not have political power, the only structures available to them to work across multiple villages are religious ones. Sometimes a cultural committee may be formed that is not explicitly religious, but if that committee does not have the blessing of the religious structures, then its role is very limited. Thus, those villages which have already entered into some kind of religious organization are the best suited for language development. In fact, it is exceedingly rare that non–government supported language development succeeds outside of a religious structure.

The history of the Lisu and Lahu was one of progressive Christianization which was followed by progressive literacy. In fact, for decades the dominant form of literacy instruction was in the churches. The organizational unity provided by the Christianization process greatly assisted the process of language development.

11.4 Case Study III: LR

The third case reported on is a group that has recently been engaged in extending literacy among its communities. This is a border group with significant numbers on both sides of a national border. In deference to one of the governments, they developed a separate orthography based on the national script. However, for decades this group had their own script that was not based on the national script. The existence of this script over a number of decades has not led to significant language development. Interestingly, the request for the national script was from a large Protestant group. As a result, the Catholic groups wanted their own script—a Roman-based script. Thus, there were requests for three different scripts: (1) a national-based script, used by Protestants; (2) an historical, quasi-indigenous script, with no religious affiliation; and (3) a Roman-based script, used by Catholics.

In this case, each requesting group represents a regional structure (spanning more than one village) that has a tradition of authority and consensus. The putative distribution of the scripts appears to be something like the diagram in figure 1. The obvious choice for an orthography is the historical one, but external pressure for the national script created the need for three scripts.

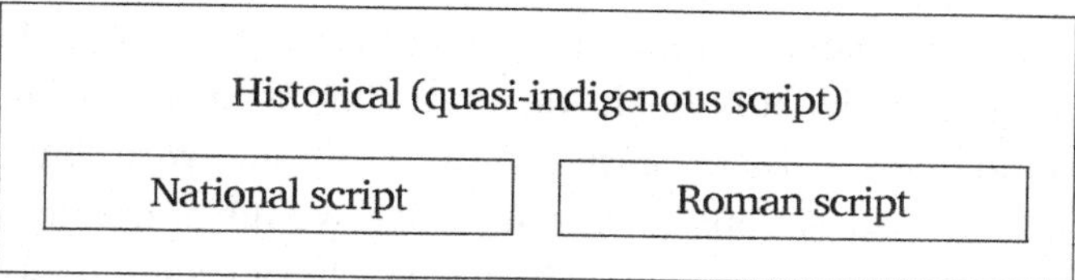

Figure 1. Distribution of scripts in LR.

For this language group, modern technology is enabling people to avoid an authority-consensus-based decision. Software exists that allows output into all three orthographies (there is no need for dialect-based choices in this case). The general idea is to make all orthographies possible and let "market forces" determine the winner. It remains to be seen how effective this solution will be.

However, there is reason to doubt the long-term success of this "multi-decision." As previously noted, orthography is often the map where people track their unity or disunity. When unity exists, orthography and literacy can solidify that unity. When unity does not exist, orthography decisions often sharpen people's awareness of disunity and the group fragments further. Having three orthographies encodes the separateness of each group into different writing communities. In effect, it is a vote for disunity. If however, the multi-scripts are not representative of actual internal groups (if they are merely to pacify external policies), then they might be harmless—since no one will really use them. It seems that these are the two most likely outcomes—perpetual disunity or ignoring all but one script, thereby reflecting an underlying unity. However, one outcome that is *not* likely is the creation of a new unity. This leads to Observation 9.

Observation 9: "Both and" is a vote for disunity.

In a situation with two language varieties, choosing both options is ultimately to encode the distinction between the two varieties into two different orthographies, thus encoding dialect "difference." Initially, taking a "both and" approach may reduce conflict, but ultimately this conflict needs to be resolved if the group is to move forward with a single identity.

11.5 Concluding notes

The most basic point of this paper is that once we as linguists cross the line from mere documenters of a language to activists in support of the future of a language, we suddenly begin to run a significant risk of doing harm even as we do good. Perhaps *harm* is a rather strong word, but sometimes our well-intentioned actions have effects we would prefer to avoid. The most significant effect is to create situations where group identity is more threatened than strengthened.

As a modest guide for linguists engaged in the activism of language development, the following list of observations was developed and is repeated here for convenience:

Observations of language development in Mainland Southeast Asia:

- Observation 1: Size matters.
- Observation 2: Unity matters.
- Observation 3: Know who you are working with.
- Observation 4: An orthography cannot extend group identity beyond any pre-existing political or social organization.
- Observation 5: Literacy and orthography decisions are often a proxy forum for other social, religious, or political issues.
- Observation 6: Most of the time money creates more problems than it solves.
- Observation 7: Language development demands regular compromises.
- Observation 8: Always work with a religious body if it exists.
- Observation 9: "Both and" is a vote for disunity.

References

Fishman, Joshua A. 1991. *Reversing language shift.* Clevedon, UK: Multilingual Matters Ltd.

Hasselbring, Sue. 2006. Cross-dialectal acceptance of written standards: Two Ghanaian case studies. Ph.D. dissertation. Pretoria: University of South Africa. http://uir.unisa.ac.za/xmlui/handle/10500/715 (accessed November 21, 2012).

Nida, Eugene A. 1987. *Intelligibility and acceptability in verbal communication.* Georgetown University Round Table 1987. Washington, D. C.: Georgetown University Press.

Robbins, F. E. 1992. Standardization of unwritten vernaculars. In S. J. J. Hwang, and W. R. Merrifield (eds.), *Language in context: Essays for Robert E. Longacre.* Summer Institute of Linguistics and University of Texas at Arlington Publications in Linguistics 107, 605–616. Dallas.

UNESCO. 2003. *Language vitality and endangerment.* Document adopted by the International Expert Meeting on UNESCO Programme Safeguarding of Endangered Languages, Paris. http://unesdoc.unesco.org/images/0018/001836/183699E.pdf (accessed 13 June 13, 2012).

Author's Biographical Information

Larin Adams received his Ph.D. from Northwestern University in 1999. He has been teaching at Payap University in Chiang Mai, Thailand since 2007. His primary role is helping students and colleagues write descriptions of under-documented minority languages from the Tibeto-Burman, Mon-Khmer, and Tai families. He has helped several students from this area work on descriptions and orthographies of their own languages.

Michael Cahill received his Ph.D. from Ohio State University in 1999. He developed the Konni orthography in Ghana while working in a multidisciplinary language project for several years under the Ghana Institute of Linguistics, Literacy, and Bible Translation. He served as SIL's International Linguistics Coordinator for eleven years, and currently is the Editor-in-Chief of SIL's academic publications. He is a member of the Linguistic Society of America's Committee on Endangered Languages and their Preservation, as well as a member of its Ethics Committee.

Leanne Hinton received her Ph.D. from the University of California at San Diego in 1977. She is a specialist in Native American languages, with a focus on language revitalization. She is a Professor Emerita at the University of California at Berkeley, and a founder and advisory board member of the Advocates for Indigenous California Language Survival. She has worked with a number of indigenous groups on orthography development.

Gwendolyn Hyslop received her Ph.D. from the University of Oregon in 2011. She is currently a Research Fellow at the College of Asia-Pacific, Australian National University, and is engaged in oral literature and language documentation projects in Bhutan.

Elke Karan received her M.A. in Linguistics from the University of North Dakota in 2006. She is a Literacy and Education Consultant with SIL International. She has developed several distance learning courses. Her experience in francophone Africa as consultant and as instructor at various formal and non-formal literacy-related courses resulted in research interests in orthography development and standardization, mother tongue–based literacy instruction, instructional methodologies, and language acquisition.

Constance Kutsch Lojenga received her Ph.D. from the University of Leiden in 1994. She is a Senior Linguistics Consultant with SIL International. Since 1975 she has been involved in grassroots linguistics and language development in many countries in Africa. She specializes in phonology and morphology, tone, orthography and primer design, developing methodology for linguistic discovery procedures in these domains, and particularly participatory-research discovery methods for awareness raising of basic linguistic structures among native speakers.

Pamela Munro received her Ph.D. from the University of California at San Diego in 1974. She is a Distinguished Professor of Linguistics at UCLA. Her publications include dictionaries and grammars of Cahuilla, Chickasaw, Kawaiisu, Mohave, Wolof, Zapotec, and UCLA student slang. Currently she is also working on Gabrielino/Tongva/Fernandeño, Garifuna, Q'anjob'al, and Quichua.

Keren Rice received her Ph.D. from the University of Toronto in 1976, with a thesis on the phonology of an Athabaskan language of northern Canada. She is currently University Professor at the University of Toronto. She was actively involved in a committee that sought to standardize the writing system of Slavey, an Athabaskan language, in the 1980s, and she has co-taught a workshop on orthography development at InField/CoLang. Her *Grammar of Slavey* won the first Bloomfield Book Award of the Linguistic Society of America.

Keith Snider received his Doctor of Letters in African Linguistics from the University of Leiden in 1990. He is a Senior Linguistics Consultant with SIL International. He has been consulting in the field of orthography development for over twenty years. His main areas of interests are tone analysis, general phonology, and historical and comparative linguistics.

Mary Ruth Wise received her Ph.D. from the University of Michigan in 1968. She is Editor-at-Large and a former International Linguistics Consultant with SIL International. She did field work among the Yanesha' in Peru in 1953–1957 and 1959–1964; this allowed her to observe bilingual education from its initial establishment by the Peruvian Ministry of Education in 1953. At the invitation of the Yanesha' bilingual teachers, she is currently serving as Linguistics Advisor to their NGO called CORINDES, and as a consultant in workshops organized by the Ministry of Education in which teachers prepare educational materials in their mother tongue. Her most recent publications and papers presented at conferences have been Arawakan comparative studies.

Language and Language Family Index

A

Akan [aka] 19
Algic 154
Alur [alz] 53
Arabic, Colloquial 124–125
Aramaic 218n
Arawakan 192ff.
Attié [ati] 57–58, 64, 100
Avokaya [avu] 55

B

Bantu 53, 56, 66–67, 69, 70, 77, 78, 79, 80–81, 87–89, 90, 91, 94, 95, 96, 98, 100, 101, 104
Betawi [bew] 108
Bidayuh, Biatah [bth] 125–127
Budu [buu] 66–67

C

Cebuano (Visayan) [ceb] 130
Central-Sudanic 53, 55, 57, 60, 63–64, 93, 94, 95, 97, 102, 103, 104
Chali [tgf] 212
Cherokee [chr] 165, 171–172
Chöke (see Tibetan, Classical) 217
Chumburung [ncu] 38–40, 42–43
Cree [cre] 165
Creole, Haitian [hat] 108
Cupan 181

D

Dayak Ngaju [nij] 108
Dioula [dgd] 51
Dogrib [dgr] 147
Dutch 114, 119n
Dzongkha [dzo] 212, 214, 226

E

Ebrié [ebr] 17, 61–62
English 19, 29, 30, 34–36, 37, 78, 121, 141, 142, 148, 150, 153, 156, 157, 159, 160, 162, 166, 173, 180, 217n

O

P

Q

R

S

T

Y

Z

General Index

I

K

L

M

N

O

P

U

V

W

Z

SIL International Publications
Additional Releases in the **Publications in Language Use and Education** Series

5. **The early days of sociolinguistics: Memories and reflections**, reprint, edited by Christina Bratt Paulson and G. Richard Tucker, 2010, 259 pp., ISBN 978-1-55671-253-1
4. **Language contact and composite structures in New Ireland**, by Rebecca Sue Jenkins, 2005, 275 pp., ISBN 1-55671-156-5
3. **The in-between people: Language and culture maintenance and mother-tongue education in the highlands of Papua New Guinea**, by Dennis L. Malone, 2004, 263 pp., ISBN 1-55671-147-3
2. **And I, in my turn, will pass it on: Knowledge transmission among the Kayopó**, by Isabel I. Murphy, 2004, 235 pp., ISBN 1-55671-155-8
1. **Reading is for knowing: Literacy acquisition, retention, and usage among the Machiguenga** by Patricia M. Davis, 2004, 343 pp., ISBN 1-55671-094-3

SIL International Publications
7500 W. Camp Wisdom Road
Dallas, TX 75236-5629

Voice: 972-708-7404
Fax: 972-708-7363
publications_intl@sil.org
sil.org/resources/publications

CPSIA information can be obtained
at www.ICGtesting.com
Printed in the USA
LVOW04s2142230116
471998LV00024B/390/P

9 781556 713477